The Development of Play
Third Edition

Why do children play?

What can children learn from playing?

What have psychologists learned from 150 years of studying play – usually a bit too seriously?

The Development of Play explores the central role of play in childhood development. David Cohen examines how children play with objects, with language, and most importantly with each other and their parents. He explains how play enables children to learn how to move, think, speak and imagine, as well as to develop emotionally and socially. Incorporating much of the recent research in this area, including that of John Flavell, Henry Wellman and others, *The Development of Play* shows how play encourages children to grasp the difference between appearance and reality.

This new edition updates and builds on the previous two editions, to include new research on pretending and the theory of mind, autism and how parents can play creatively with their children. Play therapy, the history of play and how play is dealt with in the media are also covered. The book addresses the often ignored subject of adult games and why adults sometimes find it difficult to play. *The Development of Play* offers a fascinating review of the importance of play in all our lives.

David Cohen is a filmmaker and psychologist. He runs *Psychology News*.

The Development of Play
Third Edition

David Cohen

LONDON AND NEW YORK

First published in 1987 by Croom Helm

First published in 1987 in the USA by New York University Press

Second edition published in 1993 by Routledge

Third edition published in 2006
by Routledge
27 Church Road, Hove, East Sussex, BN3 2FA

Simultaneously published in the USA and Canada
by Routledge
270 Madison Avenue, New York NY 10016

Routledge is an imprint of the Taylor and Francis Group

© 1987, 1993 David Cohen, 2006 Routledge

Typeset in Times by
Keystroke, Jacaranda Lodge, Wolverhampton
Printed and bound in Great Britain by
TJ International Ltd, Padstow, Cornwall
Paperback cover design by Lisa Dynan

British Library Cataloguing in Publication Data
A catalogue record for this book is available from the British Library

Library of Congress Cataloging in Publication Data
Cohen, David, 1946-
  The development of play / David Cohen.– 3rd ed.
    p. cm.
  Includes bibliographical references and index.
  ISBN 0-415-34702-5 (hard cover) — ISBN 0-415-34701-7 (soft cover)
  1. Play–Psychological aspects. 2. Child psychology. I. Title.
BF717.C63 2006
155.4'18—dc22

2005033449

ISBN10: 0–415–34701–7   ISBN13: 9–78–0–415–34701–7 (hbk)
ISBN10: 0–415–34702–5   ISBN13: 9–78–0–415–34702–5 (pbk)

Contents

Acknowledgements

This book is partly based on my doctoral thesis. The late Professor Brian Foss was very supportive as was my external examiner Rom Harre. I also benefited from the support of the Leverhulme Trust. My thanks to them all.

More personally, my love and thanks to my children – Nicholas and Reuben – who, 25 years ago, let me watch and be delighted by what made them laugh.

If it had not been for Aileen La Tourette, their mother, I would never have had the good luck to be able to observe, and learn from, Nicholas and Reuben. I dedicate this book with love and gratitude to her.

1   Introduction

When I came to London as a boy of 9, I was baffled by some of the games English children played. Cricket was a total mystery but, at least, it didn't seem dangerous. Far more threatening was a game called *Double or Quits*. The fat boy who lived in the flat above ours insisted I play this game with him. New to England, I didn't dare refuse because I wanted to be accepted. I didn't dare admit either that I never understood the rules as FatBoy wielded them. The way we played the game I could never quit and never win. Often, at the end of an hour's playing, I was seething with frustration while FatBoy grinned in ecstasy. I never discovered how to play *Double or Quits* and so, in the end, I avoided meeting him. I mention this experience because psychologists who write about play tend to lapse into a kind of romantic smugness. Playing is wonderful, fun, golden, innocent. Play is how we learn to handle the world and our social roles in it; play teaches and heals. The way some psychologists write, you would imagine that what the children in William Golding's macabre *The Lord of the Flies* (1954) needed was a good dose of play therapy. Then, they would have acted out their fantasies instead of, well, acting out their fantasies.

Playing is, of course, often fun and light but this romantic attitude has given the extensive psychological literature on play an odd feel. More than most psychology, studies on play report naturalistic behaviour in detail. There are extended accounts of life in playgroups and in 'warm home-like laboratories' (a phrase from a study) of children doing charming things. To read of 3 year olds playing doctors, nurses, fire engines, space adventurers and so on is entertaining and some children can be sharp as pins. One wily boy refused to pretend a colander was a shoe 'because that's too silly to be a shoe'. All this yields good data. Since psychologists have often been blamed for providing too little raw data from real life, it may be churlish to complain.

However, these reports also contain many questionable assumptions. Usually, play is seen as something children do and adults don't. This is specially odd when in 2003 entertainment economists suggested that the worldwide market for video games was now worth more than the combined film, video and DVD market. Many of those who buy and play video games are adults. Then, while children are presumed to think that play is good fun, wiser adults (especially psychologists) know there's more to it than that. Play is a learning experience. Piaget argued that as children get older, they reject the sillier games of childhood in favour of more realistic pursuits. Fantasy is a stage one grows out of.

Most texts on play do not investigate the origins of such assumptions even though it is quite clear that historical attitudes both to children and play have changed. Unusually, Brian Sutton-Smith (1983) has claimed that western societies have used play to make children conform and prepare them for their role in capitalism. It is certainly odd that there seems to have been no attempt to link a text like Marcuse's (1959) *Eros and Civilisation* to the subject. Before flower power, Marcuse claimed that capitalism did not dare allow adults real pleasure. Surplus repression was used to keep us in check. The notion that play is sinful stems from the Puritans and has influenced research. Psychologists certainly seem to accept that while play may appear frivolous, it has to have a proper, serious explanation. It cannot just be; it has to have a purpose. Sutton-Smith considered the nature of the play ethos. In other work he has argued that play does not just help the child mature and master but that it also has some immediate benefits.

The paradox – let's be serious about play – has not been commented on much since Groos (1896) claimed that we had a long childhood so that we could play and that we played to 'pre-exercise' skills we would need as adults. Groos originated the idea that we play in order to learn and, as we shall see, few people understand now what a reversal this was. Groos made specific links between some games and some skills. This prompted one of the few jokes by the great Genevan psychologist, Jean Piaget. It was unlikely, sniped Piaget, that when a baby dropped a rattle, it was pre-exercising its grasp of gravity and the laws of physics. Did Newton play much with apples? The growth of psychoanalysis, and the start of child analysis, gave Groos' ideas a new twist. Emotional skills rather than cognitive ones were being rehearsed. Freud made only fleeting references to play but from the 1920s, analysts like Susan Isaacs, Anna Freud and Melanie Klein saw it as a crucial process and useful tool. In free play, children could express their anxieties. Guide them right and they could use play to conquer these. Klein and Freud were to quarrel about the way analysts could use play but both believed it was important. For both, though, it was a phase; Freud said there was a clear 'development line' which was *from play to work*.

Return to the paradox. Play cannot just be; it has to have a purpose. Otherwise, biology would not have permitted its evolution. The task, therefore, brave psychologist, is to burrow beneath the play for the real meaning. Sutton-Smith (2003) in *The Ambiguity of Play* was inspired to look at play in ways suggested by William Empson's Seven Types of Ambiguity (1949). Sutton-Smith suggests seven different rhetorics including play as progress, play as fate as in gambling, play as power as in sports, play as identity, play as imaginary, and play as merely frivolous. He argues that the rhetoric of progress has taken over the way we see play – the child must play to master skills – and that this has perhaps obscured other aspects of play. Impressively Sutton-Smith lists over a hundred uses of the word play from playing with fire to playing Shakespeare to playing charades. (He omits though the sexual dimension of play as in playing with oneself.)

A further assumption is that all children play. Well, they would all have to play if it is such a major developmental process. Current orthodoxy argues that autistic children are very poor at pretend play. In fact, there are non-players and they don't turn into monsters necessarily. J.S. Mill's father wanted his son to be educated from birth which meant there was no time to play. The son could never remember playing. In his autobiography, the philosopher noted: 'Of children's books any more than of playthings I had scarcely any, except an occasional gift from a relative or acquaintance.' This deprivation does not seem to have hampered Mill except that he reckoned it made him bad with his hands. He could deal with people, politics and philosophy but – probably – not with the plumbing.

These assumptions and paradoxes may affect psychologists more than they admit. As it is a science, they/we are meant to be objective. But these cultural legacies prompt awkward, and often unasked, questions. Should one be playful about studying play or should one treat it with scientific seriousness as if we were studying the aggressive behaviour of the well-conditioned pigeon? A review in *Contemporary Psychology* snapped that it wasn't necessary to be humorous about humour research. On the whole, play researchers have been conservative and grave but all this argues that we need to look at play from a variety of perspectives.

To show how serious I am about being playful about play, there will be an interlude before getting on to the introductory ritual of explaining what is in this book and why it is necessary to add to the literature. A few quotations will reveal not just the contradictions and confusions surrounding play but the range of writers who have bothered to think about it without satisfying themselves (let alone others) that they have cracked the problem:

> The function of play has been commented on for many centuries, to little avail.
>
> (Erving Goffman, sociologist, 1976)

> Play is a child's life and the means by which he comes to understand the world he lives in.
>
> (Susan Isaacs, psychoanalyst, 1933)

> Animals are young so that they may play.
>
> (Karl Groos, comparative psychologist, 1896)

> We can be sure that all happenings, pleasant or unpleasant, in the child's life, will have repercussions on her dolls.
>
> (Jean Piaget, psychologist, 1952)

> In attempting to interpret the play of infants one must bear in mind the love of nonsense and tomfoolery.
>
> (C.W. Valentine, psychologist, 1942)

> [Play] is one of those concepts that Wittgenstein might have said is wrapped in so much toilet paper, it looks round. The cutting edges have been dulled.
>
> (Gregory Stone, sociologist, 1973)

> The motives of play are various and, often, complex, and they cannot be characterised by any brief formula; nor can any hard and fast line be drawn between work and play.
>
> (William MacDougall, psychologist, 1919)

> Generally speaking there is continuity between a child's play and work.
>
> (Jean Piaget, psychologist, 1952)

> [In] play, the ego aspires to its full expansion.
>
> (E. Claparède, psychologist, 1913)

> Fantasy play can reveal a great deal of material but any kind of play can be used defensively.
>
> (Anna Freud, psychologist, 1984)

> Play therapy was able to reduce hyperactivity in rats suffering from attention deficit.
>
> (J. Panksepp, psychologist, 2005)

And we must not forget:

> The play's the thing
> Wherein I'll catch the conscience of the king.
>
> (Shakespeare, *Hamlet*, Act 2, sc. 2)

The Bard was clearly an early advocate of play therapy.
  And let's finish this fandango with

Play originated from boredom and deteriorated behaviour, an outrageous speculation that may, after all, be true of the writer and his thesis.

(Gordon M. Burghardt, psychologist, 1984)

I could go on and on. I cannot tell you how concerned I am about hyperactive rats and I do wonder if Wittgenstein ever played. I suspect he did since he worked some time in a school.

I deliberately finished with Burghardt's provocative words for two reasons. First, he provides an adequate set of working definitions for play and, second, he has mainly studied animal play. This book examines play in humans and does not consider, except very occasionally, animal work. It seems generally agreed that detailed studies of chimpanzee play such as Jane Lawick Goodall (1968) reveal that they use play both to improve manual skills and to practise social skills. Fagen (1981) stressed that play leads to many encounters in which apes learn to co-operate. He concludes that 'it is most fruitful to look for social play as a source of certain kinds of flexible skills'. Research on human play has examined many aspects that animal studies did not touch – such as the use of toys, the role of pretending and the impact of cultural fashions. But now we have ethologists looking at first two of these with work on whether chimps can pretend (2001 Savage Rumbaugh). In the second edition of this book I quipped that the smartest chimp going does not seem to act out being King Kong because he is nervous of how well he'll do on the rugby field. I now have to revise that quip and do so in Chapter 7.

Looking both at animal and at human play, Burghardt (1984) offers the following useful defining characteristics. Play has

- no obvious immediate function
- a pleasing effect
- is sequentially variable
- is stimulus seeking
- is quick and energetically expensive behaviour
- involves exaggerated, incompetent or awkward movements
- is most prevalent in juveniles
- has special 'play' signals
- has a background in role relationships
- is marked by a relative absence of threat or submission
- is marked by a relative absence of final consummatory behaviour.

Some of Burghardt's points fit animals better than people, in fact. Children do not always move awkwardly when they play, for example. In a Wendy House or clambering up a climbing frame, children can move normally or, even, gracefully. Pouring sand into containers also does not seem to be expensive in energy terms. Burghardt (1984) makes something of the lack of real threat or submission. With human beings it is more complicated. Freud suggested long ago that jokes allowed real hostility to surface in a socially acceptable way. The bitchy repartee is a real put-down but acceptable. Observations of children indicate that they often are hostile in their play but they know that the veneer that it is a game makes it likely they will get away with it. Despite such quibbles, Burghardt draws attention to some useful boundaries between play and 'not-play'. It seems possible to accept that play does involve a varied set of activities and behaviours. Not every instance of play needs to fulfil all of Burghardt's criteria. Many kinds of behaviour that are recognised easily as play will score only some of the criteria.

Burghardt also does not help much in describing moments of transition such as when a child shifts from walking down the street to galloping like a horse. Usually, there is no difficulty in recognising when children are playing. An interesting article by Dunn and Youngblade (2003) suggests that mothers give babies signals from the age of 3 months which make it clear that 'kiddo we are now larking about'.

I doubt if it is possible to fashion a perfect definition of play precisely because it is such a wide behaviour. There are many ways of playing play.

Despite the variety of quotations – and, of course, many more could be culled – the literature on play tends to one of three traditions. The most influential today is probably the Piagetian one. As McCune-Nicolich and Fenson (1984) noted, Piaget was one of the few psychologists to map in detail the development of imitation and play in his children over a long period of time. Piaget's (1952) *Play, Dreams and Imitation in Childhood* is both accessible and fairly short on observations compared to most of the master's books. In plotting the growth of intelligence, Piaget seemed to make notes virtually every day – certainly every month – on new things his children did. With play, there are huge gaps between observations. Piaget notes the play behaviour of J and L at three-month, even six-month, intervals. Interesting as the material is, it is not as thorough as his cognitive work. Nevertheless, as McCune-Nicolich pointed out, it is a seminal contribution. Psychologists who approach play in the Piagetian tradition tend to focus on what children do with objects, the point at which they can use an object for something else (say, an eggshell to be a spoon) and the relationship between play and exploration.

Piaget commented on Freud's ideas about play and accepted that, for the very young child, play was totally gratifying to the ego. The demands of reality did not intrude. Play should fade away, Piaget believed, as the child became more competent with real objects, and real situations, in the real world.

The second tradition has been closely linked to psychoanalysis. It concentrates on what emotions are expressed in play and on how play can be used to heal. These two traditions have tended to function in isolation – few studies even now ask how a child's cognitive 'level' of play is linked to his or her emotional development – but they do share one prejudice. For Piaget and for Freud, only children play. Any adult who larked about in a funny hat would be a candidate for the funny farm or, in Piaget's case, for a severe dose of logic. Freud claimed the human task was to learn to be able to love and to work. Not much room for play there. Piaget went to some length to explain why some adults persisted in playing organised games. But, of course, to play tennis is not to play in quite the same way. Nor is to play the Stock Exchange. There are cultural changes in the way we think of play among adults. The rise of computer games, for example, shows that many adults love playing. So do the large numbers of apparently sane grown-ups who spend their weekends pretending to be Vikings or 'pretend fighting' old battles from the Civil Wars. The Brits act out Naseby; the Yanks act out Yorktown.

The third tradition in play research is educational. Much of the early work on play was done not by psychologists but by educationalists like Froebel and Montessori. They wanted to see what play could be used for. Initially, many of these workers wanted to liberate what was best in the child through free play. But, as Sutton-Smith (1984) observed, $100 million was spent in the United States on building playgrounds between 1890 and 1920. That was not because American society wanted to foster the sweet bird of liberty in its young. Rather, social leaders hoped to train youngsters, especially working-class youngsters, to take their place in American society and become productive members of it. Studies of playgroups since 1920 have tended, usually without much awareness of it, to accept the fact that play ought to be used to certain ends. Children ought to learn how to co-operate, to share things and, of course, to obey wiser adults. There is much descriptive literature on what happens in playgroups but rather less writing on why adults have created and run corrective playgroups. There were social engineers on the swings.

In Britain, the government has invested hugely since 1998 in a programme called Sure Start whose aim is to give 'deprived' toddlers a good start – and those programmes aim to give children chances to play among much else. In his spending review (July 2004) Gordon Brown, the Chancellor of the Exchequer, announced 120,000 new places for deprived toddlers in nursery schools where there would be great emphasis on play. In 2005, however, it emerged the government was trying to hide research which showed Sure Start was not working so well.

In fact, the literature on play has tended to be rather fragmented. There are some useful introductory texts such as Millar's (1968) *Play* (now a little out of date) and Garvey's (1977) *Play*. More recently Singer and Singer (1990) *The House of Make Believe*, Moyles (1989) *Just Playing?* and Pellegrini's (1995) *The Future of Play Theory* have added the literature.

But most books on the subject tend to be collections of essays in which authors with different special interests concentrate on them and offer few connections to the rest of the literature. An early example was Yawkey and Pellegrini's (1984) *Child's Play, Developmental and Applied*. There are chapters on pretend play, the play of handicapped children, humour, exploration, the uses (and misuses) of objects, playschools and, even, play in the hospital setting. The list may be comprehensive but Yawkey devotes just 7 out of 370 pages to a general introduction and most of that is taken up with listing what the following chapters are about.

I believe it's both possible and useful to offer a coherent account of the state of our knowledge about play – and the implications of that.

I also wanted to write this book because of two previous pieces of research. First, I did my PhD thesis (Cohen 1985) on the development of laughter basing most of it on following what made my children laugh over four years. Second, in a critique of Piaget in the early 1980s (Cohen 1983), I argued that his theory, valuable as it is, focused far too much on how children reacted to things and far too little on how they reacted to people and, especially, to their parents. We need to integrate different approaches. Play is not either cognitive or social or emotional. When children play, they often combine all these faculties.

Psychologists have played the game of play research in some curious, even defensive, ways. I'm not being offensively flippant in describing it as a game; much work in the philosophy of science since Kuhn (1962) has stressed that science is a game with its own rules. Two of the traditional approaches emphasise research in controlled situations, either the laboratory (which can be dolled up to look playful) or the consulting room. The playgroup is somewhat less controlled, of course, though researchers often impose their own restrictions on what slices of play they study. More than most psychologists, students of play have ventured into homes but they often feel compelled to turn these into mini-labs, bringing with them a bag of approved toys (in case the ones people have don't suit) as well as much techno-baggage such as video cameras, tape-recorders, electronic bleepers and so on. Mothers are sometimes given bells to ring to signal the start of the experimental period. The experts, as Belsky and Most (1981) admitted, are rarely content to observe playful behaviour as it happens. They catalyse it or limit it. McCune-Nicolich and Fenson (1984), for example, often do a 'warm-up' visit to set mothers and infants at ease a week before they actually do their video with toys they provide. The observation period lasts 30 minutes. Psychologists control to an unnatural degree the setting and tools with which the play they observe occurs. Is 30 minutes enough? Why not use the toys on site? Belsky and Most (1981) even constructed a twelve-stage model of the development of play using such short bursts of observation.

The way that children develop their play in their own home with parents, siblings and neighbourhood friends has barely been studied. The convenient assumption is that play in the lab or the home or the nursery class is much the same. My observations on laughter show clearly this is not entirely true with laughter. Over four years, Nicholas and Reuben played far more complexly at home than in their nursery school – where I observed them together with Vicki Hayward Cripps. Their home play incorporated and dealt with far more emotional material. Their mother, Aileen LaTourette, and I played with them in ways that their teachers didn't. This is no criticism of their teachers but a fact of family life.

The first edition of this book was published in 1987. Since then, there have been a number of important practical and theoretical developments which have made play research actually more central to developmental psychology.

First, the availability of good, cheap video recorders – everyone is a camera-person now – has made it easier to acquire large amounts of observational data in naturalistic settings. Many studies still appear to prefer bringing children into the laboratory to study what must be fairly artificial forms of play, as Haight and Miller (1992) complain in their analysis of everyday play. One perhaps unintentionally amusing study, for example, observed how children responded to a non-reciprocating robot in a lab and noted, oh the great discovery, that frustrated children tended to hit the thing. Despite such continuing eccentricities, there has been some move towards observing real behaviour in real settings. Data have become more complex, messier and more revealing.

Naturalistic observations make it clear that parents and siblings play an important role in teaching children how to play. It seems staggering – and reflects the extent to which Piaget dominated those parts of developmental psychology he hardly attended to – that there should ever have been doubt of the importance of parents. There have been a number of longitudinal studies like Haight and Miller (1992) and Howes and Matheson (1992) which outline how that develops. Youngblade and Dunn (1995) have looked at how mothers signal to kids when they start to play so that babies start to learn what is real and what is pretence. Pictures of the fetus at 18 weeks even show the yet to be born is smiling. The importance of parents in creating the setting for play and using it to teach young children has also been made clear by the work of Ladd and Hart (1992) on how American parents organise playmates for their children. It turns out that you're never too young to network.

Perhaps the most important development has been the link between play studies and what has come to be called the child's theory of mind. In the 1987 edition, I devoted a large central chapter to pretending. I argued that there was evidence that children as young as 2½ could pretend and knew they were pretending from 3 years of age. Children can know they are pretending only if they have some sense of their own mental states and can compare real feelings with unreal ones that are put on. As I shall show in Chapter 5, there is now a lively literature on young children's ability to deceive, to induce false beliefs and the various strategies they master at different ages (Sodian 1991; Flavell 2004).

Pretend play, which once seemed a slightly esoteric interest, has come to occupy a central focus in developmental psychology. Knowing the difference between appearance and reality is a crucial mental leap. There is now growing evidence for some form of quantum leap in children's cognitions between the age of 3 and 4½ – a leap that seems to require the revision of key elements in Piagetian theory. Pretend play seems to be a key skill in social and cognitive development. Baron-Cohen (2003) has also suggested that children who suffer from autism and Asperger's syndrome also do not seem able to pretend. Mark Haddon's (2003) bestselling book *The Curious Incident of the Dog in the Night-Time* offers a wonderful insight into the doggedly literal mind of the autistic child who is brilliant at prime numbers but really struggles with pretending and the point of pretending.

Another interesting change has been in research on how children understand the media, on how they distinguish reality and fantasy on television and in video games. Two very different kinds of experts operate in this field. On the one hand, there are meta-analysts inspired by work on deconstruction; on the other, American TV companies commission endless market research to ensure that the latest cartoon doesn't stretch little Timmy's attention span too much because he might then not pay attention to the adverts. What emerges from all this is that children are much more sophisticated in understanding media and media games than one would have imagined (Kinder 1992).

There is a further oddity of the play research game. It rather peters out round when children are 11 or 12. Do teenagers never play? Perhaps we don't study how children play with their parents enough because adults are not meant to play. Peter Pan today is seen as pathological rather than charming.

But who decided that play ends so abruptly? Is it a biological fact or a cultural convention? If it is the latter, is it changing? In the chapters that follow I give an account of play research in its cognitive, emotional and social perspective. But it seems important also to ask a few historical questions. The French historian of *mentalités*, Philippe Ariès (1914–84), claimed that childhood is not a historical absolute. In the Middle Ages, children had no 'childhood'; they were seen as miniature adults and, as soon as physically possible, integrated into adult life. Parents saw children die young too often, Ariès (1962) believed, to invest emotionally in them. There was no protected period of innocence. Pollock (1984) has argued that Ariès is wrong. She found examples from the sixteenth century onwards of children who were doted on by their parents and a few scattered accounts of games they played together. Nevertheless, play was not considered a subject for study until the late eighteenth century. Rousseau's (1759) *Emile* waxed lyrical about its joys. The Victorians adopted some of his romantic views of childhood and believed that childhood was the best days of our life. Victorians, however, also sent their children down mines and into factories. This dichotomy is interesting and I consider some of its origins in Chapter 2, which looks at some of our historical attitudes to play. Most developmental psychologists do wrong to ignore such issues. It stops them asking important questions about how adults play with their children and, also, about whether adults go on playing.

Digging is work; digging about in the playground is play.

I want to argue that psychologists are still too apt to accept the dichotomy the Victorians set up of work versus play. In his *Hard Times*, Dickens (1854) gave the definitive picture of the awful Victorian school where Mr Gradgrind ground facts into his poor pupils. Play was sin. The good child worked all the time. Dickens did not criticise Mr Gradgrind for drawing too sharp a distinction between work and play but because, for Gradgrind, there ought to be no play at all. Dickens accepted, nobly, like most Victorians, that work was one thing and play another. He wanted children to have more play. It has been argued that one reason for the Victorian accent on work was that industry needed to persuade the labour force that it had to work its guts out. Anything else was immoral.

Since Dickens, the industrial world has changed. We have to live with more leisure for the lucky and more unemployment for the unlucky. In the chapter on adult play I want to raise the issue that, in some jobs, it is hard to work out where work stops and play begins. Doing the same task month after month on a car assembly line may be work but what about writing computer programs? Or running a small business you like? Or doing psychology? Many people (especially middle-class people) can enjoy their work now in a way that would have been inconceivable in Dickens' day.

Is writing a new book work or play? Especially difficult if the book is about play!

We have also become, the pun is deliberate, far more used to the idea of playing with ourselves. For Freud and the early analysts, therapy was serious, perhaps even sacred. The growth of endless therapy groups, growth groups and grope groups means that there are group groupies, people who devote much of their time to personal games. You need only read the personal and therapy ads in publications like London's *Time Out* or the *New York Review of Books* to see that we are in a universe that neither Dickens nor Freud would recognise. People addicted to psychological games may be lonely and/or a small minority but the whole 'personal growth' movement has affected the way many people think about psychological change. Playing for adults has come 'on to the agenda'. Even quite conservative organisations like the British Medical Association run role-playing groups for doctors so that coldfish medics can get to feel what it is like to be the patient. Somehow, developmental psychologists have managed to ignore many of these adult aspects of playing and have failed to ask what it might mean in terms of how they play with their children.

A contemporary book on play needs to look at such issues and I intend to argue that adults need to learn how to play more. Playgroups for the over-twenties!

There is, as I said, the game, or is it ritual, of setting out what is in the book to come. Chapter 2 looks at historical attitudes to play and how they have influenced play research. Chapter 3 looks at the way children play with objects and toys. It analyses Piaget's views and tries to incorporate the fact that often children play with toys with other children or adults. Chapter 4 discusses the social games and pretend play of young children, focusing mainly on games with their peers. In Chapter 5, which looks at the ways in which children play with their parents, I try to integrate my own research material with the latest ideas in work on the child's theory of mind and autism. Dividing the research into these three areas looks rather arbitrary but it follows the pattern of most work. Connections need to be made between them because, when a child is playing, he or she is using mind, body, heart and social skills. I also look briefly at the issue of whether children can be taught to play better by adults. Ponder the irony: children are the experts at play, play is their work and yet we, long-out-of-practice oldies, think we can teach them how to play!

Chapters 6 and 7 also focus on how children play with their parents. I draw to a large extent on my research on my own children, who often laughed, while they were playing. Some observations support Bruner's analysis of how children develop their peekaboo skills. The value of long-term observations in the home is that they offer a richness of data. They also reveal what the child uses, and transforms, in everyday life and something of the interaction between daily events and the child's play. Since Nicholas is 3 years and 9 months older than Reuben, the observations also suggest much about how brothers play together and what they learn from each other. It is not all one-way traffic with the younger learning from the elder.

I often return to the paradox that psychologists don't know whether to be playful about play. Psychoanalysts have few such tensions. Play is the road royal to the child's unconscious and you would no more be frivolous about it than about dreams. Chapter 7 looks at play therapy and asks how much of it is play and how much of it is therapy. In an interview not long before her death, Anna Freud had some sceptical points to make about the use of play.

Chapter 7 also raises the question of whether research helps find ways in which parents can teach their children how to play creatively. Having stressed the point that children often start playing with their parents, Chapter 8 considers some kinds of adult games and argues there are more of them than ever before. The radical psychiatrist R.D. Laing suggested grown-ups need to play both with their children and with their lovers. I argue that adults need to play more and more freely. The growth of many sports and leisure activities indicates that we are continuing to play once we pass the age of consent but there are also many signs that we feel uneasy about it. As industrial societies become post-industrial (whatever that label quite means) adults ought to become less inhibited about playing. And psychologists ought to struggle through their Puritan heritage and become less inhibited about studying it. Finally, Chapter 9 conforms to the rules of the bookwriting game. It sums up what we have learned and points out directions research ought to go.

Over the years, attitudes to play have changed. In his delightful *Let Your Mind Alone* the humorist James Thurber berated psychologists who, in 1936, 'agree[d] that realism as against fantasy, reverie, day-dreaming and woolgathering, is a highly important thing'. Thurber pointed out:

> In this insistence on reality I do not see as much profit as these shapers of success do. I have had a great deal of satisfaction and benefit out of day-dreaming which never got me anywhere in their definition of getting somewhere.

Today, few psychologists would argue against play or fantasy but the feeling still persists that such frivolous activities need to be justified by being in the service of reality. The right games should spur the best development. I hope this book offers not just a more rounded view of play but also a less utilitarian one. To be worth studying, play does not always have to be *for* something else.

Let play begin.

2 A history of play

If rats are given the chance to engage in rough and tumble play, are they less likely to be delinquent? And if so can we treat bad boys with rough and tumble therapy to help them stay out of jail? Panskepp and his colleagues posed this question and it shows off nicely some of the paradoxes of play research (Scott and Panksepp 2003). I want to come back to that later on in this chapter.

The West Indian writer C.L.R. James, who was an authority on cricket, noted wryly: 'What do they know of cricket who only cricket know.' Upper-class romantics might imagine it was only a game with the thwack of leather on willow but James, who was poor, black and a Marxist, could see that its rules and rituals were profoundly affected by social and political events. Play too cannot be viewed in a vacuum. As long as there have been writers and artists to observe them, children seem to have played and to have mimicked adult behaviour. What commentators have made of this has varied widely.

In this chapter, I do not attempt a comprehensive history of play research; I want to pick out certain times and themes which seem interesting because they show how research into play has been influenced by different factors. Today, fretting about work stress and all too imperfect pursuit of happiness, we glorify play. It was not always thus. Plato in *The Republic* described a system of education for his philosopher-kings without ever mentioning play. That was something women did with infants and it didn't matter a jot.

As a subject for philosophical consideration, play hardly figures before Rousseau, but then the eighteenth-century Romantic movement rhapsodised play. It was, after all, what *l'enfant sauvage* got up to in the state of nature. For the romantics, play and its freedoms were normal. They discussed the subject to prove that we had lost much natural innocence. For the Victorians, the opposite was true. It is no accident that the scientific study of play began in the mid-nineteenth century with writers like Herbert Spencer. Victorian society and industry needed to define play and leisure as rare, abnormal activities, the opposite of that normal activity, work. Even an enlightened visionary like Robert Owen put few facilities for play in his model industrial villages.

We have not yet outgrown this Victorian legacy. From the 1870s onwards, research on play branches out mainly in three directions – the cognitive value of play, the emotional value of play and the social value of play. Educators like Froebel and Montessori did not see play as a good in itself so much as a means through which children could be taught formal skills. Make mathematics fun and kids will learn to add up better. Fifteen years before Freud (1905) wrote his book on jokes (which had only a few asides on play), the American 'mental hygienists' were praising its educative uses. Joseph Lee of the National Recreational Association claimed in 1910 that if immigrant children were put in 'sylvan sanctuaries' they would soon twig the American way of life. When psychoanalysts suggested that play was therapeutic for children, they were building on old foundations.

There is much paradox in this. Most writers argue that play is a free activity and one which has no clear goal or purpose. Nearly all research then contradicts this nice, free-wheeling view and psychologists try to unravel the truer, deeper, more meaningful meaning of play or to find its purposes. Freud and Piaget are the masters of this approach, sniffing out profundities in the way a child plays with a mobile or pours water about. Studies of laughter reveal the same lust for the serious. Philosophers and psychologists have tried to uncloak its deeper purpose since day 1 of metaphysics. Hobbes saw laughter as an expression of hostile triumph; Bergson saw it as our reaction to seeing ourselves depicted as machines; Nietzsche saw it as a means of subverting the ordinary. You can't just laugh – or play – for the fun of it. Truth has to be more sombre. It is worth noticing how psychology needs to make 'light' trivial behaviours the outward signs of much weightier stuff. Victorian attitudes have left their mark. Who can justify studying play unless it gets you to hidden depths?

Research into play is also beginning to be affected by two more recent developments. Since the 1960s, we have learned that we live in a stress society. To avoid ulcers, the heebie-jeebies and heart attacks, we have to relax. All kinds of sports and games have boomed. So have psychological games, including encounter groups, growth movements, self-help groups of some sorts, following-the-guru, self-therapies and all kinds of ego-fests. Television's *Big Brother*'s success reflects our interest in all this. Obviously, many people take these activities very seriously and some need help. But, for many people, going to groups has become a form of 'deep' play. We have learned to play with ourselves. Psychologists have not quite caught up with the need to study adult play.

Finally, consider the way the media have become playful. Once, advertising was content to ram home the message that Brand X was best. John B. Watson, the founder of behaviourism who went to work for J. Walter Thompson, believed that the way to sell products was to appeal to the emotions

(Watson 1925). Nowadays, many ads have adopted a deliberately playful style. Take an ad like that for one of the bacteria drinks. The woman who drinks the bacteria becomes manic, plays all kinds of pranks and finally is carted away by security men because she is just too frisky to be allowed in a supermarket. We all want to be playful, the ad suggests, so glug the bacteria! Even banks like the Abbey National use playfulness in their ads. The hard sell has become the humour sell.

In 1956, in a classic paper, Bateson anticipated such trends. He pointed out that play was a form of meta-communication. To play cops and robbers, we have to have a double dialogue. If all I say is 'hand over the money', you might imagine I really meant it. For it to be a game, I need to preface my aggressive demands with a signpost like, 'Let's play cops and robbers'. The signpost need not be so literal. Putting on a funny voice or face or a mask will do. Then, you know that what follows is not for real. Bateson's paper was well in advance of its time. Since 1956, semiotics, the theory of signs, has become very fashionable. Bateson was surprised to find that monkeys could meta-communicate and signal 'this is play', which was the title of his paper.

Yet psychologists have tended not to acknowledge fully the historical and cultural influences on play research.

The origins of play and 'the play'

In explaining the origins of play, psychologists draw analogies between human and animal behaviour, especially that of primates. Bruner et al. (1976) in their 700-page selection of writings on play devote nearly one-third of the book to animal play. The psychoanalytic tradition gets only one article by Erik Erikson. Though there are a number of short extracts from literary figures like W.H. Auden and Simone de Beauvoir, the editors entirely neglect the tradition which has looked for the origins of play and laughter in drama or 'the play'. This is a pity.

In his *Poetics*, Aristotle argued that comedy and tragedy sprang from similar religious roots. Both developed out of the improvisations that accompanied religious rites. Comedy, Aristotle suggested, began as a form of prayer. During processions in honour of the god Phales, whose emblem was a giant phallus, the 'worshippers' larked around. Aristotle believed these improvisations slowly became more formal and established the basis for the comedies that Athens was famous for. Such improvisations suggest that play was not something that only children did but that it might have important connections with very adult activities – such as ritual, prayer and drama.

Aristotle was writing about the origins of comedy rather than origins of play. This was a subject not much discussed even though Greek and Roman children clearly played and had toys. Archaeologists have found Roman toy soldiers. The Vatican Museum in Rome has a sarcophagus showing Roman boys in a piggyback fight. H.A. Harris in *Sports in Greece and Rome* (1972) shows that children in the ancient world took part in a variety of running, jumping and throwing games. In the *Odyssey*, Nausicaa tosses a ball at one of her maids and misses; the ball falls in the pond and 'they all shrieked to high heaven'. The great doctor, Galen, described how Greek children made balls out of pigs' bladders which they blew up. To improve the shape, they rubbed them with warm ashes and sang songs over them. Galen even wrote an early version of the aerobics textbook, *Exercise with the Small Ball*, in which he suggested that playing ball kept you healthy at all ages. The satirical poet Martial observed that children, and adults, used five different kinds of balls. The early Christian writer Dio Chrysostom talked of a game in which children threw the ball at one another and the one who got hit lost. Plato observed that children who dropped balls were called donkeys. The philosophical emperor Marcus Aurelius said that small children could get as obsessive about possessing balls as emperors did about possessing countries. Harris (1972) also quotes many references to children playing the game of 'hoop bowling'. They made the hoops out of the iron frames of wheels and careered along the street with them. Sextus Empricus noticed that children loved both ball games and hoop bowling. Many of the games described by Iona and Peter Opie (1969) in their catalogue of street games in Britain had parallels in Greek and Roman times, according to Harris (1972).

Ancient children played and, in a haphazard way, authors mentioned it. But no one wrote on play. Plato did not think that his philosopher-kings needed to play. The neglect of play is interesting given the evidence that children played and given also the many treatises on education. Until Rousseau's (1759) *Emile*, play did not get a bad press so much as no press at all.

This absence of early comment on play may have lulled psychologists into ignoring its historical and cultural origins. The sources Harris (1972) cites also suggest something that we would have found very odd until recently. Children and adults in ancient Greece and Rome played many of the same games. Both these points are crucial to the arguments developed by Huizinga (1949) in his classic *Homo Ludens*. In their anthology Bruner et al. (1976) give a twelve-page extract from Huizinga's book, far less space than they allow for descriptions of Balinese cockfights, let alone animal play. Huizinga was a historian and attacked the way psychologists and sociologists tackled play. All their hypotheses 'have one thing in common; they all start from the assumption that play must serve something which is not play, that it must serve some kind of biological purpose'. Huizinga complained that most of these theories 'only deal incidentally with what play is in itself and what it means for the player'. Measuring how much children played in certain situations, already a familiar form of research when Huizinga was writing, was more important than 'paying attention to its aesthetic qualities. As a rule they leave the primary quality of play untouched.'

Huizinga deployed a formidable amount of literary, historical and archaeological evidence, from Troy to the troubadours, from Chinese history to Canaan. He used this to develop a surprising argument. Play was not an activity that developed as civilisation became more sophisticated; rather, play was at the heart of the start of civilisation. Since psychologists usually assume that we can explain play by pinpointing the real activities it prepares the child for, it is worth quoting Huizinga at some length. He said:

> The spirit of playful competition is, as a social impulse, older than culture itself and pervades all life like a veritable ferment. Ritual grew up in sacred play; poetry was born in play and nourished on play; music and dancing were pure play. Wisdom and philosophy found expression in words and form derived from religious contests. The rules of warfare, the conventions of noble living were built up on play patterns. We have to conclude, therefore, that civilisation is in its earliest phases played. It does not come from play like a babe detaching itself from the womb; it arises in, and as, play and never leaves it.
>
> (Huizinga 1949: 21)

Huizinga certainly does not consider animal evidence and, at time, readers may be irritated by flights of near-pedantry. Allusions to Norse myths, Sanskrit etymology, bragging contests and Icelandic riddling feats tumble out as does much else that empirical psychology doesn't usually consider. But the very weight of this evidence makes one wonder why nearly all psychological work on play assumes it has a biological explanation. Couldn't play be either cultural or, even, truly for its own sake?

Cultural and historical attitudes to play certainly vary though the evidence both of classical texts and of medieval pictures suggest that play is as old as humankind. In his account of the sports of Londoners in the thirteenth century, William Fitzstephens noted that they went into the fields on Sunday afternoons in Lent to have mock fights. The older men used real weapons for unreal fights while 'the younger sort with pikes from which the iron heads had been taken off and they get up sham fights'. In medieval art, as in the Flemish *Hours of The Virgin* (c. 1290), children are shown playing to one side. It is not till the sixteenth century that games became the focus of any pictures, such as a few of Bruegel's. Some artists were well aware of the power of play and comedy – Shakespeare makes much of it both in *Hamlet* with the players and in *King Lear* with the Fool, who teaches that 'tis folly to be wise' – but nobody considered them sufficiently significant processes to analyse.

Recent work in communications theory has shown how certain subjects are put on the agenda by powerful groups while other subjects are ignored. It is interesting that, as the Renaissance developed, children's play and laughter never surfaced as topics. Consider, to get this in perspective, what writers did write about. Erasmus (1473) in *In Praise of Folly* made fun of human unreason. Why could we never be reasonable? Over a century later, Burton's (1609) *Melancholia* gave a long account of everything that made people miserable and why. Frances Yates (1982) in *The Art of Memory* has shown how men like Giordano Bruno spent years perfecting their memory skills and analysing how they did it. Between Erasmus' writing in 1473 and Rousseau writing *Emile* in 1759, John Locke, Bishop Berkeley, Leibniz, Spinoza, Thomas Hobbes and David Hume all produced significant treatises on how the mind developed and functioned. Hobbes (1652) briefly mentions laughter as 'sudden glory' which is 'those grimaces' we flash when we see someone in worse shape than ourselves. We laugh 'at the imperfections of others'. In the country of the blind, they guffaw at the man who has also lost his leg. The absence of comment on play is striking. Some writers like Philippe Ariès (1962), who wrote *Centuries of Childhood*, would not be surprised as he claimed that medieval parents did not treat children as special creatures to be petted and loved. Psychologically, they dared not do so because too many children died. Instead, children were treated as miniature adults.

In *Forgotten Children*, Linda Pollock (1984) argued againt Ariès. She revealed that many parents did care for their children because their letters and, sometimes, memories of a dead child are full of feeling. Pollock found that play did not often surface in the texts and, when it did, it was disapproved of. Cotton Mather (1663–1728), for example, wrote: 'I am not fond of proposing play to them [children] as a Reward of any diligent application to learn what is good lest they should think Diversion to be a better and noble Thing than Diligence' (quoted in Pollock 1984: 236). Mather did give his children paints but thought his offspring should have their minds raised 'above the Sillier Diversions of Childhood'. Another diarist, Henry Slingsby (1601–58), reflects this Puritan attitude too. When his 4-year-old son seemed dull, he said: 'I think ye cause to be his too much minding Play' (Pollock 1984: 237).

As she was interested in diaries rather than in manuals of how to educate children, Pollock did not go into much detail about John Locke's advice. Locke (1692) wrote a short treatise on education, *Some Arguments Concerning Education*, which was edited from his letters to Edward Clarke about the education of his children. Clarke was married to a kinswoman of Locke's. Locke certainly urges Clarke in respect of his son to 'Incourage his Curiosity' (letter 822) and even advocates using a game in which almonds and raisins are placed on letters of the alphabet to teach the child his letters. But Locke was no advocate of play. In letter 829, he stated:

And I doubt not but one great reason why many children abandon themselves wholly to silly play, and spend all their time trifling, is because they have found their curiosity baulked and their enquiries neglected.

Locke recommended Clarke to be honest with his children and to answer all their questions as he would those of adults. Compare the child to a traveller who has just landed in Japan! Wouldn't he be full of endless questions? Locke conceded that the child should be trained to appreciate leisure but that meant proper instruction in dancing and fencing and not in music or writing verse. Society was too full of people who couldn't rhyme and couldn't perform. There was no need to encourage such grating graces. The whole tone of the advice is lofty. Locke gave a list of books the child should read and I would guess that, a century later the father of J.S. Mill read Locke because he fed his son many of those books. Concentrating on educating the child would bring its own rewards, Locke suggested, because 'there is not much pleasure to have a son prattle agreeably as to reason well' (letter 845).

Throughout the seventeenth century, play was not seen either as valuable or as a topic for debate except for the occasional Puritan blast against sinful indiscipline. This high-minded attitude didn't always affect adults: witness Andrew Marvell's very playful *To a Coy Mistress*, as clever a piece of love play as you could wish for, or a more obscure book, *Gratiae Ludentes* (published in 1638). This had parlour games such as: a gentleman asks a lady which part of the body she would cover first if he came into a room while she was naked. 'Your eyes, sir', was the answer. The pleasures of play were wicked, a tradition we continue today for the playboy, and his magazine *Playboy* is naughty – or worse.

The educational and cognitive uses of play

The Romantic movement of the eighteenth century changed these attitudes, as Pollock (1984) noted. The French philosopher, Rousseau, was perhaps the first thinker to argue the importance of play. In *Emile* he described the ideal education for a young man. Emile should be allowed to roam freely, to explore woods and fields. Nature would fire his imagination and inspire his love of freedom. 'Let Emile run about barefoot all year round, upstairs, downstairs, and in the garden,' Rousseau recommended, 'Let him learn to perform every exercise which encourages ability of the body . . . children will always do anything that keeps them moving freely.'

Rousseau criticised those who would 'rob these little innocents of the joys that pass so quickly', blamed those who tried to force children to read and went on:

We must never forget all this should be play, the easy and voluntary control of movement which nature demands of them, the art of varying their games to make them pleasanter without the least bit of constraint. To a child of 10 or 12, work or play are all one . . .

provided, Rousseau added, that both are carried out 'with the charm of freedom'.

The attitudes are partially, but only partially, reflected in the texts analysed by Pollock. Mrs Reynolds (1770–1803), for example, took her children to the seaside where they loved standing on rocks and collecting shells. Mrs Macready (1793–1873) recorded running 'into the garden to enjoy a romping play with my dear children' (Pollock 1984: 238). The new attitude saw play as liberating the potential of children. Rousseau inspired educators like Johann Pestalozzi (1746–1827), Froebel and Montessori and has been much discussed. Less attention has been paid to the ideas of the German philosopher Schiller. Like Rousseau, Schiller (1759–1805) was a child of the Enlightenment. He developed an aesthetic theory from the work of Kant. Rousseau lamented the paradox that, though man is everywhere born free, everywhere he is in chains and he believed this was due to the 'social contract'. Schiller saw a way of turning those chains into hoops of pleasure.

Reality was the problem, Schiller (1845) believed. It tied men down so that 'man fashions himself only as a fragment'. To become whole, man had to break the physical and moral constraints of reality.

This could be done by taking a different attitude to things. Through play, Schiller said, 'reality loses its seriousness'. This could only happen once there was enough economic progress for human beings not to have to slave to feed, clothe and house themselves. But when there was enough general wealth for that to happen, play could make us whole and unserious. The aesthetic impulse – Schiller saw play as being closely linked to beauty – could transform our lives. It would make it possible to harmonise two opposing impulses – that of reason and that of sensuousness. Play and imagination could also conquer the tyranny of time, especially the need to use our time to work for others.

In *Eros and Civilisation* (1959) Herbert Marcuse argued that Schiller had offered a truly revolutionary theory of play and suggested that adult play might have its uses. Marcuse highlighted three key points. First, 'the transformation of toil (labour) into play and of repressive productivity into display'. Second, with sufficient wealth to abolish want, play could be used to reconcile the warring impulses of reason and pleasure. There would be no reason not to indulge in more pleasure. Finally, play would allow 'the conquest of time in so far as the time is destructive of lasting gratification'.

Schiller was important, Marcuse argued, because he had a vision of a society in which playing changed adults. Marcuse claimed in *Eros and Civilisation* that capitalism had to create 'surplus repression' in order to prevent the triumph of Eros or the life-enhancing, pleasure principle. Schiller offered an interesting compromise. Play did not lead to chaos and self-indulgence. It was a means for human beings to express their desire for beauty, for enjoyment, for pleasure and through 'having' those experiences, to become more whole. Marcuse was right to claim that Schiller had been unjustly neglected. Certainly, psychologists have only now started to tackle the dilemmas of adult play and, usually, when Schiller is quoted at all, it is assumed he was writing about child's play.

Both Rousseau and Schiller established their place in the history of ideas. But when their ideas, especially Rousseau's, were developed by the educators Pestalozzi, Froebel and Montessori, they could not help but be affected by Victorian attitudes. They turned play into a purposive activity. Pestalozzi even went so far as to exclude play altogether from the child's education (quoted in Silber 1954):

> The important thing in good upbringing is that a child should be well prepared for his own circle; he must learn to know and to do the things that will bring him bread to still his hunger and peace to content his heart.

Silber (1954: 44), in her biography of Pestalozzi comments: 'Even the children are not idle for one moment; they know no play, they have no leisure for work – work is essential to country folk.'

For all Rousseau's success, his influence on the education of liberal intellectuals was small. In his *Autobiography* (1924), J.S. Mill lists the formidable milestones of his education which his father, a historian, closely supervised. Before he was 12, Mill had been introduced to Shakespeare, Hume, Gibbon, Plato and most of the classics. Father and son often went walking but during these expeditions, they admired Nature and discussed Meaning. Mill's father did not want him distracted. Mill wrote:

> It was not that play or time for it was refused to me. Though no holidays were allowed lest the habit of work be broken and a taste for idleness acquired, I had ample leisure time to amuse myself but, as I had no boy companions and the animal need of physical activity was satisfied by walking, my amusements which were mostly solitary were in general of a quiet, if not bookish, turn.

> (Mill 1924)

None of this stunted the philosopher socially though it left him 'inexpert at anything requiring manual dexterity'. He was ill at ease with 'the practical details which, as they are the chief interest of life to the majority of men, are also the things in which whatever mental capacity they have chiefly shows itself'. Mill may have been the classic swot but not being allowed to play does not seem to have ruined his life. Contemporaries speak of him as a pleasant man. He married, did not behave in a socially embarrassing manner and was even quite imaginative. Mill's *Autobiography* highlights Rousseau's failure to convert even the intellectual classes to his romantic view of the need to play.

Less surprisingly, Rousseau failed to convince Victorian capitalists. 1 want to suggest that it is no accident that it was towards the late Victorian period – 1865 on – that play began to be of scientific interest. First, that reflects a growing concern for children; second, as Victorian industry developed it was necessary for it to create a division of work (the normal activity) versus leisure or free time (the abnormal activity). One of the great British scandals of the early nineteenth century was the abuse of children. While Britain was mainly an agricultural country, children certainly worked but they worked in the open at least. With the growth of factories and mines, children became cheap labour.

In the mines, children could burrow where no one else could and were, therefore, very useful. In his *English Social History*, G.M. Trevelyan (1942) noted that the children were often victims both of tyrannical employers and bad parents. By 1833, there was enough concern for children for Parliament to pass a Factory Act. This limited the amount of time a day children could work in factories. Nine years later, Lord Shaftesbury forced through his Mines Act which outlawed children under 10 working underground. This was seen as a great step forward. In 1847, The Hours Bill stopped children in textile factories working more than ten hours a day. Despite these reforms, many children were still oppressed. In his *The Water Babies* Charles Kingsley (1863) showed how a young sweep, Tom, was bullied and exploited by his master. The outcry led to an Act of 1864 which was meant to stop children being used as chimney sweeps but, eleven years later, Shaftesbury pointed out that this 'brutal iniquity' still existed and 'in many parts of England and Ireland it still prevails with the full knowledge of consent of thousands of all classes'. Shaftesbury finally managed to get an effective law through Parliament to stop that. Committed as he was to view that history was progress, Trevelyan noted that:

> This enlarged sympathy with children was one of the chief contributions made by the Victorian English to real civilisation. But such feelings were not universal as the long delay over the chimney sweep scandal testified. Neglect and ill usage of children died hard. The streets of the slums were still the only playground for the majority of city children, few of

whom had schools till 1870, or playgrounds and none of whom had Play Centres till the turn of the Century.

(Trevelyan 1942)

Rousseau had argued that children ought to play as a right. The Victorians tended to see it differently. If people had free time, they should use it to improve themselves. More surprisingly, the feeling that play had to have practical uses surfaced also in the work of 'radical' educational theorists. Two of Rousseau's most important heirs were Friedrich Froebel (1782–1852) and Maria Montessori (1870–1952). In their different ways, they show how unfree play remained.

Froebel and Montessori both had dramatic lives. Froebel was born in Thuringia in Germany in 1782. His mother died when he was small and he had an unkind stepmother. His unhappy childhood made him determined to find ways in which to make children happy so he became a teacher. Soon he became disillusioned with ordinary teaching methods, which drilled information into the child. Froebel decided to set up a *kindergarten* where children could 'blossom' as flowers did. *Kindergarten* means a garden of children. Children were to be allowed to play and were to be encouraged by interested adults rather than be fact-filled and fact-drilled.

This apparently gentle system of education was perceived as a political threat. Froebel opened his first kindergarten in 1837. Thirteen years later, he was forced to close all his schools in Germany because the authorities accused him of being an atheist and a socialist. His schools spread throughout Europe nevertheless.

Dickens was impressed by Froebel's schools. Very clearly, Froebel was fighting to allow children more freedom than usual. But, for him, play was still educational and children were not that free in the kindergarten, as Montessori noted. In *The Advanced Method* she queried how much freedom Froebel really allowed, writing:

> Some of Froebel's games are based upon similar beliefs. A wooden brick is given to a child with the words: 'This is a horse'. Bricks are then arranged in a certain order, and he is told: 'This is the stable; now let us put the horse into the stable.' Then the bricks are differently arranged: 'This is a tower, this the village church, etc.' In such exercises the objects (bricks) lend themselves to illusion less readily than a stick used as a horse, which the child can at least bestride and beat, moving along the while. The building of towers and churches with horses brings the mental confusion of the child to its culmination. Moreover, in this case it is not the child who 'imagines spontaneously' and works with his brains, for at the moment he is required to see that which the teacher suggests. And

it is impossible to know whether the child really thinks that the stable has become a church, or whether his attention has wandered elsewhere. He would, of course, like to move, but he cannot, because he is obliged to contemplate the kind of cinematograph of which the teacher speaks in the series of images she suggests, though they exist only in the shape of pieces of wood all of the same size.

(Montessori 1910: 258)

For Montessori, control was the vital issue. Montessori was born in 1870 in Chiaravalle in Italy. She became Italy's first qualified woman doctor in 1896 and turned her attention to treating mentally handicapped children. She came to believe that children were frustrated if teachers tried to get them to read and write. The child had to develop at his or her own pace through freely chosen activities. Montessori developed a theory of child development which claimed that children went through periods when they were especially sensitive to particular tasks. Between 1 and 2 years, for example, the child was sensitive to small details. Montessori noticed that such infants often perceived tiny insects which no adults bothered to spot. Other 'periods' saw the child be specially sensitive to order, walking, grasping and language. No one seems to have commented on the similarities between some of Montessori's ideas and those developed later by Piaget and Chomsky. Piaget, who must have been aware of the details of her work, never mentions her in any of his major books.

Nowadays we imagine that Montessori favoured free play and the imagination. Montessori schools are contrasted favourably with others. At these schools, children learn to concentrate and create. Montessori certainly had an almost revolutionary faith in children and turned the teacher into an observer who guided children to choose for themselves. It would be wrong, however, to believe that she valued play as a creative force in itself. She argued that toys and puzzles should be used to train children to succeed at certain skills. Much of her advanced textbook is devoted to strategies to get children to write and read better, and to master mathematics. This is not to belittle her achievement but, to the extent that Montessori was interested in play, she wanted to apply it. Nothing illustrates better how far she had moved from Rousseau, perhaps, than her distrust of the imagination. Fantasies and fairy-tales were enemies. Montessori wrote:

We, however, suppose that we are developing the imagination of children by making them accept fantastic things as realities. Thus, for instance, in Latin countries, Christmas is personified by an ugly woman, the *Befana*, who comes through the walls and down the chimneys, bringing toys for the good children, and leaving only lumps of coal for the naughty ones. In Anglo-Saxon countries, on the other hand, Christmas is an old man covered with snow who carries a huge basket containing toys for children, and who really enters their houses by night. But how can the *imagination* of children be developed by what is, on the contrary, the fruit of our imagination? It is we who imagine, not they; they *believe*, they do not imagine. Credulity is, indeed a characteristic of immature minds which lack experience and knowledge of realities.

(Montessori 1910: 267)

A close reading of Montessori shows how practical her approach was. Where Rousseau rhapsodised play, she wanted to harness some – but only some – of its aspects to make children better and more efficient. Montessori was particularly keen that children should be taught to be moral; playing together, under the eagle eye of teacher, would achieve that useful end. Her views and those of Froebel reflect the paradoxical attitudes of Victorians to play. On the one hand, children ought to be loved and cared for in a civilised society; on the other hand, any free time was a concession and ought to be used to improve oneself. Adult workers who now got an annual holiday should certainly not fritter that away having fun.

Early research into play reflected these attitudes. Herbert Spencer (1860) argued that play was just a way of working off excess energy. Spencer also suggested that children learned how to master various skills in play. For him, play was a phase. It was not much more than that for Darwin (1872) who in *The Expression of the Emotions in Animals and Men* pioneered the connections between human and animal behaviour. Darwin was interested in the smiles and antics of young babies and apes. He collected anecdotes from all over the world and this stimulated interest in animal play. Perhaps his most important follower was Karl Groos.

Groos' two books, *The Play of Animals* (1896) and *The Play of Man* (1901), seem to be the first to be entirely devoted to the subject. Groos saw play as functional. All creatures used play 'to pre-exercise their skills'. Groos suggested that animals need the practice of playing to sharpen many of their instinctive behaviours. Youthful romping, and the experience it would bring them, meant that they did not have to have too rigidly formed instincts. They could adapt better. 'Animals would certainly make no progress intellectually if they were blindly left in the swaddling clothes of inherited impulse', Groos noted. Sex and fighting were skills learned through play. In a frank chapter on love play, Groos claimed that birds and humans used teasing and cooing to boost desire. Through play we master the teasing arts. Did Groos foresee the use of the word *striptease*? Perhaps.

Both Darwin and Groos helped establish the tradition of studying animal play for itself and for the light it can shed on human play. Much loving observational research has confirmed that apes use play to master manual skills and, at times, also to learn social 'arts' such as who to threaten and who to grovel to. Though, in general, this book bypasses animal play, it is worth noting that Burghardt (1984) suggested that animal play arose out of boredom and bits of 'deteriorated behaviour' in mammals with surplus energy.

Groos certainly encouraged the notion that psychology needed to dig out the serious purpose of play. Despite his books and despite some interesting observations of Darwin such as that a child will cry if surprised by a stranger, but laugh if surprised by a parent, development psychologists were less interested in play than one might suppose. Preyer (1909), for example, looked far more at the growth of intelligence. In *The Human Mind*, the English psychologist, James Sully (1892) quotes many instances of laughter but has only a footnote devoted to play. Sully accepts Spencer's view that play sheds excess energy. It may indirectly 'contribute to health, vigour, and efficiency through its refreshing or recreative effect; but this must be seen as accidental' (Sully 1892: 135).

It was Karl Groos who had the most interesting thesis about play. Usually, his ideas have been presented in an oversimplified way. Groos certainly believed that in play animals and humans pre-exercised their skills but his view of human play was more subtle. He emphasised the role of consciousness. Take the way the child grasps, Groos argued:

> The child at first waves his hands aimlessly, and when his fingers chance to strike a suitable object they clutch at it instinctively. From a purely biological point of view this is practice of an instinct and play has already begun. Psychologically, on the contrary, it is safer to defer calling the movements playful until through repetition, they acquire the character of conscious processes accompanied by attention and enjoyment.
>
> (Groos 1896)

Not only did the child delight in its movements but also there is 'the satisfaction of being oneself the originator, the joy-bringing sense of being a cause'. When they fantasised, children were conscious of their deceptions, of roaring loudly to pretend to be a lion. Groos stressed the difference between biological and psychological aspects of play. Being conscious, even self-conscious, was a mark of human play. This view did not make him too popular with the behaviourists. However, even opponents of behaviourism, like William MacDougall, attacked Groos.

MacDougall (1919) suggested that play was more than an instinct. It had many motives, he argued in *An Introduction to Social Psychology*. He said that laughter is important because it lets human beings cope with minor crises and allows us to express sympathy with each other. Play, however, 'is activity for its own sake or, more probably, it is purposeless activity striving towards no goal'. Curiously, MacDougall also argued that motives of play included 'the desire of increased skill, the pleasure of make believe, the pleasure in being a cause . . . [and] the desire to get the better of others, to emulate, to excel' (MacDougall 1919: 96).

But though many psychologists like John B. Watson argued that it was important to establish norms for the development of children, play was not seen as a central topic of study. Piaget did not devote much attention to it till 1950; the behaviourists ignored it rather; and Arnold Gesell, at Yale in the late 1920s, hardly made it a focus for his developmental studies. Developmental psychology tended to pursue the question of how children's intelligence developed, a subject much closer to Piaget's heart. In his review of theoretical approaches, Sutton-Smith (1984) chided the researchers of 1880 to 1920 for being too interested in how to control the child. 'Control the child's muscles and you could control his mind and ethics', he noted (p. 2). Where play was studied, such prejudices influenced the research.

The social value of play

The mental hygiene movement had similar prejudices. It wanted to make use of play to mould children into good citizens. Between 1890 and 1920, $100 million was spent on American playgrounds. This wasn't Yankee idealism but social engineering. In *Education through Play* – the message is in the title – Curtis (1921) claimed play was the best medicine. First, Curtis skirmished against Puritan critics. 'It is not play but the idleness of the street that is morally dangerous', he said. He added:

> It is then that the children watch the drunken people, listen to the leader of the gang, hear the shady story, smoke cigarettes and acquire those vicious habits, knowledge and vocabulary which are characteristic. When they are thus driven from the street to play on upon the side-walk or doorstep, the only common games which they pursue are tops, marbles, kackstone, war, craps and pitching pennies . . . The politeness and ethics of a game played on the street are on a lower plane than those of the same game played elsewhere . . . play has probably reached the lowest ebb in the history of the world.
>
> (Curtis 1921)

But play could be reformed and, if that were done properly, it could produce excellent social consequences. By the 1930s, playgrounds were quite common. The next stage was to argue for special playgroups for specially difficult children, the ones who could not be persuaded into conformity just through having swings and see-saws.

The adventure playground has been an interesting extension of the playground. The first adventure playground was set up in Copenhagen in 1943; it offered facilities for 900 children. In introducing the first year's work, its director, John Bertelson (1943), said: 'There can be no doubt that in the case of so called difficult children, free play presents a solution to their problem.' In their large space, the children accomplished much. 'The children's productivity is really enormous', said Bertelson. He went on to assure his readers that play did have a purpose for they were asked to 'notice this year how much more familiar they have become with the various materials and able to express themselves'.

The success of the Copenhagen venture led to international imitations and the setting up of an International Playground Association. Its publications stress the therapeutic value of freedom and it defines an adventure playground 'as a place where children are free to do many things that they cannot do elsewhere in our crowded urban society'. In Britain, there were quibbles about whether adventure playgrounds might not lead to unruly behaviour which is ironic since their rationale is, of course, to contain any such unruliness. Joe Benjamin, a leading authority on playgrounds, noted such a complaint about discipline in letters in 1955 to the *Grimsby Evening Telegraph*. Benjamin riposted: 'Discipline as a problem hardly exists.' By 1970, the first adventure playground for disabled children was set up.

Play centres, playgrounds and adventure playgrounds were all spaces in which the child could be free within certain limits. That freedom, however, wasn't given to children only to enjoy themselves but to stop them being nuisances. They could be noisy, raucous and violent (up to a point) in the fantasy space of the playground if that stopped them being violent in real life. It's hard to find firm empirical evidence of the therapeutic value of going to playgrounds. But that has not stopped the British government being committed to play. Sure Start programmes, into which Tony Blair's government has poured massive resources, are supposed to help 'poor' children and include a large element of play.

And play is becoming more serious.
We have diplomas in play – and advanced diplomas in play.
Hallelujah – play has become an (ology).

The emotional value of play

The first child Sigmund Freud analysed was Little Hans. Little Hans turned out to be frightened of horses because he was frightened his father might cut off his willy. At least that was Sigmund's view. I might believe it more if the original analyst had ever invited the boy to play on his couch. Freud relied instead on Hans' father as a go-between to relay news of Hans' dreams and fears.

Twenty years later, by the mid-1920s, it would have been considered very odd not to see Hans and make the child play in the clinic. Psychoanalysts like Susan Isaacs and Melanie Klein were suggesting that play offered a powerful technique for individual therapy. Never mind the American dream of using play to turn ghetto children into proper Yankees, play could be used to cure infants of Oedipus and other complexes.

Susan Isaacs was one of an impressive number of psychoanalysts – nearly all of them women – who developed the use of play as a therapeutic technique. Anna Freud worked along similar lines at the Hampstead Clinic. Melanie Klein devised a slightly different approach. In their book, *Understanding Children's Play*, Hartley et al. (1952) make their commitment to the therapeutic value of play clear. Sections have headings like 'The Benefits of Water Play' – and these include 'the expression of aggressive impulses' and 'instrument for growth'. Splish splash your way to psychological health!

The only male psychoanalyst to have devoted such attention to play therapy is Erik Erikson who, in *Childhood and Society* (1981), gives an affectionate and wry account of what it must feel like to a child who comes to an adult who looks like a doctor and, then, asks you to play with all manner of toys. It is not my purpose here to analyse the uses and limits of play therapy but, rather, to note that it again involves seeking deeper, hidden meanings. Play is more than play. In the consulting room or out in the specially structured playground, it can improve the child. Good play as developed by pundits with the play-ology will help create the perfect child.

At this point, it might be nice to play a joke.

Irwin and Barbara Sarason in their *Abnormal Psychology* (1983) reprint a cartoon of a therapist talking to a baby on the couch. He says: 'So, tell me, when did you first notice you were having trouble coping with life's little ups and downs?'

The Sarasons don't leave the joke to make its point. They add that it shows 'traditional psychodynamic therapy is not appropriate for young children'. In fact, the cartoon obviously pokes fun at the pretensions of therapy. The Sarasons take it differently though, as a comment on the need to use play to help the child express what he or she is too young to express in words. They don't dare leave the joke as it is.

Given such a background, it is not surprising that, since the 1950s, research into play has developed mainly along three lines. First, what kind of manual and cognitive skills do children develop in play? This leads eventually to the thesis put forward by Jerome Singer (1973) that children who show good 'fantasy skills' are cleverer and more imaginative. Second, what social skills does playing teach? Throughout North America and Europe, in kindergartens attached to university campuses and towns, researchers are tackling aspects of that question. There is such a kindergarten at Stanford and Flavell (2004) explained to me how much fun it was to do research there. Third, how can therapists use play to understand the deep conflicts in the child and to heal them? There is nothing wrong in these serious approaches but they do seem to miss some crucial elements in play. The Puritans may have thought they lost the battle to stop children playing but they did succeed in leaving the feeling that play ought to justify itself as a means to more profound ends. Never play for its own sake.

Ironically, psychologists may now feel more than justified in the notion that children should never just play for its own sake. The growing interest in the child's theory of mind has made children's ability to pretend and deceive a central area of research. It is increasingly likely that through play children start to construct a theory of other minds. Play is becoming part of metaphysics.

In the rest of this book, I examine a number of ways in which psychologists and therapists have studied play and wonder why far less attention has been paid to some interesting aspects of play. First, play is not only an individual activity, but also a cultural one. It has the power to turn the world upside-down or topsy-turvy. Nietzsche in *Thus Spake Zarathustra* (1883–92) imagines all kinds of games that his nihilistic superstar uses to subvert the ordinary order of things. Huizinga (1949) lovingly gives instance after instance of how societies used play and parody, fun and games, to overturn conventions such as when peasants were king for a day. Le Roy Ladurie (1981) in his *Carnival in Romans* provides a fascinating account of the way a Renaissance town behaved during Carnival where all the rules (or nearly all the rules) might be broken. Psychological texts on play hardly ever mention such points or look for their possible modern equivalents. Is the urban riot or the political demonstration where people chant and bands play and activists give out badges (or toys) a kind of modern, perhaps macabre, carnival? Why rule out such questions from psychological debate?

The second omission in play research is that of adult play. I have suggested that our definition of work versus play is a Victorian one. The Victorians created most of our modern sports but, apart from such games, adults did not play. Psychology has largely failed to study adult play. This no longer makes sense in a world where leisure is big business and takes up much time. In a later chapter, I suggest that adults nowadays try to play more than ever before though it is still hard for most of us to throw ourselves into it. Researchers like Lawick Goodall have known for years that adult primates play and have tried to incorporate this into their theories. Human psychologists have been much less willing to fit adult play into theories of play because it calls into question their overarching assumption – that play exists to prepare us for adult life. Why then do adults go on playing? And why are adults, apparently, playing more than ever before?

In his *Decline and Fall of the Roman Empire* (1776–88), Gibbon noted that, as the Empire crumbled, and the barbarians threatened at the gates, there was a frenetic increase in all kinds of games. It could be argued that, under the shadow of the Bomb, still not dispelled after the collapse of the Soviet Union, we too are playing more in order not to face reality. However, I think the increase in adult play is not negative and marks, instead, a step in coping better with the stresses of industrial, post-industrial, post-Freudian life. The psychological research so far reflects this too little, partly because we have not yet freed ourselves from the idea that there must be a serious explanation for every kind of play. Before returning to this theme, one must ponder some fascinating, if sometimes ponderous, studies of play from birth on.

3 Playing with objects

Imagine a child of 15 months playing. Ben can now walk quite steadily. He doesn't speak very much as yet but he points to objects. Anything that moves he calls a 'ka'. It is four o'clock on Monday afternoon. His mother is preparing dinner in the kitchen because she has some guests. Ben's older sister, Katie, who is 3 years old, is watching *Teletubbies* on television and, occasionally, doodling a drawing.

Ben's playpen, which he is a bit old for, stands in one corner of the room. Ben tries to get Katie's attention, first, by calling her name and, then, when that fails, by taking one of his dolls from the side of the playpen and offering it to her. When Katie brushes him off informing him she is busy watching television, Ben first drops the doll on to her lap, laughs, picks it up and places it in one of Katie's carts. The cart has a long string attached so Ben pulls it away. Katie complains that Baby is taking her things but is more interested in Big Bird. Ben pulls the cart across the living room to the kitchen. His mother is irritated and tells him not to bring toys in there but she can't help smiling when he says 'doll hungry'.

His mother gives him a piece of carrot which Ben puts in his mouth. 'I thought the doll was hungry', chides his mother. She gives him another piece of carrot which Ben duly feeds to the doll. 'Did she like it?' mother asks. 'Yes', smiles Ben. By now, Ben's mother has had enough of being the ideal, play-stimulating parent and tells Ben to go and play with Katie.

This slice of play in the home resembles some of my observations of laughter in the home and classroom. But this kind of naturalistic observation is rare. Most research isolates specific aspects of play. This is paradoxical. Piaget inspired most of the work covered in this chapter. In *Play, Dreams and Imitation in Childhood* Piaget (1952) reported on how his children played at home and with their parents. He often noted how their play reflected not just their cognitive skills but also their daily lives and problems. Far more than in most of his work, Piaget tried to link emotion and intellect. Piaget claimed that a child's toys and the use to which they were put experienced 'the repercussions' of everything that had happened that day to the child. This rounded view seems to have been rather ignored.

More than most of their colleagues, psychologists who study play have gone out of the lab and into homes. They often undo this naturalism, however, by trying to adapt the home to their scientific needs, importing their own toys and instruments – and that has not changed much since the late 1970s. That criticism needs to be tempered in the light of work by Judy Dunn at the Institute of Psychiatry in London (Dunn and Youngblade 2003) and by John Flavell and his team. Very neatly, Flavell (1992a and b) has examined how well young children can tell the difference between reality and appearance. In an interview, Flavell told me he had learned that there was a big difference in that ability between the ages of 3 and 4 (Cohen 2004).

As I shall show later, Flavell's work fits in nicely with the growing interest in young children's ability to understand deception – and to perpetuate it, issues that are at the heart of the child's theory of mind.

In the early 1980s Belsky and Most (1981) included dolls, blocks, cars and the Fisher-Price® Snow Queen in their lot of 'typical' toys. But what about children who play best with cuddly toys or Cabbage Patch dolls? McCune-Nicolich had her own favourite typical toys and pointed out that one psychologist often takes the mother aside so that the child's 'pure' play could be watched. But when is play so 'pure' mothers have nothing to do with it? Almost no studies include brothers, sisters, fathers. Fein (1975) claimed: 'It is unlikely that parents play pretend games with their young children or model such games.' Fein provides no evidence of this very dogmatic statement. Yet there is even evidence in as improbable a source as Piaget. Piaget hardly ever wrote much about how he interacted with his children yet he offers one observation in which he played the fool on the hunting horn, trumpeted 'Taratara' and then found one of his children imitating him. Piaget offers a number of other instances where he, or his wife, got children to imitate them, sometimes deliberately and sometimes not. These included when Piaget stuck his tongue out at J (Observation 17) and when L blew through his nose at his cousin T. Furthermore Valentine (1942) detailed some of his games with his children while Bruner (1975) explicitly claimed that parents showed children how to play peekaboo. Why not other games?

My own research on laughter revealed many occasions when parents initiated games and, at times, intervened in ongoing games to make them more complex. These interventions included parents taking various parts, even Batman and/or Superman if in a good mood! Dunn and Kendrick (1982) found similar occasions.

Much research on playing with things focused on the child's manipulative and cognitive skills. We have been able to plot the way the infant develops from being just able to mouth objects to being able, by 30 months, to wash a doll with a block (which is a pretend mop) while cooing 'you're clean now' – and then putting the clean doll to bed in a bucket with a lullaby. This is progress. There has also been work on the relation of games to language.

In the first edition of this book, I was very critical of the way in which research on how children play with objects had been so central. There seemed to me to have been little progress over the years since workers as historic as Gesell and Piaget had laid down what was accepted as the basic evolution in the way children play with objects. I want to ask why so much work still does focus on the child's relation to objects as if that could be isolated from the social situation in which the child plays; in general, this strand of approach does not seem to go far beyond insights that Piaget, Valentine and Gesell developed years ago. Children now play with different toys but, and one can hardly be astonished, play itself has not changed that much.

Gesell (1929) was perhaps the first to develop a list of stages of play. He brought children to his centre at Yale where they were 'taken to a room with a few toys standardised in kind and arrangement'. Mothers were not allowed in. The examiner let the child play with this fixed set of toys for 15 minutes of 'convenient unobtrusive examination'. The word *convenient* is telling. These convenient examinations allowed Gesell to set out a developmental sequence, the first of many.

At 15 months, the infant walked all the time, picked up objects and threw them and put one object after another 'in and out of receptacles'. Three months later, the child was less aimless. There were now 'very rapid shifts of attention especially expressed by gross motor shifts. Moves actively from place to place and "gets into" everything'. The typical child of this age pulled toys, was carrying dolls or teddy bears and imitating many adult actions, including reading newspapers and sweeping and dusting!

At 24 months, the child could concentrate more effectively. The toddler did not shift attention so quickly. 'There was interest in dawdling and manipulating play material to feel, pat and pound.' The child also liked using dolls and teddy bears to create 'domestic mimicry', stringing beads and dropping beads through holes in the tops of boxes. Having dumped them in, Gesell noted, the child nearly always proceeded to dump them out and repeat the process. At 24 months, there was much playing with blocks and the wagon, mainly using the wagon to transport the blocks.

Gesell (1929) was aware of how playing developed as a skill. The 2 year old 'does not imitate things which he remembers but only those events which are present to his senses'. The 3 year old could combine toys into longer sequences, play a little with other children and, even, put away his toys with some supervision. By the age of 4, the child could make constructive use both of objects and of play materials like plasticine. He could use objects in dramatic play and co-operate with two or three other children. There was far more activity and interest in dressing up. By the age of 5, the child liked cutting things out, pasting them up and working in a nursery class way on a specific project. Putting toys away was now a matter of routine. Gesell worked out typical social behaviour for different ages.

Many of Gesell's observations were interesting. He warned that not all children play the same way:

> To mention just a few examples, there is the child who scatters his energies, having first one toy and then another; the child who concentrates his attention on what first comes to his notice; the child who works apparently just to please the adult; the child who demands the examiner's attentions even though he has been warned she is busy; and the child who taps gently on the hammer toy, looking up repeatedly to see if he is disturbing the observation.

How children progressed from stage to stage Gesell never resolved. Piaget approached the development of play as an extension, a late, often interesting extension, of his theory of intellectual development. Piaget argued that intelligence developed through four definite stages. In the baby, it very much depended on motor movements. As the baby starts to move itself, and things, around the world, it acquires both co-ordination and schemas. A schema is, essentially, a design or an idea. For a 9-month-old infant, grasping a bottle and putting it to its mouth is a schema. Piaget claimed that the first stage of development could be called the 'sensori-motor' period. Roughly, it went from birth to 18 months. It was towards the middle of this period that play emerged out of imitation.

In *Play, Dreams and Imitation in Childhood*, Piaget (1952) argued that imitation starts through attention to reflex. By 2 months, the baby is capable of sporadic imitation. Piaget noted that when T was 2 months and 11 days, he made the sounds *la* and *le*. Then, Piaget repeated them. Seven times out of nine, T repeated *la* and *le* after Piaget had done so. Imitation of movements occurred even earlier in J. At 1 month and 27 days, she watched Piaget while he moved his head from right to left and, immediately, J reproduced this movement three times in succession. After a pause, Piaget did it again and J imitated again. Later, she imitated him nodding. Such sporadic imitations grew into systematic imitation both of sounds and of movements already seen. Observation 9 is an amusing example:

> At 0:6 (25) [in this book colons divide years and months; therefore 0:6 = six months. The figure in parentheses represents days.] J invented a new sound by putting her tongue between her teeth. It was like *pfs*. Her mother then made the same sound. J was delighted and laughed as she repeated

it in her turn. Then came a period of mutual imitation . . . Later on, after remaining silent for some time, I myself said *pfs*. J laughed and at once imitated me.

T learned to imitate the gesture of waving goodbye from 3 months old and incorporated this into a game. J often imitated her father sticking his tongue out. There were toys, of course, but the imitations that Piaget records were often both intellectual and emotional events. A striking one took place when J was 8 months old. She saw her father hit a celluloid duck. She then hit the duck herself and went on to hit a doll. Piaget added:

A moment later she was lying on her stomach screaming with hunger. To distract her, her mother took a brush and hit a porcelain soap dish with it. J at once imitated this somewhat complicated movement.

She also imitated banging a comb against the side of her cot and shaking objects that had just been grasped. In these cases, the child was imitating what she had just seen the parents do in an emotive situation. Over the weeks, imitations became more abstract and complex. The children learned how to imitate movements they had made but were not seeing; often these involved movements of the tongue. In one sequence, Piaget describes how J learned to imitate putting her finger in her ear. The child goes on to imitate or to parody new movements such as Observation 36:

At 0:11 (6) I struck the back of one hand with another and J immediately imitated me.

At 0:11 (9) her mother hit a duck with the end of a comb and J reproduced the movement without any hesitation. Same success at 0:11 (19) when I struck the notes of a xylophone with the head of a little hammer.

At 0:11 (27) she drummed on the table in response to this stimulus.

This final observation is interesting because J has become able to perform a playful act that is not direct imitation of hitting the xylophone. Piaget did not believe that play started only when the child had mastered all the stages of imitation. As soon as the child could imitate systematically, it had enough motor co-ordination to play. Play, for Piaget, began 'as soon as the new phenomenon is grasped by the child and offers no further scope for investigation so called'. The simplest example he gives is of L who discovered the possibility of making objects hanging from the top of her cot swing. At first between 0:3 (6) and 0:3 (16) she studied the phenomenon without smiling or only smiling a little but, with an appearance of intense interest, as though she was studying it. Subsequently, however, from 0:4, she never indulged in this activity, which lasted to 0:8 and even beyond, without a show of great joy and power.

She no longer had to make the things swing to find out what she could do with them, it was pure play, 'the use of the phenomenon for the pleasure of the activity'.

The next stage came, Piaget argued, when the child could combine new elements in its play. T was 7 months, Piaget often put a piece of cardboard between T's hand and the toy he wanted. T learned to brush the cardboard aside. Sometimes, he did it to get the toy but, sometimes, he forgot the toy 'momentarily at least', and burst into laughter as he swept the cardboard to one side. The sweeping had become play. When J was 9 months, she tried to make the duck on top of her cot swing, then started shaking the cot and, then, very deliberately fell back, shaking the whole cot. J repeated this performance ten times. She also imitated, ritually, some of the things she did when going to sleep like sucking the fringe of her pillow. Piaget's stress on the ritual aspect of play is interesting as it suggests he accepted play had emotional uses.

Piaget argued that, by the end of the sensori-motor period, the toddler was experimenting actively to gain control of his world. Play reflected this progress. The child combines new sets of movements but does so as if 'to make a motorgame of them'. At 10 months, J put her nose close to her mother's cheek and then pressed her nose against her mother's cheek which forced her to breathe more loudly. J then 'quickly complicated it for the fun of it; she drew back an inch or two, screwed up her nose, sniffed and breathed out alternately very loud and hard and then again thrust her nose against mother's cheek laughing heartily'. For about a month, J did this at least once a day. She repeated other games, too, such as holding her hair while she was in the bath and banging it on the water, putting her leg through a basket and making an orange skin sway from side to side at the table. Once, she did this twenty times while an amazed Piaget watched and saw her peer each time beneath the orange skin. None of these actions had any purpose. They were acted out with a playful air. For Piaget, these primitive ritual acts were an important stage in the evolution of play.

By the end of the period of sensori-motor intelligence, children no longer needed rituals because they could use symbols. This development coincided, Piaget argued, with the ability to play.

The move from ritual to play involving symbols is not a sharp one. In one of his children, L, Piaget witnessed it round her first birthday. L fell backwards in her cot. Then, she seized a pillow with one hand and pressed it against her face. She smiled broadly as she did so. This pressing was part of her routine, or ritual, in falling asleep. After a moment, L sat up, delighted. During the day, she repeated the performance a number of times. It always began with a smile, a point Piaget dwells on for he believes that shows she was signalling 'this is play'. Then, L would throw herself backwards, turn on to her side and put her hands over her face as if she was holding the pillow. Six months later, J was an accomplished player with objects. At 1:6 she pretended to eat or drink without having anything in her hands and, a month later, she pretended to eat or drink out of a cup and then offered it to the mouths of all the others who were present.

This second 'game' illustrates an important point. At first, infants play roles themselves. L and J both first pretended to fall asleep. Two months after J had done that, she made her bear and dog pretend to sleep. L first pretended to drink out of an empty cup and then, a month later, made members of the family do it. By 1:7 J made her bear bite her mother's cheek. Piaget noted instances of his children feeding dolls, feeding giraffes and J putting a doll to bed in a pan and then covering it with a postcard for a blanket.

In all these games, the child started out from an action or cry of her own. Next, Piaget saw children begin to use scenes from their daily life. At 1:9, J rubbed the floor with a shell, then with cardboard lid, saying 'Brush Abebert' which, Piaget explained, was 'like the charwoman'. At 1:7, L pretended to read a newspaper and pointed with her finger at certain parts of a sheet of paper. A month later, she pretended to telephone and this fell into a familiar pattern. First, L pretended to telephone herself. Then, she made her doll telephone. Then she telephoned with all kinds of objects, even a leaf, though she never seems to have reached the point of pretending to be someone else telephoning. T also learned from domestic life. Fifteen minutes after he saw Piaget blow a hunting horn, he (now 1:3) picked up a doll's chair, held it to his lips and sounded as he had seen Piaget do, 'Taratara'.

Slowly, each child learned to substitute one object for another. When J was 1:9, for example, she saw a shell and said 'cup'. Then, she pretended to drink out of it. The next day, she called the same shell a glass, then 'cup' again, the 'hat' and finally 'a boat in the water'. Other shells metamorphosed into a tree, a cat on the wall and a thimble. L was slower than J at this. Only when she was 2:1 did she pretend an orange peel was a potato and, then, a noodle. Objects then became people. At 3:0, L said that a small piece of material was 'grandmother, very ill, her legs hurt'.

First, the child pretends an object is someone else. Next, according to Piaget, the child pretends he or she is someone else. This cognitive skill can be put at the disposal of the child's emotional needs, Piaget saw.

The first person J pretended to be was her cousin Clive, who was running and jumping and laughing; then, at 2:2, she pretended to be ironing like the washerwoman and said: 'It's Mrs Sechaud ironing.' At 2:8, she crawled into Piaget's room on all fours, saying 'miaoux' and, that same month, she also 'was her nurse'. These episodes merged into more complex symbolic games as she got older. L started a little later. At 2:3, she was the postman and, two months later, declared herself 'Therese with her velvet hat'. At 4:3, L engaged in a strange game where she imitated the sound of bells and when Piaget tried to stop her, she said: 'Don't. I'm a church.' The children learned to substitute objects in play. At 2:5, for example, J prepared a bath for L. A blade of grass was the thermometer. (In the Piaget household, they must have checked the water temperature.) The bath was a big box and J just pretended it was full of water. Having dipped the blade in, she went to L and pretended to undress her for her bath. Round 2:7, J often picked up an imaginary baby and told it to go to sleep. Piaget noticed near the end of her second year that J would devise long and complicated games in which her dolls were fed, bathed, put to bed, made to watch life through the window and much else beside. L started these games even earlier because, Piaget noted, she saw J play them – an interesting example of how younger children learn to play from older ones.

Piaget also noticed that his children created characters. J had the most definite one, a creature called *l'aseau*. She pronounced it very carefully to distinguish it from the proper word for bird, *l'oiseau*. J sometimes did make it a bird, flapping her arm-wings around the room but, other times, when she crawled on all fours growling, it was a kind of dog. Sometimes, *l'aseau* would scold her; sometimes, it explained strange events. A dead duck had no feathers because 'I think the *aseaux* have eaten them'. Piaget saw that its influence was profound.

'In a general way, this strange creature which engaged her attention for two months was a help in all that she learned or desired, gave her moral encouragement and consoled her when she was unhappy. Then, it disappeared', Piaget noted. Later, J had a dwarf companion and a black companion she called Cadile. By now, aged 4, J was able to create completely novel characters though Piaget was careful not to suggest children had real imagination. What charmed adults was, in fact, their lack of coherence rather than any kind of art. The child was only, through 'imaginative play, reproducing what he has lived through'.

Far more than other aspects of his work, Piaget's observations on play reflect the influence of Freud. Once the child could create complicated play situations, these became a way of coping with reality. As early as 2:4, J who was forbidden to play with water used for washing, took an empty cup, stood by the 'forbidden tub' and said 'I'm pouring out water.' J also played at carrying the baby who had just been born but 'the game became more and more secret'. These 'compensatory combinations' allowed the child to be 'exercising his present life' through play. Piaget found instances when J was angry at him and made up stories of how Caroline, her godfather's daughter, had hit her godfather. When J was put on a diet, she made up a whole scene about a meal. When she was upset because a local dwarf had died, she made up a story about a little girl dwarf who met a boy dwarf. He died, 'but she looked after him so well he got better and went back home'. When J was told to go to bed, she said that her imaginary companion, Marceage, never went to bed being allowed to play all afternoon. Fear of objects could be conquered through play. At 2:9, L was frightened of a tractor and said her doll would like to ride it. This pattern was repeated with aeroplanes and steam rollers.

Following Freud's ideas, Piaget noted that his children often re-created a painful scene. But when it was dissociated from the original unpleasantness it became a kind of coping play. Piaget called these *liquidating compensations*. At 3:11, J was scared by the sight of a dead duck. The next day Piaget found her motionless in his study on the sofa, arms pressed against her body, legs bent. He asked her if she was ill. 'No, I'm the dead duck', she said. When Piaget hurt her by knocking her hands against the rake, she insisted on redoing the whole scene after saying, 'You're Jacqueline and I'm Daddy'. Through such games, the child came to use play to anticipate difficulties such as meeting frightening animals.

Piaget argued that these symbolic games are at their most important between the ages of 4 and 7. During this period, children also become far more able to speak what is on their mind. The symbols children use cease being so private and become collective ones so that play becomes more social and more realistic. In his work on the development of the intelligence, Piaget argued that children were very egocentric and unable to see the world from any point of view other than their own. Their play was hampered by these limitations. As children got older, they became more aware of the realities of the world and of the role of other people. They demanded a more exact imitation of reality in their games. T, for example, started off with a set of imaginary characters and, then, created a country for them called 'Six Twenty Balls'. From the age of 7, he became less interested in the people in the country and far more concerned to draw accurate maps of the state. These maps, by the age of 9, were closely modelled on maps of Europe. By 10, T started to invent a history for the country. Piaget noted: 'He drew and made all the material himself with great skill and dressed tiny bears and monkeys in the costumes of Rome, the Middle Ages . . . and housed them appropriately.' It was play but very much play based on reality.

I have dwelt on Piaget at such length because his observations remain a rich source of data. He offers something like an integrated account of the development of play in his children. Their games with objects merge in with their games with each other, their friends and their family. Piaget identified stages of development in the kinds of things the children did with objects. Given that his theory of intellectual development places too little emphasis on the social and emotional development of the child, his account of play is surprisingly rounded. And it really has not been properly superseded.

Piaget's book *Play, Dreams and Imitation in Childhood* was published in French in 1945 and in English in 1952. The observations it was based on were, by then, about twenty-five years old and some of them were available in his article, 'The First Year in the Life of the Child' (1928). Since 1952, there has been oddly little advance on Piaget's description of the various stages of play. Furthermore, while critics of his general theory of intellectual development have questioned the very idea of stages (Fischer 1980; Brown and Desforges 1979), there has been surprisingly little comment on whether it is appropriate to dissect playing skills in this way. Worse, perhaps, most later psychologists have discarded one of the great merits of *Play, Dreams and Imitation in Childhood*, the way Piaget weaves in the connections between the child's play and the child's daily life. Psychoanalytical case histories don't do this as usefully because analysts are not parents and because, nearly always, the children studied are disturbed or disturbing.

This lack of fundamental critique has meant that since 1952, many psychologists have studied detailed questions as when children know they can substitute one toy for another. We know much about the different ages, and stages, at which children can use ambiguous toys or combine them. We know much less about the general context of their play. The following account of much research is somewhat dry and, in that, it is an accurate reflection. Sadly, few of those doing it seem to realise that they have left much of the spirit of Piaget's book behind for such scientists would not like to be seen with their dignities down, blowing horns and going Taratara to amuse children.

In its aim to be scientific in a particular experimental way, much of the research imposes many restrictions on the way play is studied. I ask half seriously, half playfully: has this need to be scientific been imposed on them partly because their subject looks so unserious? We must work at play research, not play at it! Discuss.

Skills with toys

The fear of the frivolous is apparent in research on the use of objects since Piaget and, especially, in the attention paid to the stages by which children learn to use substitutes in play. These stages are identified and said to show the growth of cognitive skills. The problem with this is that it tends to see play in isolation as an exercise of mind. Some of the points made are interesting and important but they remain very much in isolation.

Fein (1975) mapped the development by which the child moves from realism, only being able to use the right object for a particular purpose, to substitution. For her, the pinnacle of play seems to be when a child can feed a not very good replica of a horse with a not very good replica of a cup. More naturalistic research like that of Belsky and Most (1981) and Lowe (1975) also seemed intent on dissecting the intellectual skills of play. All this leaves many questions not just unanswered, but unasked, such as how children use their toys in the home, what they make do with in free play and why.

Stages of skill?

The most impressive-looking chart of development is that produced by Belsky and Most (1981) who conceded that it is based on tiny numbers (four children at each of the following age groups 7½ months to 21 months, each at 1½ month intervals). Belsky and Most (1981) logged the following kinds of behaviour:

- Mouthing manipulation (simple)
- Functional – the use of an object appropriately
- Relational – combining two objects, putting peg on a plate
- Functional-relational – as above except the correct use
- Enactive naming – such as putting lips to a cup without either drinking or making drinking sounds
- Pretend self – where the child pretends to, say, go to sleep himself
- Pretend other – where the child pretends to give food to an adult who is supposed to pretend to eat
- Sequence pretend – where the child strings together a number of actions into a pretending 'script'
- Substitution – where the child can substitute an object for another, making a toy horse drink out of a clam shell.

Before 12 months, Belsky and Most (1981) found no instance of any kind of pretending. The closest to a play behaviour they had was 'enactive naming' where a child might approach an object but not use it properly. There would be no sounds made. The increasing complexity of what the child can do in playing is apparent but there are all sorts of inconsistencies in the data which may well be due to the fact that Belsky and Most (1981) studied a sample of different children of different ages. At 19½ months, for example, less time was spent in substituting objects than either at 16½, 18 or 21 months. Significant, or were the 19½ month olds just not interested in that? Between 13½ and 15 months, there was a huge leap in *functional-relational* play. Was this a conceptual leap or an accident of the tiny sample? The problems in

Belsky and Most's chart dog all the studies examined in the rest of the chapter. With the exception of Nicolich (1977), there is no longitudinal study and no attempt to relate the way children play with objects to their lives. Play is studied as a desiccated skill.

Fein (1975) produced an elegant experiment to see how children became more adept at handling abstract symbols. She studied sixty-six children aged between 1:10 and 2:3. She showed them a plush toy horse which was a good replica, a far less accurate metal horse shape, a plastic egg cup and a clam shell. She pretended the horse was hungry. When the children had the chance to feed the accurate horse with the plastic egg cup, 93 per cent of them did so. When they were told to pretend to feed the metal horse shape with the authentic plastic cup, 79 per cent did so. This fell to 61 per cent when they were asked to feed the good horse with the shell. Most telling, for Fein, only 33 per cent of these infants managed to handle double substitution, feeding the poor replica of a horse with a poor replica of a cup. Fein (1975) suggests young children need realistic toys. But her study is one in which the whole dynamics of the game are out of the children's control: adults run it.

McCune-Nicolich (1981a) also accepted that a child must know an object's proper use first before playing with it. Further evidence of a progression from realism to symbolism comes from Jeffree and McConkey (1976). They looked at ten children aged from 1:6 to 3:6. Younger children played more with more realistic and prototypical toys. Corrigan (1982) found the same pattern. As they grew older, children went from playing at washing themselves with a real cloth, to using a wooden block to wash themselves, to washing a doll with a cloth, to, the ultimate symbolism, washing a doll with a toy cloth. Nicolich (1977), in her longitudinal study of five children from 12 months to 26 months, saw that they first preferred realistic toys. They then became less realistic. A child might use a doll's shoe as a hat for a doll. By 1:2, the infants could play with ambiguous objects. A twig was used as a pencil, a spoon or a chopstick. It seemed the shape mattered. It had to be approximately correct, Nicolich claimed, and this was more important than whether the child had 'knowledge of the function of real objects in real situations'. What significant cues made the twig a good pencil but not a car she did not study. Could the twig have been a rocket? By 26 months children were able to use quite dissimilar objects in play. In her later studies, McCune-Nicolich (1981b) suggested that, by 3 years of age, children could play without any objects or toys at all. It could all be imagined.

Belsky and Most (1981) would seem to accept most of these notions but their model has more stages than Nicolich's and one interesting variant. Once the baby can use objects in a functionally correct way, he moves through stage 4 *relational* which means bringing any two objects together and, then, to stage 5 *functional-relational* which means using the two objects appropriately, so that a cup is put on the saucer or the peg in the pegboard. For Belsky and Most (1981), the wrong use of two objects precedes realistic use. Otherwise, the stages they propose seem quite similar.

Other researchers have pursued the same theme. Elder and Pederson (1978) studied seventy-two children aged 2:6 to 3:11. They divided them into three groups – those under 3:0, those from 3:0 to 3:5 and those up to 3:11. All the children were asked to play with set toys that Elder and Pederson reckoned were *realistic*; *similar*, as a flat piece of wood for a comb, or an eggshell for a cup; and *dissimilar*, such as an apple for a hammer or a guitar for a cup. They found that younger children had problems with the unrealistic toys. Children from 3:6 upwards could, however, use any object in their games. Unfortunately, Elder and Pederson do not seem to have considered whether or not the younger children really understood the kind of game they were being asked to play.

Even more exotic in asking children to suspend disbelief was the study of Jackowitz and Watson (1980). They started with a toy phone and a toy cup. They found out whether children knew you could speak on the phone and drink from a cup. They then swopped the phone for a banana (same form, different function). Then, could the children still use it to talk? In a series of changes, the phone also became a walkie-talkie (dissimilar form, similar function), a block (ambiguous) and a toy car (dissimilar form, dissimilar function). Finally, the children were asked to speak on the phone with no object there at all. Children were given a modelling session and 'tested' to see how competent they were with all these various substitutes for a toy phone. No one questioned how realistic such experiments were. The infants were divided into two groups – those from 14 to 19 months of age and those from 19 months to 24 months. By 19 months, the children had mastered all these progressive steps and so could merrily telephone on the banana and drink out of a toy car. It is hard to see just why these children performed so much more symbolically than Fein's (1975) because two-thirds of her groups aged 22 months to 27 months could not manage double substitution. Fein (1984) does not explain nor did Jackowitz and Watson (1980) comment in their article on the differences.

By far the largest study of the growth of representational skills is that by Lowe (1975) and it is much less interested in substitution. Lowe studied 244 London children. Like Belsky and Most (1981), she hoped to reach developmental conclusions through looking at different samples of children of different ages. She focused on 12, 15, 18, 21 and 24, 30, 36 month olds. Again, the psychologist rigorously controlled the nature of the play. Lowe gave her subjects four different sets of objects: I – Doll (girl), spoon, cup, saucer, comb and brush; II – Doll, bed, blanket, pillow; III – Doll, table, chair, plate, fork, knife, tablecloth; IV – Truck, trailer, man, four small wooden logs. The child sat at a table usually with his or her mother and was allowed to play 'until he had indicated he had finished with it', i.e. with one set of toys. Then, the next set was shown. Usually the 'experiment' lasted 30 minutes.

The first situation showed Lowe (1975) that even children of 12 months knew the correct use of objects linked with food though they might not be able to link them correctly. For example, only 7 per cent of the 12 month olds placed the cup on the saucer. Knowledge of the comb and brush came later. Only 15 month olds knew how to handle them though a sizeable majority (29 per cent) at 24 months didn't seem too sure what the brush was for.

Lowe (1975) found a clear pattern in the persons on whom, or with whom, the child used toys. The youngest children used the objects on themselves. They fed themselves and, at 15 months, 64 per cent combed their own hair. Very few of these youngest children fed other people or dolls. By 21 months, 46 per cent of the children fed the dolls and 52 per cent brushed the doll's hair. Lowe argued that, with age, behaviour changed from being 'self-directed' to being 'doll-directed'. Two sorts of action that Lowe scored related to the other adults in the room. Between 15 months and 24 months, a small number of children (roughly 15 per cent) fed the adult present or combed her hair. But this tailed away.

The second situation offered children the chance to put the doll to bed. Lowe (1975) noted that bedtime objects, like pillows, were used correctly rather later than the food objects or, even, the comb or brush of Situation 1. Only around 21 months of age did the children relate the doll to the bed and only at 24 months were the doll, blanket and bed integrated to play putting the doll to bed. Lowe noted that the age at which the idea of putting the doll to bed first surfaced was around 21 months as was the age at which, with food, activities became firmly doll-centred.

The third situation gave the children a chance to play at a meal. Again, near 21 months, the children stopped playing feeding themselves and started instead to feed their dolls. Lowe noted, however, that after 24 months, many of the children stopped really feeding the doll. A nice middle-class touch in this experiment was that Lowe noted how many children were able to use the tablecloth correctly; 54 per cent by 30 months, as it happens.

Lowe's fourth situation was less designed to bring out behaviour related either to the child or to others. Knowledge of the truck, trailer and logs was slower to develop. At 18 months, none of the children had placed the driver in the driving seat. By 30 months, only 52 per cent of the children lined up the truck and trailer together even though Lowe did not require them to place the two objects in the right formation. By 36 months, only 53 per cent had actually managed either to join truck and trailer or to show the clear intention of doing so.

In her conclusions, Lowe (1975) argued that her findings pointed to the need for further research. She accepted that, at 12 months, all the children had grasped the idea that miniature objects stood for a real object. You had to use the miniature object in the way that you would use the real object. Note that for adults it's different. We may buy a fine miniature car to put on our mantelpiece but, for us, it isn't a practical object but a decorative one. Lowe claimed that progress in representational play depended on the understanding of the domestic situations and accepted that she was a bit puzzled as to why some actions came to be played earlier than others. The two most interesting lags were in Situation II and Situation IV (the truck). Situation II offered the child the chance to play with a doll, bed, blanket and pillow.

There is, I would argue, an answer which harks back to Piaget. He noted that children first pretended to sleep themselves, then pretended to put dolls to sleep. This progression is generally accepted. Lowe (1975) has shown that even 12-month-old infants have an acute sense of reality. Faced with a toy plate, infants may feed themselves. Faced with a toy brush, they may brush their hair. But they already 'know' that they can't put themselves to bed in a toy bed so they omit 'a stage'. Infants' ability to adapt to laboratory life is telling here. Piaget noted that J at 1:3 pretended to go to sleep. She did so without the use of any objects other than her real pillow. Lowe's useful study could have led to a more realistic investigation of how children use toys in their homes. Instead, Lowe seems not to have pursued research in the field and two other studies focus again in a slightly artificial way on what is technically known as 'sequence of agent use'.

Watson and Fischer (1977) studied thirty-six white children aged 14 months, 19 months and 24 months. They discovered that given a doll, a pillow and a bed, there was a pattern to play. In free play, twenty-eight of the children did some pretending though Watson and Fischer do not reveal what it was like. When they came to the experiment, they found that first, the infants tended to put their head on the pillow. The infants aged 19 months had, in general, moved beyond this and put the doll on the pillow. A third stage came when a block could be used as a doll so the block was put on the pillow and wafted to sleep. Finally, the infant at 24 months was able to 'give life' to the doll using the doll to put itself to sleep. The 'other agent' became 'active'. Watson and Fischer, McCune-Nicolich and other psychologists in the play area agree that this point is an important watershed. When the child is able to 'give life' to dolls or animals it is ready for the more sophisticated kind of pretend games we examine in Chapter 4.

Giving life to doll, blocks or other objects ought to be an experience in which the child feels both joy and power. I have tried to argue that the form of experiments since Piaget seem to have ironed out these feelings. One study, however, sheds some light on the conflicts children feel when they are put in experimental situations which demand such behaviours. Golomb (1977) had found evidence in a study by Sliosberg (1934) that children were made uncomfortable by too fantastic play – the kind, one might snipe, that requires you to telephone with a banana or make a cup out of a toy car. Golomb gave children three jigsaw puzzles, one of a car, one of a manikin and one of an elephant. Each puzzle had a part missing. Golomb found that when children came to get this final part, they wanted one which would make a coherent fit. They didn't want the tail of an elephant to finish off a car.

In a second experiment, Golomb (1977) compared the ways children played three games – feeding a hungry baby, going to the beach and going to the petshop. There were appropriate and inappropriate objects for each game and Golomb saw to it that the appropriate objects were used up. Her children were aged 2:7 to 3:8 and an older group up to 4:5. The younger children made more incongruous selections which Golomb thought reflected their lack of knowledge. But the older group became faintly uncomfortable when they could only use 'wrong' objects. 'Children's responses extended from hesitation, evasiveness, outright rejection to amusement and laughter.' But there was much common sense in these reactions and Golomb had the respect for her subjects to listen to what they had to say when forced into such odd choices.

Golomb (1977) gave one example of a boy who, when there were only balls from the beach available to feed the baby, evaded by pretending, 'Baby is asleep.' Another said: 'She's not going to eat now.' When there were no beach toys, one child moaned: 'I want to play at home.' When there were no decent food toys, a girl had to feed a hungry baby a pencil. She protested and warned: 'Do you know this is poison?' Still, in the experimental situation, she obediently fed it. Golomb interpreted her results conventionally, as proof of the fact that older children want realism. She did not elaborate on how bizarre some of the experiments appeared – from their comments – to the children. Yet, their remarks did highlight the oddity of the paradigm psychologists have used to judge progress in play. Can you pretend an apple is a car? Top marks. Do you refuse to feed your teddy detergent? You must be backward.

In some ways, Golomb's results contradict Lowe's. Golomb (1977) found children of 3 did make wrong choices where Lowe (1975) found that her 36 month olds knew the correct uses of food, combs, trucks, trailers and blankets. But more interesting is the fact that by asking for and recording reactions to these tasks, Golomb showed that children were not just laughing or being silly but feeling uncomfortable. It seems possible to argue that they were being made to feel uncomfortable by the experimental situation. Though the research since Piaget is labelled as being on play, it often owes much more to problem solving and very little research has looked at proper free play, because psychologists 'set the agenda'. (In French, Piaget's book was called *La Formation du symbole chez l'enfant*. Not much play there.) Free play and the play studied in almost all the post-Piaget studies cited in this chapter differ crucially. In free play, the children control what they do. They choose the toys. They do not feel under any kind of test or examination.

The research with things makes it possible to trace one sort of developmental sequence. The baby learns to mouth and, then, to manipulate objects. Towards the end of the first six months, the baby can look, grasp and reach quite confidently. Babies begin playing with things by experimenting on objects that are near to them like pushing the mobiles near their cots. Piaget observed these playful pushes were usually accompanied by smiles, of triumph or glee. The later studies of play with things have identified a sequence of stages. At 12 months, most children have grasped the idea that toys replicate things in the real world. Some of these replicas are best if vague so that a stick can become any manner of things. On the whole, young infants find it easier to play with realistic stuff where there is no confusion as to what the toy stands for. They become skilled, first, at using ambiguous objects to do things to less ambiguous objects and, eventually, at using dissimilar objects. By the age of 2:0, most children can manage to handle double substitutions so that they can use something which is not much like a cup to feed something that is not much like a horse if they have decided these should stand for cups and horses. Around 2:0 or a little later, infants also begin to 'give life' to objects so that the doll becomes an active being that can talk, put others to bed, feed children and so on. This is an important stage opening the way to more pretending.

Symbolic progress seems nicely mapped out. But just look at it from a different perspective, from outside the paradigm. Would we say that an adult who claimed a banana was a telephone and proceeded to land the fruit in a soup plate he called an airport was particularly *bright?* It would depend. He might find himself in front of a psychiatrist who might wonder if he had trouble distinguishing the real from the unreal. The rules of the game developmental psychologists play are very special and rather zany. Do children always understand them? Being able to perform such substitutions is certainly proof of cognitive skills of a certain sort but not too much should be read into them out of context. And, paradoxically, psychologists have studied the context in which play starts (the home) far less than infinite variations on toy telephones. Piaget argued that, usually, children under the age of about 7 were trapped by immediate sensations and could not conceive of a difference between appearance and reality. Research by Flavell is challenging that (Cohen 2004) because he has found pretence is well established by the age of 4.

Also this theme of research was produced before Siegler produced his influential critique of stages and his notion that it would be wiser to think of development in terms of overlapping waves, but no one has yet worked on how children play with objects in the light of what Siegler said.

Appearance and reality

Children aged 3, 4 and 6 were shown a rock which an experimenter held. They were then allowed to feel the rock. The rock was in fact a clever visual creation. The rock-like object turned out to be really a sponge on which a rock had been painted. The children were then asked what it felt like. There was a telling difference between the 3 year olds and the 4 year olds. The 4 year olds said it was a sponge but also knew it still looked like a rock. In other words, they could distinguish between the appearance of an object and its reality. Flavell and his co-workers found, however, that the 3 year olds could not manage this feat of separating the look of an object from its feel. Appearance determined reality for them. Once the 3 year olds knew the object was no rock but a sponge, they said it looked like a sponge. The way the object felt created a new reality for the 3 year olds.

Flavell argued that this result supported the notion of some dramatic increase in competence between 3 and 4. Children of 4 are no longer so bound by their perceptions. They can appreciate that things can exist on two levels. What sight and touch reveal does not need to be the same. It doesn't take too much imagination to argue that this has parallels with experiments on how children perceive other people and their capacities. People often behave, after all, like Flavell's rock-sponge. They act in one way but are thinking something else. Usually, 4 year olds can grasp that. Flavell has also done further work using a very similar design with people to test whether 3, 4 and 5 year olds are influenced by changes in appearance of a storyteller – a study considered in Chapter 5.

Harris et al. (1991) conducted an ingenious experiment to test the conditions under which very young children can tell fantasy from reality. Their experimental procedure centred on monsters. Fairy-tales and empirical studies agree that children are often scared of such monsters. Jersild (1943) claimed that fear of monsters in children increased between the age of 2 and 4. But do children really believe in the monsters that are alleged to scare them?

Harris and his colleagues gathered together a group of 4 year olds (mean age 4:5) and a group of 6 year olds (mean age 6:7) to study this idea. In the first experiment the children were told that the experimenter was looking at a cup, a balloon, scissors or a monster. They were asked if what the experimenter was looking at was real or if she was imagining them.

All the 6 year olds and half the 4 year olds made no mistakes. Of the 4 year olds who did make some mistakes, only a small number made frequent errors. There was little evidence to show that these very young children had difficulties in separating reality from imagination.

There was one odd finding, however. Even though children didn't think the monsters were real, they showed some signs of being scared of them. In a second experiment, forty-eight children were brought in a room which had two boxes. They were asked to imagine that there was a puppy in one box and a monster in the other. The children saw that there was no real monster and no real puppy but they were much more wary of the monster box. They approached it far more cautiously.

Harris and his colleagues were aware of the fact that the children might be colluding with the experimenter, showing fear where they felt it was expected of them. In a further variation, therefore, the experimenter said that she had to leave the room. The children were left in the room alone and their behaviour was filmed. Four of the twenty-four 4 year olds became very nervous indeed and said they were too frightened to stay in the room. Others also showed very real signs of fear.

Harris concluded that though children could tell what was real and what was imaginary, they showed traces of magical thinking. They remained scared.

But the essential finding was robust. Children of 4 and upwards are unlikely to confuse what is real and what is imagined when they play with objects. The work of Flavell and Harris fits in well with work on how children play with each other and how they pretend, since the trend of recent studies has been to suggest that, in such games, children begin to reveal that they understand other people have other wills, ideas, beliefs, plans and other minds.

The meaning of toys

Settling questions about the conceptual skills children use with toys has meant that many questions about how children use toys, and what they mean to them, have gone unanswered. Imagine – which is part of play – some of the questions psychologists might have pursued as well.

In ordinary life, what sort of toys do different kinds of children prefer? Analytically inclined psychologists have sketched some differences in the toys that boys and girls prefer but the research is fairly small.

How do children turn ordinary objects in the home into things they play with? Reading the play research, and remembering how one's own children used toys, one is struck by how ordered the toys used in research are. Yet the process of turning a real carrot into something you use to feed a doll or into a gun is an interesting one.

How do children use toys to enter a particular role? I will show later on that, for one of my children, putting on a rough piece of blue material nearly always signalled the start of his playing a Batman game. How does that happen? This kind of question raises an important issue. In normal life, children run their own plays and games. In psychological experiments, they hardly ever do. What are the consequences of that?

How do children see the toys that parents give them? How do parents play with their children? It may be anecdote but there certainly are fathers who adore playing with their children's toy trains.

Two final questions that might have been answered: in what ways has television and the growing 'toy industry' affected the toys children want? And does class affect the kinds of toys children like and how they use them?

There are, of course, many other questions that could be asked about the role of toys but the point is that we have rather little information about the meaning that toys have in a child's life. One area of research which has been pursued to some extent is the different kinds of toys that boys and girls prefer.

The feminist movement spotlighted the way in which many child care manuals like Dr Spock's tended to reinforce conventional sex roles. Boys had to be discouraged from playing with girls' toys because, oh calamity, the 2 year old who plays with dolls and a sewing set may become a homosexual. In case you might be deluded into thinking this is antique thinking of the sort that no sensible psychologist would endorse, consider Bates and Bentley's (1973) article, 'Play Activity of Normal and Effeminate Boys'. The authors drew up a list of sixty-four games which were divided – by them – into feminine games and masculine games. The games that were labelled as feminine included playing house, playing doctor, sewing, playing nurse, singing 'London Bridge is Falling Down', playing donkey and playing with stuffed animals. Why singing 'London Bridge is Falling Down' should be 'female' the article never explains! The proper games for boys were playing baseball, playing with guns, with trains, with telescopes and playing king of the castle. Bates and Bentley (1973) recommended that children (especially boys) should be watched so that if they played too many effeminate games, their teachers and parents could take steps to prevent 'gender deviance'. There is no record of these psychologists continuing their research.

A rather different strain of research into play preferences dates from when psychoanalysts started to deal with children. There are two quite different sets of questions involved. First, do children naturally and instinctually prefer different kinds of toys and, second, do we condition them to love the toys that we think are sex appropriate?

Psychoanalysts have tended to see the different toys that different sexes like as a reflection of their fundamental biology. Erik Erikson (1977) observed that boys and girls played very differently with blocks. Boys tended to create tall, long shapes – the Lego phallus – while girls tended to make dumpier structures with enclosed spaces. John plays at making rockets; Jill at building a house. Erikson suggested these were biological differences and, also, reflected the basic male/female divide. The boy thrusts aggressively into the world while the girl envelops it with love.

Bruno Bettelheim (1965) who studied the lives of children born on kibbutzim and published a study of fairy-tales has claimed that the play of children reflects their basic concerns. He comments on a report by Paley (1973) which has the fiery title, 'Is the Doll a Sexist Institution?' Paley ran a playgroup and found that the mothers of the children complained she was running a sexist playgroup because all the domestic toys (kettles, pots, pans, beds, etc.) were in the doll corner. Paley then took away these toys and found that equality did not bloom. Instead, the girls started to make housekeeping games under the table and even served breakfast at the sand table. 'I was witnessing a spontaneous underground movement', Paley noted, in which the girls were asserting their femininity. Neither Paley nor Bettelheim consider though how much taking dolls away could alter the basic conditioning in society.

More feminist writers see in the toys children choose nothing more than a reflection of social conditioning. After all, many toy shops have separate sections for boys' and girls' toys. You don't find cuddly toys on the rockets or Cindy dolls on the tanks. In a study in 1957, Pitcher found that fathers tended to discourage their boys from playing with female toys. It was sissy. Wolf (1973) used a playgroup to model children the use of the wrong-sex toy. Wolf called a fire engine a male toy and a doll a female toy. Connoisseurs of the psychoanalytic literature will know that a fire engine has hoses and the water-spurting hose is the phallic symbol to end all phallic symbols. Wolf found it much easier to get girls to play with the fire engine than to get boys to play with the doll.

Pitcher and Schultz (1983), building on Pitcher's earlier work, report that in their school when boys had to play with dolls, they played quite differently. The boys would treat the doll as a thing to explore. They pushed and prodded it. Sometimes they stuck it in a car. Very rarely did boys use the doll to play any kind of parenting games. The psychologists never saw a boy wash, bathe, feed or put the doll to bed as an integrated sequence. They found also that boys and girls turned a neutral space – a table with chairs, a toy phone, carpentry tools and rope into quite different environments. So, boys would turn it into a construction site or a space ship, shooting each other and using the rope to organise pulling toys about. The girls played with the telephone ringing people up to organise parties and making a Chinese meal. Pitcher and Schultz (1983) saw stereotypes at play. They recognise that biology may influence play. They quote an article by Middleton (1980) in which he fantasised that if 'a mad sociologist' gave 1000 boys dolls and 1000 girls footballs, most girls would soon be babying the footballs and most boys would soon be booting the dolls as footballs. Pitcher and Schultz offer the story as an anecdote and don't say whether they think this means boys are 'naturally' destructive or are conditioned so to be. In general, their argument in *Boys and Girls at Play* is that the toys and games that boys and girls prefer are heavily influenced by society's view of correct sex roles. Hostility to women by men is acute and they blame that for fathers' determination to stop their boys playing girl-games. Since the mid-1970s a clear cultural swing to greater sex equality has taken place. Some wonder if girls should be brought up with a taboo on toys like guns and trucks. And why not encourage boys to play with dolls? Whether fashions in toys have changed, and what psychological meaning that might have, is an issue research has not yet tackled.

Toys parents buy

It seems clear that children use toys for fun and, also, to practise both certain motor activities and certain social ones. There has been little academic research on what seems to me an important reality in all this – the toys that parents choose to buy for their children. When both our sons were young, we were determined in best *Guardian* reader style not to encourage aggressive impulses in our boys. No guns, more dolls. We found we couldn't stick to this ideal because the boys insisted in having all kinds of space weaponry, especially after *Star Wars*. To balance this, though, we did buy them cuddly toys and found absolutely no rejection of these.

Both of the boys used these soft toys to play babying games, and Nicholas's mother, Aileen, was very surprised once to find him putting the baby doll to bed when he had never seen this done in real life. Nicholas at 4:10 spent a long time pretending he was a baby after seeing a cartoon which involved Deputy Dawg yelling at a baby to go to sleep. But the cuddly toys didn't become footballs; they were often held and often took part in make-believe games. The toys we bought were influenced both by our wish to help our children to grow up to be less sexist and, also, since we never managed total dogma, by what the children wanted. Try going to a toy shop with a 3 year old you love (who isn't too greedy) and refusing him a *Star Wars* Demon-Blaster because it doesn't fit your ideology. This whole area – why parents choose to give certain toys and how children negotiate for the toys they want – is almost entirely ignored. I will argue later, in dealing with laughter, that there is some evidence that parents teach their children what to laugh at. Almost no theorist has approached play in this spirit. Playing with toys springs out of the literature as if it's something that children do naturally by themselves, either to practise their motor and intellectual skills or to express their conflicts and 'inner space'. But you would never really guess from the literature that I might buy my son a train set because he has been nagging me to do so and, though it brings back uncomfortable memories because I lost my train set when my parents moved house, I want to please my son and suspect we might have a good time playing trains together. Toys are springboards for fantasy. Children do not just use toys as intellectual tools as most of the research would have us believe. They're part of the child's life. Piaget observed that a child's doll would feel and suffer all the repercussions, good and bad, pleasant and unpleasant, of what had happened in the child's life that day. It's an insight much subsequent research has forgotten in its pursuit of an accurate description of developmental stages. As a result, we have theories of play which describe the progress to different cognitive and motor levels of play. However, these theories remain divorced from the real life of children and do not take into account the fact that most children learn to play, not in a vacuum, but in their families. In Chapter 4, I begin to look at the games children play with each other before moving on to the neglected heart of this topic – how children learn to play with their parents and siblings.

I have claimed in this chapter that, after Piaget's pioneering research, too much effort has been devoted to isolating the cognitive aspects of play without any consideration of the actual environment it blossoms in. I have sniped that many psychologists have been too narrow and too concerned with a scientific dissection of levels of skill. It's worth ending this chapter playfully by remembering that there are many different perspectives on toys. The French semiologist Roland Barthes (1973) saw in toys the stunted hallmarks of a materialist culture and, in an essay, accused:

> The fact that French toys *literally* prefigure the world of adult functions obviously cannot but prepare the child to accept them all, by constituting for him, even before he can think about it, the alibi of a Nature which has at all times created soldiers, postmen and Vespas. Toys here reveal the list of things the adult does not find unusual; war, bureaucracy, ugliness, Martians.
>
> (Barthes 1973)

For Barthes, such literal toys not only condition the child to accept the adult, 'bourgeois' world but also force him to be passive. Faced with these objects, 'the child can only identify himself as owner, as user, never as creator; he does not invent the world, he uses it; there are prepared for him actions without adventure, without wonder, without joy'.

Barthes did not write as a psychologist but as a social and political critic. Nevertheless, he does make one crucial psychological point – that children ought to be allowed to create their own games and play, not have them devised by adults. For all the skill of the research on playing with objects since Piaget, it has denied children this right. Instead of looking at how the child within the family context makes up games and uses toys he or she chooses, work has concentrated on picking out the cognitive levels of play. This gives only a very partial view. In the next chapter, I look at the considerable research on how children play with each other which has usually been done in nursery schools rather than homes.

4 Playing with other children

Sara Smilansky's (1968) research on disadvantaged children in Israel was a landmark study. She claimed that dramatic play (sociodramatic play) and games with rules provide the most opportunity for cognitive development. Dansky and Silverman (1973) tested the notion that play furthers a measure of creativity known as associative fluency. They measured 4- to 6-year-old children's ability to form associative elements into new combinations that met certain task requirements. One group of subjects was allowed to play with a particular set of objects, another was asked to engage in an equivalent amount of imitative behaviour with the same objects, and a third group was shown the objects but given experiences that did not involve contact with them. The study found that the subjects in the play configuration produced significantly more non-standard responses for every object than subjects in either imitation or control conditions. Later work by the authors suggests two important principles: first, play creates a set, or attitude, to generate associations to a variety of objects, whether or not those objects are encountered during the play activity, and second, make-believe is one form of play that contributes to the enhancement of associative fluency.

If prior play experience facilitates associative fluency, then does it also help children solve specific, goal-oriented problems? Sylva, Bruner and Genova (1976) found that prior play experience gave preschoolers an advantage in solving certain kinds of problems, such as retrieving a piece of chalk in a box that is out of reach without getting out of your chair. This was true even when the play subjects were compared to subjects who were given a demonstration of the solution. Pepler and Ross (1981) later showed that, among preschoolers age 3 to 4, experience with play that had no single correct solution led to greater flexibility in problem solving and more imaginative solutions than single solution play or controls.

Although studies show that play can change the way people solve problems, they do not necessarily demonstrate improvements in problem-solving ability.

Specific outcomes of play, such as practice with skills, social communication and problem solving, may not fully explain its overall function. Rather than primarily training specific motor or cognitive skills, Fagen (1981) suggests that play may provide the generalised ability to adapt to environmental novelty. He finds strong evidence for the claim that enrichment through play enhances behavioural flexibility, including the ability to solve novel problems and to respond effectively to novel environments. In this light, play experiences facilitate generalised learning and problem-solving skills, such as seeking multiple solutions to problems, adjusting problem-solving strategies to the task, and adapting to changing environmental or problem conditions.

When Reuben was 2:1, he created his first truly incongruous joke. I begin this chapter with the incident of the Flying Cucumber because it seems to illustrate some of the more interesting aspects of play that much current research bypasses.

Reuben is in the kitchen and picks up a cucumber. He says: 'Cucumber fly.' He grins at this. His brother Nicholas who is 5:10 picks up the joke. That week, we had watched a performance of *The Flying Dutchman* on television which had mesmerised Nicholas. He insisted on staying up. Now, Nicholas declaims: 'Tonight, instead of *MASH* and *The Flying Dutchman*, we present The Flying Cucumber. This woman is in love with the image of a cucumber.' (Oh, Freud, what would you have given for this observation!) Nicholas laughs and says he likes being silly. In the next few weeks, the Flying Cucumber recurred a number of times. Sometimes, Reuben brought it up himself. He knew it was well received. Sometimes Aileen, Nicholas or I brought it up knowing it would make him laugh. Both Reuben and Nicholas elaborated on the theme, turning the flying cucumber into a flying carrot or a flying potato. These aerial vegetables were put into all kinds of games. That month Reuben was also much taken with Superman and Batman. Reuben would often whirl about energetically being, or pretending to be, the flying cucumber. Reuben uses the game sometimes when he is made to feel inferior by Nicholas. At 2:2, R is having to listen to Nicholas asking him testing questions about where we are. We happen to be in the dining room. Nicholas is showing off his superior knowledge. After this, Reuben gets up on the chair, laughs as he makes a few gestures and says: 'Flying cucumber'. Reuben laughs and knows quite well he is going to make us laugh. The next day, I am lying down by Reuben's side on his bed. After a while, he says: 'Flying cucumber' and laughs. Five days later, Reuben tells us again he is a flying cucumber and whirls around. He also pretends to drive a bus around the kitchen. Then, he says, 'Swimming bus' and laughs.

Reuben's pretence of being a flying cucumber started off when he seized the object. It then became a useful technique both to get laughter and, also, to protect himself against his brother's superior wisdom. Being the cucumber became entangled with playing Superman or Batman. There is no way of testing whether 2 year olds when they play such games are actually pretending to be these things or, somehow, because their sense of their own identity is fluid, become them. My intuition – and intuitions are notoriously wrong – is that Reuben knew enough of the world to realise that first, he was not a cucumber and second, he could not fly even if, as he did once, he stood up on his chair to be more in the air, and that third, cucumbers couldn't fly. Nicholas responded to Reuben's pretence and so did his mother and I.

Before examining the issue of pretending, I want to look at the most basic kind of play that children engage in with other children – rough and tumble play. Psychologists usually define this as very physical play which can sometimes appear to be quite aggressive.

Rough and tumble play

Getting the objective play counter out, psychologists estimate that 15 per cent of vigorous physical play consists of activities such as play fighting, hitting, wrestling, and chasing and pseudo fighting. Pellegrini and Smith (1998) suggest that such rough and tumble stuff allows children, and particularly boys, to establish their status within a dominance hierarchy. Chimps use rough and tumble to establish who is top monkey so this seems a plausible hypothesis. There is a neurological aspect to this too. I have tended to ignore brain development because there are so few human studies of brain and play but Panksepp et al. (1995, 1997) have made some interesting findings in both animals and humans. The results of their work suggest there is a correlation between the appearance of this activity and the maturity of the frontal lobes of the brain. Frontal lobes help, facilitate and contain reflection, imagination, empathy and play/creativity. As the frontal lobes mature, the frequency of rough and tumble play goes down, and damage to the frontal lobes is associated with a higher level of playfulness. If one surgically reduces – whatever that means – the frontal lobes of young rats, they play more and show signs of hyperactivity. If these 'frontally reduced' rats are given the chance to rough and tumble, the decline in such play with maturity is even more dramatic than the decline in the normal rat. Panksepp and his colleagues speculate that rough and tumble play not only is correlated with frontal lobe development but also may actually promote it.

Spontaneous rough and tumble play may be increasingly seen as a sign of pathology, rather than as an ordinary childhood activity, a growing intolerance corresponds that with one of the more intriguing trends in the diagnosis of childhood psychological problems: the dramatic increase in the diagnosis of attention deficit hyperactivity disorders (ADHD) in the late twentieth century (Panksepp 1998). It has been estimated that in the year 2000 15 per cent of American children (about 8 million) were so diagnosed, up from 1 per cent at the beginning of the twentieth century and 5 per cent at the beginning of the 1990s. It seems unlikely that there really has been an increased prevalence of genuine neurological disorders in the United States; a more likely interpretation is that we have redefined what we consider to be 'normal' childhood behaviours, and spontaneous energetic physical play is sometimes interpreted as a form of pathology (Panksepp 1998).

There is evidence that genuine attention deficits in children are correlated with reduced frontal lobe size and activity, although brain-imaging data are obviously not a prerequisite for a diagnosis of ADHD. Whether or not a neural disorder is present, however, findings from animal research suggest that rough and tumble play not only reflects frontal lobe development but also promotes it. In other words, active, energetic, spontaneous physical play may facilitate neurological development. If this is the case, the inhibition of play through the use of behavioural restrictions or medication might actually contribute to developmental abnormalities. Indeed, while psychostimulant medications such as Ritalin are quite effective in focusing children's attention, another of their major effects is to reduce the urge of young organisms to engage in rough and tumble play (Panksepp et al. 1998).

Since learning requires attention and focus, vigorous physical play may appear to be antithetical to the educational process. Teachers may believe that opportunities for physical play may make children, and particularly those diagnosed with attention disorders, even more difficult to teach. Panksepp (1998) maintained that, as is true of other appetites, the need for rough and tumble is a self-regulating process. Once the need is satisfied, the organism will return to a relatively quiet state. In fact, there is evidence to suggest that if children are deprived of physical play, they will play with even greater vigour when given the opportunity to do so (Pellegrini et al. 1995; Smith and Hagan 1980). If there is an appetite for rough and tumble play, and if such play not only reflects but also promotes neurological maturity, it seems that it would be counterproductive and possibly harmful to try to prevent it.

In general, boys are simply more physical than girls. Far more boys take part in rough and tumble play than do girls (Humphreys and Smith 1984). Boys also tend to enjoy physical activities on the playground, which reflects the fact that men are, in western culture, more physical. But this is not just a matter of culture, it is neurological as well. The brains of boys develop slower than those of girls, even before birth. Boys tend to be more aggressive than girls, a trend that appears in many cultures (Whiting and Edwards 1988).

Studies of girls and rough and tumble play are more rare. In 'Super Cat Girls: Girls' Engagement in Rough and Tumble Play', Jennifer Somerindyke (2000) argues that girls have been usually excluded from the study of rough and tumble (R&T) play because it is believed that they do not enjoy physical play activities. Her study showed, however, that girls do engage in rough and tumble play. Somerindyke encouraged a mixed group to create a new game Super Cat Girls. This study suggests that R&T combined with sociodramatic play can provide cognitive, physical and social benefits for both girls and boys. The Super Cat Girls allowed the children, both boys and girls, to experiment with their levels of creativity; for example, the girls invented 'poison' in the form of sand. The children developed elaborate rules for Super Cat Girls which provided opportunity for higher level cognitive functioning through R&T play.

Playing Super Cat Girls also helped the children to develop social skills. A key part of that was that the children learned *role reciprocity* because they had to take turns chasing and being chased. For the girls the game had the merit of teaching them what it meant to be the ones in positions of power.

Somerindyke (2000) concluded that the game showed how both boys and girls

> integrated R&T with sociodramatic play, creating opportunities for mixed-gender interaction and mutual cognitive and social benefits for both boys and girls. Pellegrini and Smith (1998) note that often researchers face conflicted coding situations because of a tendency to separate R&T from sociodramatic play. Our study supports their call to establish more complex coding schemes that account for the interaction of R&T and sociodramatic play.

But there is another unexpected sexual politics aspect to rough and tumble play. Reed and Brown (2000) argue that 'One less-researched aspect of R&T is the affective dimension, more specifically, the way in which boys care for one another through R&T.' Their qualitative study examined preadolescent boys' rough and tumble play and the way the boys expressed care and intimacy through that. The authors videotaped the boys playing their favorite R&T games in their natural surroundings. Then the subjects saw the videotapes and were asked about the experience. The surprise was that subjects were clear on where and when it was appropriate to express care and intimacy for one another. The authors suggest that teachers need to reconsider the importance of R&T as one way boys express care, fondness and friendships towards other children.

Most of the research on the pretend games that children play is very different. Nearly always, outside playschools, it is the psychologists who set the agenda for play. They initiate proceedings by saying, 'Now, let's pretend this . . .'. Though McCune-Nicolich (1981b) in an article for *Beginnings* stresses the need for parents to play with their children, the bulk of our knowledge of pretending comes from observations and experiments in play-schools. The need to be scientific has pushed research into certain directions, notably dissecting pretending as a skill. As with substituting objects, the assumption has been that one of the main tasks of research is to tease out the development of the various stages of pretending. Singer (1973) takes a slightly different view as a result of his work on fantasy and day-dreaming, rather than play.

This accent on stages of pretending is muddled, furthermore, because the literature often seems to assume that perspective taking, role playing and pretending are the same thing. Piaget argued that young children were completely egocentric and could see the world only from their own immediate point of view. Critical experiments (Hughes 1975; Donaldson 1979) have suggested that children can do rather better if they are made to see that what the experimenter wants them to do is to take the perspective of another person. Such experiments have nothing to do with pretending and not much to do with role playing but psychologists often comment on them as if they did. Light (1979), for example, looked at children who could imagine what a game board would look like from a different position; Hughes (1975) considered a problem in which children had to decide whether a policeman could see a robber from different vantage points. But these are studies of adopting different perspectives, not different roles or identities.

Pretending is also philosophically more controversial than psychologists assume. The model of it as a skill with different stages presumes children accumulate make-believe capacities and learn to pretend ever more elaborately. No moment of revelation exists when children know that it is within their control to think one thing and do another. Most psychologists appear to accept Ryle's (1947) views in *The Concept of Mind* where Ryle argued that pretending was parasitic. A child had to know what a real duck or a real party was like to play with a toy duck or pretend to be at a play party. First, you visited ponds; then you quacked in your living room. Traditionally, dualistic philosophy claimed that human beings were physiological machines with souls attached. The link between the material and the spiritual was, according to Descartes, the pineal gland. Pretending was an important faculty in this tradition. Creatures who could pretend did not reveal themselves entirely in their behaviour. Each of us has special access to his or her mind. Only I can know if I really love you. The appearances may be all there. I give you flowers, shower you with serenades but, at the witching hour of the night, I know my dark truth. I'm after your money or just doing what my analyst said would be good for my ego. But only I can know that and know that I'm pretending. In such a theory, pretending is an all or none experience.

Ryle was out to debunk dualism. He argued throughout *The Concept of Mind* against what he called 'the ghost in the machine', the ghost being the creature inside the head who guided our actions, spoke our innermost thoughts and knew we were really pretending. It was important to Ryle to show that pretending was rare and, fundamentally, unimportant.

There is an opposite view, however, and a dramatic one. It could be argued that when children know they can pretend, they cross an important barrier. Children know that you do not have to show what you feel. There are parts of your thinking you need not reveal. More, you can look and say the opposite of what you feel 'inside'. These are treacherous areas to write about but some accounts of consciousness such as O'Keefe's (1985) seem to accept that we can hold two separate things in consciousness at the same time. There has to be point where the child can do that and, even more important, one when he knows that he can do that.

The success of Ryle (1947) has meant that no one has discussed whether there might not be a revelatory moment when the child grasps that he or she can pretend, and can intend to pretend. Yet some of Piaget's observations – remember how L pretended to fall asleep many times – and some of the observations of when children first animate dolls, giving life to them, have something of that 'Eureka' feel to them. Afterwards, nothing is quite the same. Obtaining evidence of such moments should not be easy but developmentalists have assumed the stage model is the best fit.

A key factor in Piaget's theory is the inability of pre-operational children to understand the reality beneath external appearances. Piaget claimed that children didn't begin to understand that other people had inner thoughts, ideas and feelings till about the age of 7. The infant was a complete behaviourist.

Much of the work of Henry Wellman and his colleagues (Wellman 1985 and 2000) contradicts this. Wellman has studied many aspects of children's cognitions. Some of it is amusing, such as asking children what they need a brain for. But slowly Wellman has built up evidence which, like Flavell's work (see Cohen 2004), illuminates how children from 3 onwards grasp that other people have brains – and ideas, motives and feelings of their own. Surprisingly much of this work has now centred on play.

First, Wellman has looked at how young children understand cognition. Even 55 per cent of 3 year olds understand that the brain is not visible. You can't see the brain while you can see the head. A majority of them believe that the brain is a rather mind-like entity. You need it to think, to remember and to dream with but you don't need it to wiggle your toes. Most 4 year olds judged that while a doll had eyes, hair, ears and a mouth, it did not have a brain – unlike a human being.

Second, Johnson and Wellman (1980) showed that 4-year-old children can describe mental states that have nothing to do with object reality. In one study, children were tricked. The experimenter showed them an object that was hidden in one of two boxes. The boxes were manipulated. The child was asked in which box the object was. The child got it wrong, of course. When the box was opened, there was no object. The object turned out to be in the wrong box. Yet though the children could see they got it wrong, they insisted – using the correct mental language – that they knew where it was and remembered where it had been. What they saw didn't limit how they described their mental states.

Shatz et al. (1983) investigated the acquisition of mental terms in 2- and 3-year-old children. They looked in particular at the child's natural use of mental verbs such as think, dream, remember and pretend. Children started to use these words regularly when they were 30 months old though the use increased in their third year. Wellman (1985) cites instances such as a 2 year 8 months child saying, 'It's not real I was just pretending' or 'I thought the socks were in the drawer except they weren't'. The child is able to contrast two states. In the first case, his own external behaviour – claiming the socks were in the drawer – with his own internal state, knowing quite well they were not there.

Wellman (1985) has always been careful not to make too lavish claims for young children. Their conception of the mind is confused and growing. They often make mistakes. But there is no doubt that from 3 years on, young children begin to grasp that other minds exist – and this is often seen in their play.

Knowing that you can pretend might well seem to be a landmark on the road to being self-aware. Wellman (1985) found that, by the age of 4, children know what saying 'I pretend' means and what it implies. All this suggests a sea-change which developmental psychologists might look for. The analysis of the conflicting positions I have offered is a rather crude one. As we grow older, we may do things for real, we may pretend completely or we may carry out sequences of actions which are largely sincere but which involve some exaggeration. I may desire you rather than love you but, who knows, love may grow. Still, for the child, knowing it can act not 'for real' would seem to mark a crucial change in its sense of its own identity and of its secret power.

On the whole, developmental psychologists have ignored these possibilities. They have accepted Ryle's arguments, often without referring to him, and, as a result, have been happy to seek the stages of development of pretending skills. These skills have to depend on more realistic skills assembled slowly like learning to write. But there is evidence from Bruner (1975) that children learn very quickly, over less than three months, to take the initiative in peekaboo. And there has to be a first time for when a child puts on a play or pretend face and knows what he is doing. Reuben first put on a play face at 9 months and first declared he was pretending to be Batman at 2:2. Wasn't his world changed forever when he knew he could do that and take control of his own actions?

Whether pretending is, or is not, an important ability in the evolution of the sense of identity, its origins would seem to lie in the home. But psychologists have focused on the playschool and on play between children of the same age. Drawing on research by Garvey (1977), Dunn and Kendrick (1982), Fein (1984) and my own observations, I want to argue that children pretend earlier than is generally believed. Young children may be able to co-operate younger and better than has been supposed. They may also be able to carry out intentions and plans earlier. Analysis of the development of language (Wells 1981) has shown that from 18 months on children are aware of the need to take turns, to listen, to interrupt and to signal that they are about to interrupt. Wells' transcripts suggest that 18 month olds 'know' of the existence of others and can accommodate to it. Might they not perhaps manifest this skill in play too?

The attempt to identify the stages of pretending goes back to Gesell and Piaget. For both, young children could not play with each other. At 24 months, Gesell (1929) notes 'parallel play predominates when with other children though he obviously enjoys being with other children'. By 36 months, there was some 'co-operative activity'. A year on, the child liked to play in groups of two or three of the same sex. Piaget put such co-operative play later. By the 1970s, there was still little criticism of this nature of the whole enterprise. No one seemed to pay much attention to children's personality. Did different children play the same way? Did they play differently in different contexts? If you studied birthday party behaviour would you arrive at different conclusions from playschool behaviour? Such commonsensical questions were seen as much less interesting than arriving at a typical profile of the typical play of the typical child. It would be a mistake to think that this approach has now disappeared. Curry and Arnaud (1984) provide a profile of the playgroup. Ignoring personality, social and class differences, they sketch the typical play of the 2 year old, 3 year old, 4 year old and 5 year old.

Before the age of 2, Curry and Arnaud (1984) find little social play. 'Much of the play of 2 year olds appears to parallel or to be tangential to that of other twos.' Parents did say that 2 year olds paid more attention to other small children at home or among friends but Curry and Arnaud (1984) never saw such advanced precocious behaviour in the group. They did notice 'intense watchfulness of each other with an almost compulsive tendency to imitate'. They remained convinced that the 2 year old was solitary.

By the age of 3, 'children are obviously aware of each other' and will 'moderate their egocentric stance'. They do this to maintain the goodwill of other children though Curry and Arnaud felt they sometimes did it 'in a quixotic and arbitrary way'. One 3 year old, more despotic than quixotic, said: 'Okay, you can come to my party but you have to wear running shoes.' An arbitrary child indeed! Nancy Brown, who worked at the same centre as

Curry and Arnaud, added that 3 year olds often reproduced family themes in their play but they often swopped roles instantly. They would veer from being the family dog to the mother at the drop of a hat (Brown et al. 1971).

Most 3 year olds tended also to be fascinated by gathering objects and to enjoy repeating some play actions almost ritualistically. One example was a 3-year-old boy who always began his day in the playschool by building with blocks. Curry and Arnaud (1984) noted that 3 year olds 'seem awestruck by bolder, braver or more experienced peers' and may imitate what they have done. They even saw instances in which children of this age 'will persist in pursuing children whose play ideas parallel their own interests and concerns'. Friendships develop and the authors suggest that, even at 3, they are genuine friendships based on interest in the same kinds of activities.

By the age of 4 and 5, 'children are extremely sensitive to each other and acutely attuned to what interests, pleases or provokes another child'. Curry and Arnaud (1984) gave a more descriptive account of typical 4-year-old and 5-year-old play. The 4 year old, as she saw him/her then, seemed very concerned with aggression. Many games included portraying aggressive TV superheroes or monsters. Chases were common. Children exaggerated masculine and feminine traits. Boys wanted to don whole outfits to be cowboys while super-fem girls wanted to play 'the alluring feminine side of the mother' with all accessories from veils to high heels. Children did not restrict play to home themes and were more stable in their roles.

The typical 5 year old played using far more subjects. Pretend roles include nurse, teacher, policeman, groom, bride. Curry (1974) spotted 'a heightened interest in romance' with 'exciting' boy–girl chases, acting out fairy-tales and much 'bride and groom play'. Children often parodied adult actions nicely, a point also noted by Brenda Crowe (1982) in her lyrical book *Play is a Feeling* where boys and girls often reproduced domestic rows. One girl talked on the phone, tapped her heels and moaned she was 'bored, bored, bored'. She wanted some sherry. Her mother, Crowe presumed, was pretty miserable.

Any attempt to arrive at stages of development ignores individual differences. Curry and Arnaud's (1984) fairly informal approach may be contrasted with a more rigorous one which still has similar problems.

Acknowledging her debt to Piaget, McCune-Nicolich (1981) has elaborated the most useful stages through which pretending develops. The first level of pretend play is *presymbolic schemes*. The child who is well under 1 year old knows, for example, that a cup is used for drinking, and will eventually bring an empty cup to the lips. Belsky and Most (1981) called this stage *enactive naming* and found it as early as 7½ months. The child then moves to Level 2, that of *autosymbolic schemes*. The child knows what it is to drink or to sleep and can skip in and out of reality and pretending. The child here pretends only with respect to himself or herself. So, the child will pretend to eat, pretend to drink, pretend to use the potty or to go sleep. Belsky and Most (1981) also accept that this *self-pretend* is the next stage and that it is limited to the child pretending to do things. They saw evidence that this had started by 12 months.

From 12 months onwards, the infant moves into the realm of *decentred symbolic games*. Instead of pretending to eat, the toddler takes a cup and hands it round to adults, who have to pretend to drink. McCune-Nicolich (1981) warns against supposing that the baby which offers a bottle to the mother is playing the role of mother. A more conservative view, she suggests, is that the infant is 'still insufficiently detached from the interpersonal matrix of mother-object-self to differentiate these roles'. Between 12 and 24 months, though, the toddler acquires the ability to play with others. The child pretends to feed a doll or the mother or to mop the floor. Part of this decentring involves being aware.

One development evokes general comment. Around 2 years of age, children begin to be able to 'give life' to their dolls. As reported in Chapter 3, the doll is now allowed to do things such as hold a cup or, even, feed other dolls. Pretending games that involve this skill may require, according to McCune-Nicolich, 'a symbolic capacity' similar to that needed to use substitute objects.

Once children are *decentred*, they can advance to the next level – that of *sequencing pretend acts*. The jargon explains itself really. The infant is able to link a number of pretend actions either in relation to toys such as putting a doll to sleep after washing it or in response to fantasy. Children may, for example, play chasing games which can involve a chase, a shoot-out and putting on a cowboy hat. Fein (1984) describes a sequence in which Harry and Alan who are 2:6 cradle a doll-baby, get it out of a pram, notice it has a broken arm, show that to their mother and then feed it. Eventually, they take the Baby to the doctor and, when they bang on the door with the spoon, play that he's been on vacation. This is a sophisticated pretending sequence. Such joining together of actions first appears, according to Belsky and Most (1981), at 13½ months. It is then quite rare but they found a progressive increase in it at 15, 19½ and 21 months. At 18 months, they found very little sequencing but that may be a sampling error.

The next level of play McCune-Nicolich (1981) posits has been described only by herself because hers is the only recent longitudinal study – and even that lasted only till the children were 26 months old. After putting things in sequences, the child becomes able to plan sequences of playing. McCune-Nicolich (1977) observed children searching for absent objects they needed to complete games when they were between 18 months and 26 months. Such searching suggested that the child had a game in mind and was not dependent on those toys that were at hand to spark a particular game. Such *planned pretend*, Nicolich argued, emerged when the child could substitute one object for another.

In her classification, McCune-Nicolich doesn't differentiate between solitary pretending (the toddler pretends to be Batman), pretend games played with other children (Batman chases Robin) and pretend games played with adults. She seems to accept the general position that, under the age of 3, children do not pretend with each other. Piaget claimed that till the age of 5 this was essentially impossible, children being egocentric. This view has certainly dogged most of the research. Watson and Fischer (1980), for example, offered yet another stage model of the eight stages of social role playing. But none of their eight steps involved children playing together. Rather, the solitary child moved from making a doll do something, to making the doll perform a sequence of acts, to making the doll pretend it was either a doctor or a patient.

This focus on identifying the stages of pretending has meant that there has been less attention paid to the detailed contents of children's play. Creating a general model of pretending play with a orderly sequence of stages has taken priority. Studies from a different perspective offer rich data.

Emotions and false belief

In the context of both McCune-Nicolich's and Wellman's thesis, it's important also to examine the work of Smiley and Huttenlocher. Summarising about ten years of research, Smiley and Huttenlocher (1991) claim there are four distinct phases in learning about emotions.

First, parents use words like sad or scared to describe the behaviour of the infant. The mother sees the child crying and says 'Harry is sad'.

Second, the infant associates that description with his own internal state. Mother says Harry is sad. Harry feels like this: feeling like so is being sad.

Third, the young child sees that other people also display the kind of behaviour that he does. My friend John is smiling. When I smile, Mother says I'm happy. If Johnny is smiling then the right way to describe Johnny's behaviour is happy. At this stage, the child doesn't have any insight into how Johnny is feeling.

Finally, the child realises that it is not just the external behaviour that he shares with other people but the internal states. If I cry when I'm sad then when Johnny displays the behaviour of crying, Johnny must be sad too.

Smiley and Huttenlocher (1987) found a crucial change in young children – between 24 and 39 months. At 24 months, few children use emotional words spontaneously. By 30 months, many are fairly competent in the use of the word *happy*. *Sad* and *scared* follow soon after. If they are given videotapes to watch, after the age of 3, they can infer the internal state of a character in the video. If they see a crying puppet, children know that when characters cry they are sad.

It is after 39 months, Smiley and Huttenlocher claim, that children make the important switch that allows them to recognise that other people also have thoughts and feelings. After 39 months, they have some insight into what these might be. There has been other work which examines the way in which children learn about emotions through play. Ariel (1991) has argued that children's play reflects interpersonal goals and that these can be teased out through semiotic analysis. He argues that certainly by the age of 5:6 'the child interprets the behaviour of playmates attempting to understand or guess their purposes and intentions' (Ariel 1991: 122).

Again the most interesting development is a set of studies which suggest young children can tell the difference between appearance and reality – and that play is one of the central activities where this skill is first to be seen. In many ways, the key experiment should be called the Yeti experiment for it is all about disappearing footsteps.

Chandler et al. (1989) found that children aged 2:6 removed tell-tale footprints that a doll had left behind when they were told to conceal the fact that the doll had been seen. This simple experiment suggests that children understand what clues can suggest to other people. The experiment has met with some scepticism because the children were so young that critics have claimed that perhaps the children didn't understand the relevance of removing footprints. This seems a little too sceptical. What is true, however, is that the Chandler experiment is hard to square with other results.

Joan Peskin (1992) and others studied 3 and 4 year olds. The children had to get a toy they wanted from two puppets. One was wicked. Peskin told the children, 'The Dark Blue puppet never chooses the one you want because he doesn't want you to be sad. The Light Blue puppet always chooses the one you want.' Children had the chance to induce a false belief in the puppet by hiding the particular sticker which they wanted. Only 29 per cent of 3 year olds could manage this whereas 87 per cent of 5 year olds could. Yet, there was no doubt that the children wanted to stop the Light Blue puppet getting the sticker they wanted by physically attacking it. Peskin argued that this study showed children of 3 had great difficulty in understanding the notion of inducing false belief. If so, why did Chandler and his colleagues come up with the result they did?

Sodian (1991) found that 3 year olds could predict the next move an adult or a child would make in a game but found it hard to induce false belief.

One explanation for the different results lies in the nature of the task. To remove clues may be simpler than to create a false belief by lying as to one's own internal state. Leslie (1987) proposes an interesting mix of information-processing and introspection to account for the complexity of false belief.

Flavell et al. (1992b) has also found evidence that suggests 3 year olds find it hard to grasp the reality/appearance distinction in people. Flavell altered the facial appearance of characters who were telling a story. He found that characters who looked deformed or nasty were not believed by the children just because they had had an accident happen to them. It didn't matter that the characters had been previously established as nice and truthful. However, 5 year olds were not so influenced by the mere physical appearance of the storyteller. Flavell notes that these results fit well with the results of his work on the appearance of objects.

The interest in trying to identify the stages of the development of play continues. Howes and Matheson (1992) have followed in the footsteps of McCune-Nicolich. They studied forty-eight children from infancy through preschool. Unfortunately they started late: they didn't have any subjects who were younger than 10 months old. Some subjects were 23 months old when they were first observed. Howes and Matheson's team visited the forty-eight children at six-month intervals – this again seems to be something of a methodological flaw. Six months is a long interval with such young children. On every observation day, each child was observed for two hours by two observers.

Despite the methodological problems, Howes and Matheson (1992) found a not very surprising pattern to the development of different kinds of play in their sample. They propose this sequence:

- parallel play – two children play alongside
- parallel aware – and are aware of each other
- simple social – and make simple contact
- complementary and reciprocal – which becomes more parallel
- co-operative social pretend – and leads into pretending
- complex social pretend.

Howes and Matheson (1992) also studied 259 children who attended what they called a 'minimally adequate' child care facility. These children followed the same kind of stages. Howes and Matheson were very concerned to validate a scale called the Howes Peer Play Scale. They seemed rather less interested in drawing out the implications of this work.

This continuing interest has led to some useful findings. Doyle and Doehring (1992) found that children of 6 who are more frequent pretenders have more strategies for entering into social pretend play. Ladd and Hart (1992) have found that until the age of 5 parents tend to determine the opportunities children have for playing with other children but that, after that, children increasingly start to set up more of their own play contacts. Ladd and

Hart found too that parents used inviting children over as a means of teaching their own young how to act the host and be sensitive to others' needs. Neither of these findings are very surprising but they again reflect the way in which play research is branching out to encompass other areas.

Contents of play: content to play

Matthews (1977) studied 4-year-old middle-class children to find out just what they could, and could not, pretend. They certainly could animate objects. A child held a doll and explained, 'My baby is crying because she wants to take a nap.' They could pour out imaginary substances, 'coffee' from an empty jug. They could give certain objects properties. Boys would screech like sirens as they raced around in cars. Making one object stand for another was, by the age of 4, child's play. They could pretend a block was a building and incorporate that pretence in their games though, like Golomb (1977), Matthews (1977) found that children did have standards of realism. If she told them to pretend that a flowerpot was a telephone, she would be asked to explain why.

Usefully Matthews' article did not deal differently with pretending with objects and with social pretending. Her subjects would certainly pretend any object they liked existed but they could also pretend any situation they liked existed. They could make-believe they had reached a store. They could act out various parts with, she noted, a fair degree of accuracy. The middle-class 4 year old has good patter as a patient, a doctor, even a teacher! The gist of Matthew's work was that by the age of 4 children did have a surprising level of pretending available to them.

Also in 1977, Garvey showed that far younger children, 2 year olds, could build on their pretending skills to play social games. In these games, they had to listen to each other and act on that. They were not taking part in isolated, egocentric scenarios but acting together. Garvey (1977) studied children in their homes. We have seen that by 18 months, children can ask adults to drink out of an empty cup and then may learn to pass it along. Mothers, fathers, older siblings may well elaborate such games and the child learns from them.

Garvey (1977) found that 2 year olds were able to introduce a sequence by putting on an exaggerated 'act' to signal This isn't for real. Learning to do that must occur in the home and seems to stem from the games that mothers and fathers play with their children. Garvey found that her 2 year olds would produce and react to such an exaggeration. She then offers an extended transcript of a play episode between a girl aged 3:3 and a boy aged 2:9. The girl leads the play but the boy makes 'right' responses throughout. The girl begins holding a baby doll. She tells the boy, 'Say, go to sleep now.' The boy does so. The girl then whines, becoming the baby, 'Why?' The boy says 'Baby' and the girl repeats why. The boy says 'Because'. His performance doesn't satisfy her so she suggests: 'No, say "Because"', and does so emphatically. The boy responds saying 'Because' very emphatically. The girl still doesn't think that's good enough. The dialogue reported by Garvey goes on as follows:

GIRL	BOY
	Not good. You bad.
Why?	
	'Cause you spill your milk.
No, 'cause I bit somebody	
	Yes, you did.
Say 'Go to sleep. Put your head down' (*sternly*)	
	Put your head down (*sternly*)
No.	
	Yes.
No.	
	Yes. Okay, I will spank you. Bad boy (*spanks her*)
No. My head's up (*giggles*) I want my teddy bear (*petulant voice*)	
	No, your teddy bear go away (*sternly*)
Why?	

At this point, the boy, who had already shown some initiative in spanking her, told her that her teddy bear would walk away and took it with him. The girl then demanded matter of factly if he was going to pack up the teddy bear. Garvey (1977) notes that in this exchange the girl plays herself, the Baby and, almost, the director of the play telling the boy what to say and how to say it. For his part, the boy assumes the role of the parent when he says he will spank her and, then, part-parent/part-fed-up-child, withdraws the teddy bear. Garvey notes that these children can switch in and out of familiar roles with ease. They also take proper turns to speak and to start off various elements of the game. At 2:9, the boy is perfectly able both to respond to the girl's directions and to set off on a tangent of his own which isn't a flight into egocentricity but a twist appropriate with the script of this game. Garvey's research makes it clear these achievements weren't unusual at that age.

Fein (1984) introduced her descriptions with a number of remarks on the work of George Herbert Mead. Writing in the mid-1930s, Mead (1934) suggested that children moved through a series of perspective and role-taking stages. Fein noticed that some children were able to create quite long games such as 'I'm going fishing' with another toddler where they did little but watch. Others as young as 2:6 played complex games together. Harry and Sarah (both 2:6) are typical. They start by playing close together physically but quite different games. Sarah is combing a stuffed animal's hair; Harry is placing objects in a buggy. When Sarah puts the comb down on the table, Harry picks it up and then combs his hair with a bottle. Sarah protests it's her comb. Harry says it's now his and then tries to comb Sarah's hair. She pushes him away. Harry goes to get his spoon and the bottle and says: 'Take this for medicine in, okay?' 'Okay, put my spoon,' says Sarah. Harry feeds her with the spoon saying 'It's goop, it's for your nose. Take more.' Yes, Sarah says, telling him to put the poop in her mouth. She continues to accept medicine which then becomes lemonade till she picks up the spoon and starts to feed Harry saying: 'It's medicine, it's medicine, look.' Harry then tries to take the spoon and bottle back. The children continue this with a pause while Sarah picks up her own bottle which Harry has told her is on the floor.

Harry then reiterates that the medicine is for her nose, he dips the bottle on to the spoon. Sarah sits, takes it, says 'Thanks.' 'You gonna be all right,' assures doctor Harry. (In a previous game with another playmate, Harry had taken a baby to the doctor.) Sarah says: 'I will, I will be all right.' The children then vie for which one is going to feed the other. First, Harry does the feeding; then Sarah plies him with medicine and then drinks some Kool-Aid from the bottle. 'Want some Kool-Aid,' she asks Harry. He nods yes, takes some and leaves.

In this sequence, Fein (1984) notes the children swop roles and draw on common symbols. Sarah knows that when she is being given medicine, Harry is the right person to assure her that she is all right and he does, indeed, give that assurance. The episode shows again very early interactive play.

The kind of playing described both by Garvey (1977) and by Fein (1984) is a considerable achievement for children who are so young. In a study of *shared pretend* among 3 year olds, Stockinger Forys and McCune-Nicolich (1984) give probably the most meticulous analysis of how such games evolve. The researchers brought into the laboratory playroom three pairs of children who did not know each other. They videotaped the proceeding of two 30-minute lesson sessions over two days. The study was designed to see both how the children played and, more generally, how they coped with being put with a strange child. Rather to their surprise, they found that in five out of six cases, the first pieces of social interaction between the children were pretend games.

At first all the children explored the room. In one pair (L and A), as soon as the adult left the room, A said, 'I see some fish.' L ignored at first and fiddled with her jewellery. A moved close to L and said: 'C'mon girl, let's get going.' L ignored her and continued to ignore her when she put a flashlight off and on. A walked away and played with kitchen equipment while L watched. Then, L said the goldfish were pretty and 'came to life'. She went into the kitchen play area, opened cupboards and said to A, 'Anybody have a baby?' Then, they made for the doll area and played a lengthy game of twenty-seven turns in which they cared for, groomed and put the dolls to bed. For the rest of the hour, the two girls played a variety of games. The second day, they fell into playing almost immediately. For most of this session, L's mother sat inside the room and, on a number of occasions, L tried to stop playing because she was upset and wanted her mother's attention. A's reaction to that was interesting. She tried to lure L back into their game. On a number of occasions, A tried to comfort L. Once she said: 'Now don't be so crying. Don't be sad' and, later on, 'If you cry too much, you'll be sick.' Make-believe was much healthier.

Not all the pairs were as playful, Stockinger Forys and McCune-Nicolich (1984) found. But all six children seemed quite sensitive to the others. The more familiar the children became, the more they played. At first, the solitary dominant child seemed able to wait while the other one warmed up. A was not too obtrusive, for example, but gently persisted to get L playing. By the second session, L was quite able to provoke by tossing in such remarks as 'your baby [the doll] likes me but she doesn't like you'. The children were able to act out the correct roles of a driver and passengers and L and A slipped much social observation into some of their games. All the girls devoted much time to adorning themselves with jewellery. In one of the most articulate exchanges, L and A set out to go to a fancy party and L insisted that A needed her 'fancy things' which included her brushes and her hat. They then climbed into their car, 'with hats on, holding hair brushes, combs and mirrors and continued with their journey which functioned for the observers as our most fascinating sojourn into the private world of 3 year old players'. The level of skill, throughout, was high.

But what is the limit? How young can children play together? Rubinstein and Howes (1976) studied eight children aged 18 months. The children were from professional families and, although they were watched for 75 minutes, the psychologists analysed only 75 chunks of behaviour, each 20 seconds long. Two-thirds of that play was left on the cutting room floor and never looked at! The chunks were scored for when a toddler started an interaction, talked to another child responsively, made physical contact, offered objects, imitated or just talked spontaneously. Toddlers paid quite a lot of attention to each other and this did affect their play. On their own, playing solo, toddlers were most creative in the use of objects; using an object meant that, if two children played together, they played more creatively than when neither of them had an object. Rubinstein and Howes (1976) were disappointed in how little the toddlers played together. They did not often play with each other but they were clearly affected by the presence of others. Ross and Goldman (1977) found that only one-third of their sample, aged 2, knew how to take their parts properly in a game that required them to take consecutive turns. Bronson (1972) in a long monograph was as pessimistic. She observed children aged 18 months to 24 months and found little evidence that toddlers played together. But she acknowledged that her children hardly knew each other and that she only scored interactions without a toy as play. But she also wondered if psychologists might not be looking in the wrong place. Bronson (1972: 111) wrote: 'most of the experience required to develop enactive mechanisms will be acquired, not with peers, but with older persons'. She went on to argue that there might be reasons why 'the incidence of truly social interactions among unfamiliar peers remains remarkably low'. These children not only were very small but also did not know each other. In homes, older siblings might lead younger ones into interactions including games. Bronson (1972) suggested, in fact, that a more realistic answer required psychology to look more realistically at where play starts.

Playing with brothers and sisters

It seems likely that children first show their play behaviours in the home. Valentine (1942) certainly found that with laughter as well as play. My own observations which included contrasting the way Nicholas and Reuben played at home and in the playgroup (where they knew I was observing but I did try to stay distant) found similar trends.

Furthermore, play in the lab or playschool appears often to revolve around some set themes like putting dolls to bed and play doctors. There are few mentions of roaring like lions as Valentine (1942) did or of Action Shows like Nicholas evolved, which are described later. Lab plays are usually quite anodyne. The analytic literature suggests that children deal with conflicts about their bodies and parental jealousies in play but few experiments report such dramas. Take obscene play. There were some set games where Nicholas pretended to be my Daddy, where Nicholas and Reuben pretended to have vaginas and frequent bawdy games that revolved around going to the toilet; by contrast, in the Greenwich playgroup, there were only occasional outbursts of bawdy in the Wendy House, including one game where children who knew each other very well stripped and one girl was ironing a little boy's penis. This was part of being a doctor! In general, though, research on pretend play has failed to tease out the depths and elaborations that children seem capable of.

The absence of much research on play between siblings compounds this problem. Yet, scattered, there are studies which suggest that very young children can get involved in pretend play. Dunn (1981) has claimed that 60 per cent of her sample of 2 year olds engaged in pretend play either with their mothers or with a sibling. She offered a detailed description of how Kelly, aged 3, directed a birthday party game involving other children which included pretending to have a party. Dale (1982) found that children as young as 2:0 became involved in complex pretend games within the family, involving siblings. MacKeith and Silvey (1983) have examined the imaginary worlds that some children create and found much the same. Often, an older child involves a younger child in the dreaming up, and running, of a fantasy world like the Brontës' Angria or C.S. Lewis's *Narnia*. MacKeith and Silvey (1983) learned that some children as young as 5 or 6 created elaborate fantasy worlds with their older siblings, a finding which has since been built on, as we shall see. Dunn and Kendrick (1982) found that at 6, siblings said that one of the best things about having brothers or sisters was playing with them. One pair mentioned playing 'flying objects'. Much of Chapter 6 describes my longitudinal observations of Nicholas and Reuben's play. But some aspects of that are relevant here.

When he was 9 months old, Reuben could laugh at Nicholas's physical actions. Nicholas stamped his feet on the seat of a chair, which made Reuben laugh. Nicholas repeated the stamping and made his brother laugh again. Nicholas then slid down the back of an armchair and nearly hit Reuben, who might have been hurt – but who laughed. The two brothers often played around Reuben's playpen. Nicholas charged around the outside of it pretending, he informed Reuben, that he was being an elephant. To pretend to be an elephant Nicholas walked very slowly and heavily. Then, he pretended to be a bird and flapped his arms to prove it. This was done, quite clearly, for Reuben's benefit and Reuben laughed.

Nicholas, who was 5:0, would also play peekaboo and tickling games with Reuben. When Reuben was 9 months, Nicholas got hold of his feet and banged them together. He got a laugh and, then, elaborated the game by holding Reuben's arms and waving them up and down forcing him into a gymnastic exercise. Reuben giggled at this. Clearly, in both these instances, Nicholas took the lead. As early as 7 months old, Reuben liked to be tickled by Nicholas and, once, lay on a rug close to Nicholas and enjoyed Nicholas tickling him.

When Reuben was 1 year old, he started to laugh enormously in what became a ritual called Nicholas's Action Show. Every evening before going to bed, Nicholas would go up to Aileen's and my bedroom and jump around on the bed entertaining us with all manner of somersaults and would-be acrobatics. Nicholas had seen a lot of gymnastics on the television and seemed to be imitating them. He also provided a running commentary on what he was doing and christened some of his leaps 'Super Jumps'. Usually Nicholas did not let Reuben on the bed but Reuben liked to watch and crawl around. One evening Reuben (at 12 months) became very excited. Aileen then held him by his arms and, holding him, got him to jump up and down just like Nicholas did. Being 'trampolined' made Reuben laugh a great deal.

Between 12 months and 24 months, Reuben slowly worked his way into the Action Show. By 24 months, Reuben was devoted to Batman and trans-formed him, as we shall see, into all kinds of odd characters. Reuben also brought Batman into the Action Show. Both boys now would leap about on the bed, Reuben often saying that he was Batman and laughing. Nicholas was by this age (5:10) more interested in showing off his jumping prowess. He peppered jumps with comments like 'This is a Super Jump.' Reuben watched these jumps with attention and, often, when Nicholas jumped, he laughed. This laugh had the effect often of making Nicholas jump. Despite the age difference between them, both children could laugh when Aileen told them to jump into her arms.

Just as Reuben learned to take part in the Action Show through watching Nicholas, he also learned to take part in chases at a young age as a result of the games that Nicholas played with him such as being an elephant and a number of 'play attacks'. When Reuben was 1:4, he and a friend called John could chase each other, laughing while they did so though it was neither a long, nor a fully committed chase.

As shown, Nicholas quite often ran around outside Reuben's playpen and, sometimes, play-attacked him either with a soft toy like a hippo (at 9 months) or by saying he was a bison and charging. Nicholas fell in love with bisons after reading a book in which some prehistoric Swedes visited prehistoric America which was full of bisons and Stone Age skyscrapers. By the time that Reuben was 11 months old, he had absorbed enough to be able to take the lead in charging Nicholas. The first time he did it, Nicholas was under the kitchen table when Reuben charged. 'Here's Reuben storming the castle', laughed Nicholas. By 1:4 Reuben was able to start both chasing games and, as would be predicted by Bruner's work, peekaboo games. The first time he did it with me, he snatched a magazine out of my hand and covered my face with it. By 1:11, Reuben started chases and fighting games regularly, pinioning Nicholas on the floor and poking his tongue out at him. Then, at 2:6 after Nicholas had been chasing Reuben into my study, Reuben told him to go away. Both boys tumbled onto the carpet and Reuben assumed a serious look. A moment later he wanted to restart the game which had begun as hide and seek. Reuben said: 'You get up and I'll look for you.' Nicholas obliged and it began again. At 2:6, Reuben had the skill and confidence to rekindle a game.

A good example of how Reuben learned and joined in with Nicholas took place when Nicholas was 5:6 and Reuben 1:9. Nicholas had begun listening to pop music and started to dance. He quite often laughed as he danced and, sometimes, deliberately over-contorted his body. He would pretend to be holding a microphone. At 5:6, Nicholas announced that he was going to do a funny dance. He began to skip and hop from one leg to the next, knowing that wasn't a proper dance. Aileen laughed at this and added Booing noises. They 'made' Nicholas hop more. Reuben then joined trying to hop. Both children laughed until, quite suddenly, Nicholas rushed out of the room. Outside the living room, the brothers began to shoot at each other till, after two minutes, leader Nicholas said he wanted to do the funny dance again. He pulled Reuben back into the room and Reuben started to stamp his feet in a kind of dance. Nicholas made painful noises which made Reuben laugh.

In these games, as in their chases, Nicholas was very much the senior, initiating partner but, by 1:9, Reuben was able to join in very actively. By the age of 2:6, Reuben could even take the lead in some games.

Reuben was very easily toilet-trained. From 18 months to 24 months, he had often joined in Nicholas's 'dirty' jokes. By the age of 2:3, Reuben was beginning to produce his own dirty jokes such as turning a rendition of 'Happy Birthday' into 'Happy Aaah', the grunt he used when sitting on the potty. At 2:4, Batman suffered the sacrilege of being turned by Reuben into 'Aaah-man'. Sometimes, while running about as Superman or Batman, Reuben would sing 'Aaah-man', and laugh. One evening, Reuben started a game in which he dropped Aaahs all over the living room floor. The process lasted a long time, Nicholas followed Reuben and imitated him, dropping his own Aaahs all over the floor. Both boys laughed at each drop. Reuben's interest in excrement offered Nicholas a chance to regress too. When Reuben was naked at my mother's house, 5-year-old Nicholas asked if he could also take his clothes off. When Reuben sat on his potty aged 1:7 flying a little piece of silver paper round which he called a *Buff*, Nicholas laughed and added how funny it was that Reuben was 'doing pooh pooh and flying around in his buff'.

One final example may show how, in real homes, such games can be intermingled. By the time Reuben was 1:7, he was practised in longish chasing games. One evening a game started when Nicholas laughed as Reuben peed outside his potty. Nicholas then encouraged his brother to draw in the pee. For no clear reason, then, the game turned into a chase. Nicholas started to hide from Reuben and to call 'Buff'. Reuben rose from his potty to give half-hearted chase. Aileen told them they must stop and eat. After a pause, Nicholas said: 'Do you want your food cooked in your bath?' We all three laughed. Then, again, Nicholas and Reuben began chasing each other and becoming quite hysterical with laughter with Nicholas teasing Reuben during the chases. Though Nicholas could tease Reuben verbally, Reuben was certainly by now able to start chasing games.

This brief sketch of some of the games Nicholas and Reuben played suggests that Reuben picked up some key ideas about playing and pretending from Nicholas and that he did so, inside the home, very young. The idea that there was a definite start to a game and that this often went with an exaggerated noise or face or a statement like 'I'm going to charge' were tricks that Reuben often saw his brother perform. Drawing on Garvey (1977), Dunn and Kendrick (1982), Bronson (1972) and my own observations, it seems reasonable to conclude that the earliest social games of children involve both their parents and their siblings. The texture of these games is more complicated and personal than most of those studied in the playground. In Chapter 6, it becomes clear how children often use play in their relationships with their parents – a point Howes and Matheson (1992) miss because of their methodology. Equally, despite the ingenuity of Stockinger Forys and McCune-Nicolich (1984), most of the games they witnessed were fairly direct imitations of adult life. The children did not know each other well enough to comfort each other through play as Nicholas and Reuben often did, even though once A warned L against crying too much.

Much of the work on pretending – and its stages of development – would seem to have been carried out in the wrong context where pretence is least complex. And that remains the case at the start of the twenty-first century.

Class play

This idea that play evolves in the home also perhaps throws a slightly new light on an old controversy. Are there children from different social classes who suffer from a *play deficit*? You didn't imagine, unless you were a psychologist, that you could have a play deficit. Since 1968, there has been a serious debate on this issue but, before reporting it, I want to highlight an observation on class and play by Brenda Crowe (1982) who suggests that, in games, children can weave together class barriers. I particularly like her tale of a working-class boy and an upper-class girl who, happening to be in the same playgroup, decide to give a dinner party. The boy said he'd get the spam while the girl sauntered off to get the canapes from Harrods. Never mind the class differences, the game could go on.

To concerned students of the effects of 'sociodramatic play', Crowe's anecdote may just sound silly. Since 1968, when a book by an Israeli psychologist, Sara Smilansky, *The Effect of Sociodramatic Play on Disadvantaged Schoolchildren*, was published, much research has been devoted to showing that certain children suffer a 'play deficit' and that this has considerable negative consequences. Smilansky herself pioneered methods of 'curing' the children of this deficit.

Smilansky (1968) argued that sociodramatic play had to involve imitation of roles, make-believe, two or more children playing and verbal exchanges. She counted as instances of such play only episodes which lasted ten minutes or more. She found that children with North African and Middle Eastern parents (who in Israel tended to be working class) played this way far less often and far less ably than children with European parents. As a result, these children suffered both intellectually and socially. They tended also to be more aggressive and more passive than middle-class 'playing' children.

Though it was Smilansky who first received major attention for these findings, she acknowledged her debt to an Israeli colleague, Dana Feitelson, who had started work in the field in the 1950s. Politically, in Israel at this time, there was great concern about equality between western and eastern Jews. Feitelson went to work in the United States and in a study in the early 1970s (Feitelson and Ross 1973), she found that Boston children exhibited similar patterns. Lower-middle-class children tended to engage in very little thematic play and fantasy. The whole field of research was, bizarrely, dominated by Israeli psychologists: the first study to question Smilansky's view was that of Rivka Eifermann (1973). Eifermann found that the kinds of games Smilansky had found to be lacking in 3 to 6 year olds emerged round the age of 6 to 8. But the criteria Eifermann used were far less rigorous. For her, sociodramatic play didn't require the long elaboration of themes (over ten minutes) or, even, much word play. Playing bus stop in the school playground was a sociodramatic game.

Despite Eifermann's (1973) results, Smilansky (1968) and Feitelson and Ross (1973) succeeded in putting 'play deficit' on the agenda of psychology and may have helped spur research into links between that and autism. Smilansky (1968) found in Ohio and Illinois that working-class children turned out also to be lacking in sociodramatic play. This made them less skilled at those performances 'necessary for successful integration into the school situation or full co-operation in the "school game"'. Without such games, the children did not blossom. They were poor at creativity, poor at intelligence skills and poor at social skills. Smilansky recommended a series of play tutorials. Her recommendations both fitted the political mood of the times with the Head Start programme and echoed old faiths in the power of play. In Chapter 2, we saw that in the 1920s, social reformers advocated play as a way of bringing immigrants up to American standards; in the 1940s and 1950s, the adventure playground movement was, in some European countries, almost evangelical. As a result, there was much interest in how adults could facilitate play both in working-class children and in all children.

Arnaud and Curry (1976) claimed that teachers could promote play. They had to make lots of toys available, especially toys that allowed children to play 'family' games. Teachers also had to provide 'unstructured materials', like clay, and enough of each so that the very young children wouldn't have to cope with the agony of waiting to play with them which might be too much at their age. A permissive atmosphere had to be created. Later, Curry and Arnaud (1984) went on to recommend 'some specific ways' in which adults can 'facilitate play'. With 2 year olds, the teacher should help the children become more aware of each other, saying aloud what the child is doing. For instance, look at Fred who is building a tower with the red blocks. Can we make the tower into part of an airport? Teachers have to 'accommodate to the slow, deliberate pace of the 2 year old'. At 3 years old, Curry and Arnaud recommended 'the teacher becomes an unequivocally central figure' who will clarify the roles children are playing. An example they give is of the teacher reminding a child who is playing father to say goodbye before he leaves for the office or directing what the next part is such as by saying, 'Who's going to drive the car to the haunted house?' Most 3 year olds can appreciate the teachers briefly taking a part themselves. At 4 years of age, the 'channelling becomes a major adult function with the high energy level and strong emotionality' of the child. The teacher suggests Fred uses Margaret's idea or that they play together or that they could both be doctors. In all this, there is no doubt, according to the authors, that the children will benefit by being taught play. Given the way psychologists see play as a skill, this isn't surprising.

There is, however, a different view of all these interventions. The authors who describe them, with the exception of Sutton-Smith (1983), are not very aware of the politics of the situation. Two approaches, McLoyd (1982) and Schwartzman (1984), highlighted some of the assumptions behind all this. McLoyd pointed out that many of the assessments of how well children played depended on how well they expressed themselves. Language skills rather than play were being 'tested'. P.K. Smith (1978), Simon and Smith (1983) and Smith et al. (1985) questioned the design of Smilansky's (1968) and similar experiments. They claimed that a more rigorous design shows that it is attention rather than play tutoring which boosts a child's performance. There is nothing surprising in this especially if you claim that play develops originally within the family.

Apart from such technical criticism, Schwartzman (1984) launched an ideological attack on Smilansky. She suggested that Smilansky and her followers imposed all their prejudices on the data. Good play is what middle-class psychologists of western origins think is appropriate. If North African Jews didn't play the way children from Russia, Poland and Germany did, that's why they're inferior. Schwartzman (1984) deployed this case skilfully.

The anthropological literature suggests that children play everywhere. They don't need toys and they don't need playgrounds. They certainly don't need teachers. She quoted a study by Maretzski and Maretzski (1963) of Taira children in Okinawa. They praise their subjects for their ability 'to meet the minimum of equipment with the maximum of inventiveness and enthusiasm'. Outside the protected environment of the middle-class west, children make their own toys, link work with their play and act far more creatively than adults allow. Schwartzman (1984) seems unaware of Barthes (1973) on toys but she would probably echo his sentiments. Children are robbed of the freedom to create their own play not only by adult pressures but also by the very form of toys. 'The bourgeois status of toys', fulminated Barthes (1973), 'can be recognized not only in their forms, which are all functional, but in their substances.' Chemical, plastic toys have taken over from wooden ones. Wood 'is a familiar and poetic substance which does not sever the child from close contact with the tree, the table, the floor'. And wooden blocks can be turned by the child into anything. They have been for ages. Schwartzman argued that children make toys and games out of anything. It is absurd for one culture to impose its specific ideas of what is better play or to talk of play deficits. These exist only in the mind of the psychologist.

Schwartzman (1984) whips up a good polemic. Politically, I have some sympathy with the attack she makes. It seems prudent to snipe at the label play 'deficits' which suggests, ever so maturely, that my play is better than your play, it doesn't follow though that there are no differences in styles of play. When psychologists have studied it, they have found that play develops in the home before it develops elsewhere. Children at 24 months, certainly, can engage in sophisticated pretending games with their siblings and their parents. It would be very strange if the environment in which play developed did not affect that play – especially if some parents go out of their way to follow the advice of child care experts since Dr Spock and play with their children. I have argued in this chapter that we now have partly useful descriptions of the stages of pretending that children go through. Unfortunately, most of these studies have been based in nursery schools (with children of very similar ages) or on relatively artificial observations in the home. They do not give a complete picture but they do enough to alert us to the fact that we need to study what happens in the cot, in the bedroom and in the living room if we are to understand the origins of human play.

These generalised functions may be particularly important in explaining adult play. Apter and Kerr (1991) find evidence of play in nearly everything adults do: sports, games, sexual behaviour, gambling, even some forms of religious experience. They view play as a state of mind rather than a series of behaviours, distinguishing 'telic' or serious states of mind from 'paratelic' or playful states. In the paratelic state the individual is able to explore, develop and elaborate a variety of skills, and test them to the limits in a free and imaginative way. He or she is able to build up a stockpile of habits, skills and knowledge that is more extensive than it would have been in the goal-oriented telic state alone. In the latter state, the individual learns to select from these, to articulate them over time in a way that may demand anticipation, foresight and planning. It is the transitions or reversals between the two states that allows learning to occur. This serves as the basis for what the authors call 'reversal theory'. Overall, play or paratelic thinking creates a means for adapting to one's environment by providing self-confidence, new ideas, and relief from stress, and by reinforcing social relationships.

5 Pretending

Before you start this chapter and switch into serious academic mode, try to remember at least one game that you played with your parents. Was it fun? Was it something you felt they did out of duty? Was it something they did to show off? My father didn't play with me but devoted much time when I was about 5 to explain to me the details of his stamp collection. For years afterwards, I felt I ought to collect stamps even though they didn't interest me much. He felt, I'm sure, we were having fun.

I don't mean to give that anecdote too much (or, even, any) weight but just to focus on what is a complicated and rather neglected area – the way that children and parents play together. If you were to go to Blackheath Common in London on a summer's evening, you would witness scenes that few psychologists seem to bother with. There is a fairground next to the park. Many older children go out on their own but the fairground is also packed with families. Often, the parents have resisted going and some, now that they are here, are sulking at the waste of time and money. But others are pleased their children are having a good time. Some fathers decide to teach their children how to drive dodgems and smash coconuts on the shies. Since not many fathers are coconut shy experts, they often laugh at themselves to their children. Some mothers dare their boys to go on the ghost train which won't be as terrifying as the plastic skeletons suggest. There are pauses for hot dogs and candy floss. On Sundays, in Greenwich Park by the Common, you find simpler games, parents running about with their children, helping them dress up or playing hide and seek under the big cedar trees of the rose garden. The children are having a good time – and, so, often are their parents. For them, it's a chance to act the child with their children.

The radical psychiatrist, R.D. Laing, who published a book of his conversations with his own children, pointed out that being with them gave him the opportunity to stop being an adult. It was fleeting, it was a game, but it was precious. Observe the fairground and the Sunday afternoon games on Greenwich Park and you would see many adults behaving in ways that Laing would have recognised: grown-ups being a child.

It's easy to conjure up childhood idylls but what's the point? The point is that there is a paradox in the psychological literature. Ever since Freud, psychologists have been claiming that the relationship between infant and mother is the most crucial of all human relationships. The English psychoanalyst, John Bowlby (1975), developed attachment theory which claimed that a child who had a good relationship with his mother developed the confidence needed to explore the world. Most theories of child development point out that very young children spend most of their time playing. Since children play so much and since their early life is spent largely (still) with their mothers, you would expect a vast amount of research on how mothers and children play together. Under the impact of social changes, some literature might focus on how fathers and children play together. Potentially interesting questions abound such as what kinds of styles of play different families have and what specifically children learn from play. There is also now a body of work arguing that infants who go to nurseries and are looked after by child minders become more aggressive as they have to fight for attention in the group. They don't get one to one love toddlers get from their doting parents.

It's interesting to look at this last finding in the light of the challenge that Kaye (1982) slapped down. For him, in the 1970s, psychologists became besotted with the abilities of the young infant. Freeman (2004), a well-known expert on gifted children, has now turned her keen eye to helping parents get the best out of more ordinary children.

Once the infant had been nothing but a bundle of reflexes; then, it became orthodox to imbue the newborn with myriad abilities from being able to stick his/her tongue out in imitation of adults to being social skilled almost as soon as the umbilical was cut. Kaye (1982) argued that this was an overreaction. Babies do not have many skills and, graphically, Kaye suggested that they do not even become an 'apprentice' to social life till about 1 year. Parents, however, had to pretend that their infants under 12 months were whole, real people. One technique is to play certain games in which the parent takes all the roles; the parent acts what the child could do if he or she were competent. Kaye offered interesting analyses of face to face play between mothers and 6-month-old infants in which the mother asks a question and then answers it for the baby. Few specialist play researchers refer to his work, however, even though it has direct implications.

There have been studies of how infants and mothers vocalise and look at each other but there are few in-depth studies of normal children or how mothers and infants play. There are far more descriptions of family games when the family is or the child is in therapy than when the child is well. As Erik Erikson has observed, however nice the therapist is, play therapy is a strange enterprise and, for the child, often threatening.

Even when an account is more integrated than usual, the psychologist-parent tends not to put himself or herself in the forefront of the text. In *Play, Dreams and Imitation in Childhood*, Piaget (1952) usually effaces himself and one needs to be reminded that Piaget and his wife were living there, too, playing with the children.

This relative lack of research means that an analysis of what we know about how parents play with their children cannot hope to be full. I begin by examining the work on exploration and attachment. This shows that children who feel secure about their mothers or fathers being there are likely to explore and play more creatively. Next, I focus on the work of C.W. Valentine, an English psychologist who observed the growth of his children. Valentine was far more willing than Piaget to indulge in 'sheer tomfoolery' which makes his comments on the growth of play and laughter in his child specially useful. Third, much work since the mid-1970s has emphasised that children can learn some basic social rules through play. One major driving force has been Jerome Bruner. In a study of peekaboo, Bruner found that the game allowed parents to teach children to take turns and to initiate episodes of play. Bruner's interesting work led to much experimental research that examined the social rules that could come from playing.

Fourth, with social changes due to feminism and the questioning of sex roles, fathers do spend more time with their children, both in the context of families and when they are alone with their children. Research on contact centres suggests that fathers tend to be very inhibited in playing with their children under supervision.

Some research has looked at the styles of play of fathers with children. The ways that children play with their parents suggest two other major questions. What kind of things do parents consciously try to teach their children through playing? For example, do fathers encourage boys to be manly? (Teaching rules about turn taking isn't conscious, of course.) Do some homes help to create particularly playful and imaginative children? These latter questions need to be looked at in the light of what current research on pretending has thrown up in terms of theory of mind.

Confidence to play

Paediatricians like Dr Spock long ago suggested that playing with a child is an essential part of bringing him or her up. Dr Spock sympathised with fathers who had had a long day at the office, but he still urged them to spare enough energy for a little roughhouse play with their children when they got home. Pollock's (1984) *Forgotten Children* suggested that since the sixteenth century some parents, at least, have played with their children. Early analysts like Melanie Klein (1955) studied play but not with the mother. The crucial importance of the mother–child bond became accepted only after Bowlby (1946), who argued that forty-four juvenile thieves had suffered from the prolonged absence of their mothers. Weaving together psychoanalysis with animal behaviour experiments that suggested there was a key period for imprinting the young of various species, Bowlby showed how much children need mothers.

Since the early 1970s, a sort of consensus on good parenting can be detected. No one recommends now that the child should be plonked for 20 minutes on the potty until he or she has finished. Rather, the ideal pattern is as follows. Until 6 months or so, the mother needs to treat the baby with almost constant love and attention. As soon as the baby can crawl, it ought to be encouraged to exercise its powers. It should have a stimulating environment to crawl around, explore and play with. As soon as the child can walk, it needs to walk out a little from its mother. A balance between keeping the child too close and giving him or her freedom is the aim. The toddler needs to toddle away a bit, secure in the knowledge that mother is there if something goes wrong. The good mother (her again) is out to achieve a delicate balance. Too much control will hinder the child; too little control may suggest nobody cares. Following Bowlby, psychologists have suggested that once the young infant feels secure, he or she can explore and play much better.

Analytic ideas on play were also developed by D.W. Winnicott, who suggested that there is, between mother and the baby, a potential space. Its boundaries are very flexible and, within it, the baby can explore the possibilities of playing. Winnicott (1949) recognised in a short essay, 'Why Children Play', the primacy of the home. He wrote:

> Children at first play alone or with mother; other children are not immediately in demand as playmates. It is largely through play, in which the other children are fitted into preconceived roles, that a child begins to allow these others to have independent existence.

Winnicott (1949) goes on to argue that 'play provides an organisation for the initiation of emotional relationships and so enables social contacts to develop'. Winnicott clearly would not have been surprised by the research which suggests that nurseries are damaging infants.

These powerful ideas have been relatively little studied empirically before the 1980s. The studies I go on to report, with the exception of Kaye (1982), Valentine (1942) and Bruner (1975), are all too often based on exploratory play in the lab with a correlational design. Children are tested to see how they play. Do they touch things too much (obsessive) or too little (no concentration)? What does the mother report about how she plays with her child? Studies then correlate observable behaviour with mothers' attitudes or behaviour in the lab and attempt to draw large conclusions from such methodology.

An example of this approach is Sorce and Emde (1981), who put 15-month-old children in a room either with their mother or with a stranger. The mother was told either to be available to her child or to be unavailable to her child, burying her head in a newspaper. Sorce and Emde found that when the mother couldn't be 'used' by the child, the child's play and exploration were both limited. The point about this kind of design is that the psychologists direct the behaviour. In some studies mothers are sometimes asked to do things they might find unnatural. The design of such studies leaves much to be desired and differs from language research, which has come to rely more on naturalistic observation (Wells 1981; Kaye 1982; Wellman 2000).

Play is not as easy to observe as language but more effort needs to be made – and not just by empirical psychologists. Despite Winnicott's advocacy of the role of play and the importance of the mother, the psychoanalytic literature has very few records of play in the home for normal children. If experimentalists prefer the lab, analysts prefer the clinic.

The exceptions are valuable and one of the best is C.W. Valentine's study, even if it was published in 1942!

Valentine's children

In general, therefore, the presence of the mother helps exploration. But the studies are, as I have stressed, few and rather flawed. In Chapter 4, I also suggested that because psychologists have concentrated on play in the 'play-room', they might often see it developed quite late. The psychologist C.W. Valentine (1942) reported on how his own five children developed. Valentine was aware that he was going over ground already covered by Piaget but he seems to have been far more willing to record instances of family life and of play as it emerged there.

At 0:2½, Valentine's son B was getting his dress between his fists and raising it up to his face repeatedly. At 0:5, B learned to strike the notes of the piano 'as I held him on my knee and I have a record that he struck it forty nine times in three minutes with cries of joy'. A month later, Valentine was experimenting with a variation on peekaboo. Again, he noted of B: 'Greatly amused (day 165) at my repeatedly covering him with eiderdown which he knocked back each time with one motion of his arms. On day 182 this was done 100 times in quick succession until I tired.'

Social play had begun by 9 months. Valentine argued: 'Social play is, of course, more likely to take place first with a loved mother or father but it may soon extend to others if known and liked.' A visitor to the Valentines' house, Miss L, picked up some sugar tongs that B had thrown on the floor. B laughed at that and they repeated the performance some fifty times. 'In such elementary social play, however,' Valentine said, 'it is usually an adult cooperating with the child in something which itself delights him.' Infants together were a different matter.

Valentine emphasised the role adults played in teaching children some aspects of play, even 'enjoyment in sheer nonsense'. Valentine had been teaching B how to draw a triangle and a circle. Then, he drew a tiger and said 'that it was going to eat the little boy'. His son mimicked the whole procedure but drew a triangle instead of a tiger and said that the triangle was going to eat the little boy.

By the age of 2½, Valentine's children were capable of making demands of their father:

> Thus several of my children would love me to 'play at lions'. Roaring like a lion (somewhat), I would chase the child up the stairs until when I nearly caught him he would scream in real earnest, tears rolling down his cheeks. Then at once I desisted, only to be begged a few moments later to play like lions again.
>
> (Valentine 1942: 58)

Valentine marvelled at the eagerness of children to experience such emotions. He also noted, as did his infant psychologist son, a phenomenon I describe in Chapter 6 in some detail – the game of contradictions where a child repeatedly says 'no' to irritate its parents to questions like 'Does B love Mummy?' Or 'Will Nicholas brush his teeth?' But while these sophisticated games were being tried out in the home, Valentine noticed that not until 3 years of age did children in kindergartens begin to show a consistent interest in playing with other children as old as they were.

Valentine emphasised the normality of playing. He criticised the fantastic interpretations of play put forward by psychoanalysts and suggested that much research 'on the play of problem children in clinics has been of little value for lack of a comparison with a control group of normal children'.

The rules of the game

Valentine's approach was often impressionistic but the impression he created was a powerful one. All his children had slightly different personalities which expressed themselves in slightly different 'plays'. The age at which they managed certain kinds of games differed, too, and partially reflected differences in intelligence. Valentine recognised the importance of the home in all this but did not offer any detailed theory about how parents developed their children's playing. Two research programmes did that in the 1980s (Kaye 1982; Bruner 1983). Deliberately, I report them not in chronological order but to present an evolving picture of how the child plays with parents.

Kaye (1982) believed that the pendulum in child psychology had swung too far. Once, the baby was regarded as a helpless bundle of reflexes. Then, following work such as Bower's (1977), the baby was credited with all kinds of skills. The baby was born more or less able to imitate, follow objects and respond socially. It wasn't quite clear why such a baby didn't talk at once. In his radical book, *The Mental and Social Life of Babies*, Kaye (1982) argued that babies are not that competent. At first, they are not 'persons' at all but, for the health of the species, parents treat them as such. Though a mother sees only a squirming cooing mess, she behaves as if this living object were actually a subject with ideas, feelings and plans of its own. Kaye noted that the mothers of 6-week-old babies spend much time apparently talking to them but the impression is a false one. The mother is actually taking both parts in the dialogue. He writes: 'In a sense, the mother is not really talking.'

Kaye (1982) called this work an examination of 'face to face play' though, in fact, it is a study of all the conversation between mother and child. Some of the lines do not look at all playful like when the mother asks if the baby needs to shit or if the baby is going to be a bastard. But there are many stretches of the dialogue which are playful such as when the mother tries to tease a smile out of her baby, or asks if the baby wants the 'puppy dog to give you a kiss'. Kaye said that he and his team recorded 13,574 utterances from 36 mothers – more than anyone else. Many of these were clearly playful.

The maternal monologues followed some interesting patterns, and, though there were individual differences between mothers, the similarities struck Kaye most. Comparing how mothers talk to their 6 week olds and to their 2 year olds, Kaye found that mothers spend an enormous amount of time talking to and playing with their tiny babies. Twenty-one utterances a minute was the average to the 6 week old. By the age of 2, this had declined to fourteen or fifteen utterances a minute but the child was now producing about six utterances a minute himself/herself. The child was taking the pressure off the mother. The similarity in the combined speech rate suggested to Kaye that, with the 6 week old, the mothers 'were essentially doing the speaking for both partners'. About 16 per cent of the utterances were pure repetition of the previous one; by age 2, that had dropped to 3 per cent. Kaye believed that these repetitions and the frequent use of one word utterances were a way of 'keeping the channel open', of keeping up the appearance of communication. Mothers often used one-worders like 'Hi' or 'Hello' or 'Yeah' when they managed to catch their baby's eye. At 6 weeks, these *phatic* utterances took up 25 per cent of all speech; at 13 weeks, 22 per cent; at 26 weeks, only 17 per cent.

Kaye (1982) also plotted the way the infant by 26 weeks becomes both less interested in the mother and more responsive to her. The paradox is explicable. On the one hand, the baby spends much less time just looking at the mother's face. Kaye and Fogel (1980) found that 6-week-old babies spent 55 per cent of their time just looking at their mothers; at 13 weeks, it was 36 per cent of the time, at 26 weeks, 29 per cent. But these looks were not responses. Kaye and Fogel also compared the spontaneous and responsive reactions of infants. They found great change between 6 and 26 weeks. At 6 weeks, the infants hardly react and, if they do, they respond to the mother's behaviour. By 13 weeks, they respond to greetings much more and there are a few greetings that the infant initiates. At 26 weeks, the child produces as many spontaneous greetings as the mother does. The same pattern is true for smiling and vocalising. The proportion of cooings, smiles and laughs when attending to the mother is much greater both at 3 months and at 6 months than the numbers when not attending. But at 6 weeks, there is no difference.

For Kaye (1982), the evidence points up two important facts. First, parents, especially mothers, behave even to their newborn infants as if they are real persons. They engage in what looks like a monologue with them from birth on, but it's an odd monologue because the mother speaks both her lines and the baby's. Kaye called infants 'apprentices' to social life and suggests that parents have, at first, to create their babies as people. In reality, the baby can do very little. It would not be healthy for the mother to behave as if the baby is just a semi-animate lump so mothers pretend, without knowing it, that babies are real people. That helps motivate them to look after the baby properly but it is only a healthy delusion.

For the student of play, Kaye's (1982) work has some interesting implications. First, it shows that we need to pay attention to the way parents create the conditions and, probably, the themes for much of the child's play. Second, Kaye showed the way in which the skills of even his less than competent babies grew by 26 weeks, especially their skill at learning some rules such as to initiate a greeting to their mother. Kaye said that babies do have a lot from which to learn. He calculated that the average infant will, by the first birthday, have been on the receiving end of half a million utterances from the mother which gave, if nothing else, plenty to imitate.

The analysis of face to face play leads well into Bruner's work (for a review see Bruner 1983) on peekaboo, other games and their role in language development. Bruner noted that for all the rough and tumble play of the apes, none of them has the child games 'that are the staple and delight of human immaturity – the peekaboo variants, Ride a Cock Horse, This is the Way Ladies Ride and the rest' (Bruner 1983: 45). No psychoanalytic explanations for Bruner: what makes these games fascinating is the way they offer basic training both in social rules and 'the use and exchange of language'.

Bruner gave two long case histories of boys aged from 3 months on. These were taken from his Oxford Project and were in no way special. Jonathan's mother first played peekaboo with him when he was 3 months old, either by hiding her face or by hiding his face. This is a very early start to peekaboo reflecting that things happen earlier in the home. By 5 months, Jonathan's mother had elaborated a game involving a toy clown and a cloth cone. The clown could be made either to disappear into the cloth cone or to rise out of it. Bruner dissected the game into ten units and four main stages; the italics are speech.

1 Preparation
The mother first calls attention to the clown either by jiggling it or by calling something like *Who's this?*

Then, who is to be the agent is established. Bruner gives quotations of two different possibilities. *Shall mummy do it, hide him?* Or *Jonathan do it.*

2 Disappearance
Start. *He's going. He's going to go.* Completion. *Gone! He's gone.* Search. *Where's he gone?*

Then, Bruner notes, there is a long pause which is followed by the start of the reappearance phase. This can be either slow or quite explosive.

3 Reappearance
Start.
Completion. *Here he's coming.* Or, *Boo! Jonathan, here he is.*

4 Re-establishment
Arousal. *Bababoo.*
Constraint. *Don't eat him.*

Bruner noted that the basic structure of the game remained stable. He found that Jonathan was initiated into it gradually. Between 0:5 and 0:9, he became slowly more interested. Jonathan learned to know what to expect and would wait for his mother to speak familiar lines, 'looking up at her from the clown and cone and smiling either in anticipation or after she spoke'. As he got more familiar with the pattern of the game, she skipped some utterances and elaborations. But the skeleton always remained – the fast withdrawn clown, his explosive reappearance, and, often, more warnings not to gobble him up.

Jonathan also evolved. At 0:5, he tended to try to grab the clown. A month later, he would add in some 'undifferentiated vocalisations', which happened throughout the game. By 0:7, he began to respond to the predictable rhythm of the game and produced, at the appropriate times, the appropriate smiles and laughs. A month later, Jonathan was keen to start taking a more active role. He was ready at 0:8 to take the clown out of the cone. His mother gave it him and also made the game easier by condensing it to two essential stages, disappearance and a reappearance.

To use Kaye's (1982) term, the apprentice is first allowed to make the easiest models. Jonathan, the apprentice initiator of peekaboo can play the most basic form of the game. At 0:5, Jonathan touched the clown in only 36 per cent of games; by 0:9, he touched him in 75 per cent of games. Towards the end of the ninth month, Jonathan began to get bored with the peekaboo clown game but the lessons Jonathan had learned in taking part, responding and starting had taken root. When he and his mother began to play 'human' peekaboo, he was no longer passive but active and skilful. Bruner pointed out that Jonathan now regularly looked away immediately after his mother reappeared from behind a chair, that he waited on the other side of the chair, smiling as he expected her to burst forth and that, in his twelfth month, Jonathan began hiding behind the chair to start the game off himself. By 1:2, the clown and cone returned to favour but mother and child had to negotiate now for who would take the lead. Jonathan had even learned 'not to monopolise' the active role though he preferred it. He had picked up his own form of cries to accompany the game. *Boo!* became *ooo!* while his mother's *he's gone* became *a ga*; 'He had become master of the game both as agent and as experiencer', Bruner declared.

Bruner offered a shorter analysis of the peekaboo games of Richard from 5 months on. The pattern was very similar though Richard evolved a version of peekaboo in which he made objects reappear and then greeted them as if they were people, calling *hello house* when he spied his toyhouse in a pot. Both sets of mothers and children

> established a ritualised game in which they shared interchangeable roles. The game diversified and provided a place for the child's increasing initiatives as he learned both how to initiate the game and how to execute the moves. Both children learned easily how to keep the deep structure of the game constant while varying the surface structure.
>
> (Bruner 1983: 59)

It is no accident that Bruner uses the terms *deep structure* and *surface structure*. They were popularised by Chomsky (1957) to explain different constituents of language. Bruner believes that the form of such games helps the child to learn how the handle 'the sorts of social convention upon which language use is based'. That old English motto that you have to play the games to learn the rules of life is not a stiff-upper-lip Etonian code but a psychological law, according to Bruner.

Bruner's emphasis on the changing behaviour of the child leaves one to wonder just what mothers do do when playing with their children. Few studies have directly addressed this. N. Cohen and Tomlinson-Keasey (1980) in studying how toddlers played together noted that mothers did quite often initiate play episodes. Three studies offer some preliminary data (Belsky et al. 1980; Dunn and Wooding 1977; McCune-Nicolich 1981b).

Belsky et al. (1980) studied eight children at each of four ages: 9 months, 12 months, 15 months and 18 months. The children were visited in their homes and observed for two 45-minute play sessions. The observer had an 'inconspicuous' bleep in his ears. The actions of mothers were divided by the researchers into a total of six: pointing and repointing at an object; demonstrating its use; when mother moved the baby's hands; instructing or questioning the child; highlighting the object; and naming the object. Were there any links between how mothers used these actions and how their children played?

Belsky et al. (1980) found that, between 9 months and 18 months, the child spent more time attending to the mother. The mother's behaviour changed. She pointed rather more to objects and, very markedly, instructed the child more and named objects. Mothers named objects nearly twice as often when their child was 18 months as they did at 9 months. The children's play also changed. They imitated far more at 18 months and also juxtaposed two objects or played functionally with them, i.e. dragging a toy cart along. Mothers had a good sense of the capacities of their children. With the younger children, they used far more physical strategies such as demonstrating an object; with the older ones, they relied on words. Since the psychologists scored both what each mother did and what her child did, they were able to suggest that the mother's style affected the child's play. The children whose mothers did most to focus their attention on to the environment, on to what the toys were and what could be done with them, were the ones who played most competently. Mothers 'teach' their children not just through playing but, perhaps, how to play.

Dunn and Wooding (1977) also highlighted the role of the mothers. They studied 24 toddlers aged 18 months to 24 months. The psychologists visited the homes and scored three sorts of behaviour on the part of the mother: uninvolved; joint attention; joint play. Children played longer when their mothers were paying attention and, usually, they initiated most of the bouts of pretend play once they had already got their mother's attention. They either changed the situation into a game or, quite often sought out their mother to get them in the game.

McCune-Nicolich (1981b) told mothers to respond naturally and not take the lead, which may itself not be natural. She found that some couldn't adhere to these instructions while others became so fascinated with toys they ignored the child. When they did play together, the mother 'tended to do so at one or two levels in advance of the child', suggesting that mothers may use play to teach.

The evidence seems clear that mothers play with their children and that, through games, children pick up many basic rules both of social structure and of the structure necessary for language learning. Bruner (1983) highlights *handover*. Round the age of 9 months, most mothers give their children the chance to become active rather than passive. They ease them into the role of starting the game. Jonathan's mother made the structure of peekaboo and the clown game more simple so that he could start off mastering its simplest form. This device helps shape the behaviour of the child. At 6 months, he can't participate in any game because he doesn't have either the attention or the discipline to wait. Jonathan would just grab the clown then. Six months later, he is master of the rules of this particular game, knowing when to start, when to stop, when to take his turn and how to react to various predictable cues. It is a major achievement.

The game has always been a symbol. Bruner elevates it into a crucial symbol. By being socialised into the game, the child is socialised into many basic exchanges of life. These strands of research also confirm Valentine's (1942) hunch that psychologists will see more sophisticated playing appear earlier within the family than in any other context.

If playing in the family is so important, why have psychologists done so little to study what families play about? Chapter 4 claimed that games in the school tend to be rather literal recreations of life. The elegant analysis of the structure of games just reported does nothing much to inform us about the content of games. Indeed, Bruner (1983) writes as if the crux of games is their form, never their content. But even peekaboo, as I show in Chapter 6, has very personal variations. One would expect families to play round themes that concerned them. Piaget (1952) occasionally showed that, such as when Jacqueline played at being clumsy Daddy after he hit her with a rake. Piaget recounts how sorry he was and that just repeating the sequences, with her playing him, and he being her, 'half appeased her'. Interestingly, he did not have to be actively her or 'role play' at all. He had only to stand by while Jacqueline took both roles. Given Kaye's (1982) thesis that mothers play both themselves and fill in for what the baby would say if he or she could, it's telling that by 4:0, Jacqueline could act both characters, herself and big, clumsy Daddy. There are other worthwhile questions. Does playing with your children offer you a chance to regress? Laing (1965) suggests it might. Bruner (1983) records, but does not comment on, the way Jonathan's mother appears to let herself go in the game, especially in the *re-establishment* phase when she jiggles the clown against Jonathan and exclaims 'Bababoo'. The games we play with our children may give us, as adults, a last chance to regress. But psychologists have not explored that aspect of play much.

One of the problems is that some of the research uses fantastic – and not very lifelike – research designs. Yarrow et al. (1975) brought 5 and 6 month olds to their lab and gave them toys they called 'novel'. Did they ask individually whether babies had seen such toys? No. Babies were scored for how 'creative' they were with each toy and this was correlated with measures of maternal interest. Babies whose mothers responded quicker to cries of distress were most creative according to the rules of Yarrow et al. (1975). Older babies (6 months to 12 months) did not show this pattern.

It is hard to know what to make of the results for children aged from 2:8 to 4 and 5 years of age because the design of some of the chief experiments is so fantastic. Passman and Weisberg (1975) found that 3 year olds who were allowed to hang on to their blankets, like the cartoon character Peanuts, explored more than blanket-deprived children. Passman and Erck (1978) went on to ask if mothers had the same stimulating effect. They did not, as one might imagine, compare how children behave in the home when their mother was in the room and when, say, she was upstairs or on the phone. Instead, they brought children to the laboratory and asked them to play in a variety of conditions:

- with their mother in the room
- in the presence of a film of their mother
- in the presence of a film of a stranger
- in the presence of a 'formless' film.

In a subsequent design (Adams and Passman 1979), children were exposed also to the voice tapes of their mothers. Passman and Erck (1978) discovered that children played most often and walked most when their mother was there. They found that episodes of play lasted longest when the mother was there or the film of her was present. To confuse the situation, on questioning the children, the authors learned that half of them believed the stranger on film actually was their mother! Evidence of how children view television suggests that 3 and 4 year olds can usually recognise characters. Rather than blame the camera operator or wonder if their slightly bizarre experiment was distorting the children's behaviour, the psychologists argued seriously that, as a two-dimensional replica of the mother sufficed for children to play comfortably, a cardboard cut-out was lifelike enough. Adams and Passman (1979) then 'confirmed' this by finding that children played as much when their mother was there or on film or her voice could be heard on tape. It is hard to believe that these are not artificial effects of a very odd experimental design.

Older children ought to have the confidence to explore things whether their parents are around or not. Henderson et al. (1982) observed how children aged 3 to 5 and, in a second study, 6 to 8, behaved when they were taken to the Touch and See room of a natural history museum. Half the children in each group were accompanied by six to twelve classmates and a responsible adult; half by one or two parents. Henderson et al. (1982) saw that the children in the two groups behaved very differently. Children with their parents stayed in the room longer, moved from exhibit to exhibit more slowly, talked about them more and touched them more. His impression was that the presence of parents helped children to focus their exploration more and that parents structured what their children did. They answered questions and, also, drew their attention to interesting things.

This study leads to some interesting comparisons. Henderson et al. (1982) seemed to spot that parents were, in some ways, teaching their children how to explore a playful environment. Is the ordinary play of children like that? Second, they emphasised the way parents focused on certain things for their children. This is a surprising finding, perhaps, with children as old as 8 but, as we shall see, a study by Belsky et al. (1980) appears to show that this is just what mothers do when playing with little children. Finally, Henderson et al.'s (1982) work suggests that, if the presence of parents helps children explore and play, that is true both at 3 and at 8. It is something that doesn't develop. Older children may want to play to get away from their parents but the cosy notion of child manuals, that the good mother loves the child possessively first, and then has to free the child, may be more wish fulfilment than fact. It is how we now think we ought to bring up children. None of the research uses what might be an interesting test, the Parental Bonding Instrument (Parker et al. 1980), to correlate styles of parenting with how playful children are.

Mothers and everyday play

Haight and Miller (1992) complained that there was still not enough play research done in naturalistic settings. They argued that this lack distorts research results. They followed ninety American children from 12 months to 48 months. They videotaped them for four-hour sessions at 12, 16, 20, 24, 30, 36 and 48 months. They found that until 36 months, middle-class mothers tended to be a child's main play partner. Initially, mothers initiated most episodes of play. Mothers started nearly all of the forty-three episodes of pretend play at 12 months. By 24 months, however, this had changed. The child would set up about 50 per cent of the pretend play episodes. This balance remained until about 36 months when children started to play more regularly with other children. Haight and Miller (1992) suggested this was partly because mothers started to fix play dates for their children to spend more time with friends.

What happens in the home as a matter of routine is often the basis for play. When mother cooks, washes and cleans she often turns that into play. But again adults sometimes want to turn play into something more meaningful. Vandermaas-Peeler et al. (2001) found, in both homes and labs, that while they play, parents often are doing something else besides. They teach, comment, direct and, of these serious activities, teaching was by far the most common. When playing doctors, parents were say things like 'This is how the doctor listens to your heart'. It's a pity they did their research before Toys'R'Us released a new game in which kids get to play at surgeons. Parents differ in their ability to integrate teaching into the pattern of play. Some manage to play and teach at the same time but others have to stop the pretending to concentrate on teaching – and they seem to like that. Bornstein and Tamis-LeMonda (1989) suggest that when parents can marry the fun and the didactic, children get long-lasting social and cognitive benefits. Unfortunately we don't have a manual which can help parents who have to interrupt playing with their children so that they can bang home 'educational' messages.

Haight and Miller's work raises one intriguing possibility. The work of Wellman and others suggests that it is after the age of 3 that children start to develop some notion of other minds. If this is the time when children, having learned the basics of pretend play with mothers, start to pretend – and therefore to flex cognitive skills – with other children, is there a link between these two? It seems possible that children first get insight into how other creatures think by seeing how creatures of the same age and experience react. Do children first learn that other children have other minds? This is pure speculation – but worth pursuing.

Fathers

Feminism has obliged psychology to ask questions about the sharing of child care. It has also meant that some researchers have wanted to see how fathers use play to instil sex roles into their children. Macho daddies don't often play with dolls with their boys. Britain has also seen a great deal of protest by divorced fathers who claim that they are denied access to their children and that this damages both child and father.

The pattern of child care is changing. Takkala (1984) found that in Finland in the mid-1980s fathers spent far more time than with their children than in the mid-1970s. They spend between 73 minutes a week for farmers and 136 minutes for salesmen in outdoor play with children and between 27 minutes (farmers) and 74 minutes (workers) playing indoors. Takkala (1984) was interested in changing patterns of family life and how people spent their time so he had little specific to say about what the growing presence of fathers might mean. Some sociological work suggests quite profound changes. On the one hand, men are seen much more than before pushing prams, changing nappies and being committed to child care. This is reflected in the advertisements for quite conventional child care shops like Mothercare. Nowadays Mothercare caters for fathers as well. In a more scientific vein, Trew and Kilpatrick (1984) looked at how unemployed men in Belfast spent their time. Some men devoted far more time than before to looking after their children. Some feminist writers, like journalist Katherine Whitehorn, warned (*The Observer*, 16 June 1985) that women ought not to encourage too much fathering. They might lose the one domain in which historically they have held power. So, fathers seem to be playing more with children. But what does that achieve?

Lamb (1976, 1977) was the first psychologist to research in detail how children respond to fathers. He found that there was no tendency for the child to prefer its mother. Lamb discovered that children between 7 months and 2 years were more likely to smile and coo at their father. The father also tended to play in a slightly more physical way and Lamb claimed, perhaps, children prefer fathers because they are 'simply more fun to interact with' (Lamb 1976: 6).

This thesis has been studied by Clarke Stewart (1978). In 1972, she found fourteen families who were willing to be studied over an eighteen-month period. She observed how they played at home for six one-hour periods. Three of these periods were just with the mother there; three were with the mother and father both present. There was no point in studying the father alone with his children because that was such a rare occurrence. She divided the play episodes into twenty different sorts which ranged from the child just looking at a parent to offering toys to punishing the child. In many ways, Clarke Stewart seems ready to log the widest range of behaviours of any play researcher.

In many ways, Clarke Stewart (1978) confirmed some of Lamb's ideas. The children were observed both to play more with their fathers and to enjoy these games more. Was this because they like fathers more or because they enjoy their style of playing more? Clarke Stewart believed it was the type of play that fathers engaged in that children preferred. This was much less intellectual than the games mothers preferred. Despite the fact that men are supposed to be thing-orientated, mothers played more games with objects. Fathers tended to play both social and physical games, pretending and roughhousing. They tended to play for shorter periods and there was the strange finding that fathers who were most negative to the child were also the ones who played most. Were they the most involved?

The role of the father as a playmate also seemed to Clarke Stewart (1978) to be changing. Mothers said that when the child was between 15 months and 30 months, the father played more with it and by then, more 'play periods' were being conducted by the father than by the mother. Fathers who played the most social and physical games with their children tended to be married to women who played most games with objects suggesting, perhaps, they complemented each other. There were differences in the kinds of play mothers and fathers played but each sex could be equally stimulating and responsive. Clarke Stewart suggests that social circumstances may be about to alter the role of the father radically. But she leaves the impression that fathers are actually quite fit to deal with their children and have a lot to offer them.

Pitcher and Schultz (1983) suggest a far less flattering picture to the male ego. Fathers hardly exist for children, they claim. They dismiss evidence that progressive parents care for their children remotely equally. In Boston, 43 per cent of fathers prided themselves on never having changed a nappy. Despite being hardly present, fathers influenced their children – and especially their sons. They mainly influenced them to continue to engage in masculine play which reflected hostility to girls. In their descriptions of children's play, Pitcher and Schultz do something rare in the play literature – they transmit contempt for their subjects. Boys who are 3 years old engage in too much horse play and are only able to imitate crude heroes:

> Characters are usually stereotyped and flat with habitual attitudes and personality features (cowboy, foreman, Superman, Batman). Girls prefer traditional family roles, especially the traditional ones of daughter and mother. Even at the youngest age, girls are quite knowledgeable about the details and subtleties in these roles.
>
> (Pitcher and Schultz 1983: 79)

The girls can manipulate personalities and infer what others are thinking. Poor boys, meanwhile, just keep on shooting away. And referring to male genitalia.

There is evidence from earlier studies and also from the toys that parents buy (Newson and Newson 1979) that fathers will tend to buy masculine toys for their boys. Fathers certainly appear to worry more if their boys play with feminine toys. Will this never change? Pitcher and Schultz (1983) are very pessimistic, which may explain their stridency. They refer to Paley's (1973) work. Having proved herself unable to change the way male and female children played, Paley studied a liberated kindergarten. Here, the children belonged to families where the mother often held a full-time professional job while the father was studying for a graduate degree and took more care of the children. Despite this domestic reversal, put in a Wendy House, the old roles surfaced. Girls minded the babies and the pots and pans; boys played macho games. Pitcher and Schultz (1983) recommended that girls ought to be trained in rough and tumble play to prepare them for a rough and tumble world and lament that even progressive fathers can't change their children. And most fathers are conservative and cling to male hostility to women.

I have been very critical of Pitcher and Schultz (1983) but they do at least highlight the way parents play to mould their children. The rest of the literature does little on this theme which is odd when one considers the stress there is on children learning rules through play. Granted that Kaye (1982), Bruner (1983) and Belsky (1981) show how games are a way in which infants pick up some essential rules of life from their parents, are we to suppose that parents never use this power consciously? The models that Kaye and Bruner work with stress *competences*. Chomsky (1957) argued that, when we speak, we use competences that we are not aware of. Obviously, the peekaboo playing parents (unless they are psychologists) do not know, or think, that in playing the game, they are introducing the child to social conventions. But that doesn't mean that parents are as unknowing about all games, and as unaware about all the effects of playing with their children. The question of what parents get out of playing with their children needs far more investigating. Do certain kinds of parents go out of their way to try to make their children imaginative and playful? The first of these points I try to tackle in part in Chapter 6.

Cultural variations in children's play

As the world becomes more and more of a global village, you have to go further and further to find genuine cultural variations. In the past there was great interest in cross-cultural variations in play. Rich or poor, children find both time and materials for play but their families see the value of play differently. In poor families, Sutton-Smith (1974) has argued there is less play because families need children to work and earn.

Beatrice and John Whiting (1975) claimed children in more complex cultures play more and with more complexity. In the most complex groups, there was more play among children who had greater freedom to roam about the community – something which is changing because of concerns in the west about the safety of children.

Cultural habits also matter. What parents believe about play affects, it seems, how likely parents are to become involved in children's play. When mothers did not think themselves proper play partners, as is the case in East Indian, Guatemalan (Goncu and Mosier 1991), Mayan (Gaskins and Goncu

1995) and Mexican mothers (Farver 1993), they played less with their children than did American and Turkish mothers, who think it is fine for parents to lark about with their children (Farver and Wimbarti 1995; Goncu and Mosier 1991; Haight et al. 1997).

Older siblings can sometimes compensate if parents are too busy to play, Farver and her co-workers found (e.g., Farver 1993; Farver and Wimbarti 1995). In Mexican families, for example, older siblings play with smaller children much like the way American mothers do with their young children. American older siblings are not so helpful and play in a more 'discordant' way with their younger brothers and sisters (Farver 1993). In Indonesia, rather oddly, parents start to play less when their tiny children start to walk, at which point older siblings start to play a more active role.

Different cultures use play to promote different messages (Haight et al. 1999). European and North American mothers use play to teach independence and self-expression but Chinese caregivers use it to teach social harmony and respect for rules. Chinese parents do encourage social play but not really for itself as they often use it to teach children how to behave properly. But television executives know that somehow – bizarrely – children in cultures as different as Japan, Ireland and the United States all manage to understand at least most of *The Simpsons* cartoons.

Paracosms

The experimental work on whether children can tell reality from imagination has concentrated on young children aged under 6. But there is also intriguing evidence from older children – or, to be exact, from the memories that adults have of what they imagined and created as children.

Robert Silvey had been head of the BBC's Audience Research Department for nearly thirty years. Stephen MacKeith was a retired psychiatrist. They began to collaborate on a study of paracosms (Silvey and MacKeith 1988). A paracosm is an imaginary world children create. It can be a country, an island or a tribe. The Victorian novelists Charlotte and Emily Brontë had such an imaginary country when they were children. It was called Gondal and was full of very romantic military officers. The Brontë sisters believed that they had learned how to devise interesting characters and plots through their youthful games with Gondal.

Such worlds are not that unusual. Silvey had been interested in the phenomenon from his own youth. He had created such a country called the New Hentian States. Piaget himself had written of the imaginary companions some children create and noted once that his nephew aged 10 seemed to have invented a Ruritanian world with meticulously researched uniforms and customs. After Silvey's death in 1980 I worked with MacKeith on refining their data. Eventually, we had sixty-four accounts of imaginary worlds from fifty-seven different subjects (Cohen and MacKeith 1990). There were some pure fantasy worlds like Teddy Bearland, which was peopled wholly by bears. Other worlds were based on teenage fictions. Girls in particular were apt to embroider worlds round riding schools. Some of the worlds were very well constructed and provided a backdrop for consistent adventures. These ranged from a theatre world to Ruritanian countries. Since the publication of the book, MacKeith and I have been contacted by a few adults who have kept on with their fantasy worlds. One notable one was based on an ancient Indian civilisation. The 'fantasist' is apparently well adjusted, has a quite successful career and said that he used the world as something to withdraw into when pressure was great. The paracosms reveal how children as young as 6 in some cases can create well-defined imaginary worlds to play in. In some cases, these worlds appear to be an attempt to compensate for emotional absences or traumas. Whatever their deeper function – and that is an important issue – these paracosms prove young children's ability to construct imaginative and coherent scenarios in which to play.

Summary games

Part of the game of writing a book has become including a summary of a chapter at the end. In a way, these top and tail pieces threaten to take over far too much space. You start a chapter by announcing what you are going to say and end it by resuming what you have just said. Does that leave much for the concept sandwich in between? Till someone invents a better ritual, however, I will conform to it.

In the Chapters 3, 4 and 5, I have tried to describe the various stages in the development of play that psychologists have identified. Though most of the research has been done either on play with objects or on play in the school room, it seems clear that the earliest forms of play evolve in the home – with parents and, also, with siblings. Newborn infants are unable to play at all. Most of their first actions are reflexes and, long before play, imitation of motor acts is to be found. Between 3 months and 6 months, babies begin to be able to imitate actions they have just performed and to signal that imitation differently. Instead of pushing a mobile with total, serious attention, they push it with attention but also with gurgles of pleasure. Often, they repeat and repeat this one action. Often, they do this in the presence of a parent. Valentine saw his 5-month-old son strike the piano keys repeatedly, for instance and, earlier, at 0:2½, put his dress up to his face.

These early playful acts are isolated. The 6 month old is not capable of any kind of sustained play. According to Kaye (1982) the baby is much less able to interact than flattering psychological theories allow, and, in most exchanges, the mother plays her own part and fills in for the infant, saying what he or she ought to say. Between 6 months and 12 months, through a series of stages best described in Bruner's (1983) work, children learn from their parents how to participate. They acquire the idea of taking turns and of responding to words, smiles and coos from others. Round the eighth to ninth month, babies often begin to initiate very simple games and adults deliberately simplify the games to make it possible for the child to be the leader. Certain styles of mothering, particularly focusing attention regularly, seem to develop the child's capacity to play particularly with objects.

From 12 months on, children seem to build on their early mastery of these basic structures of games. The research has focused fundamentally on how the child learns to play with other children. By the age of 2, most toddlers are able to play in parallel with other children, making occasional contact and, sometimes, getting involved in longer sequence of play. I have claimed as a result of my own observations that, in real homes, this ability can be found earlier – especially when there is an older child to help teach the younger, as in the case of Nicholas and Reuben. By the age of 3, most children can engage in simple role-playing games. In work on playgroups, psychologists tend to stress the rather literal nature of children's games. They slavishly copy the real world or the adventures of television. They play doctor/nurse, mother/daughter, Superman, Batman and so on. I have argued that, in the home, children play – and, perhaps feel free to play – rather more complicated and personal games. Unlike Fein (1975), I claim that evidence shows that parents do play all kinds of pretend games with their children and get a great deal out of this. The psychologists' determination to study play scientifically, as a growing series of motor and social skills, makes it harder to tease out that important aspect of play. By the age of 4, children have a large repertoire of play. They can signal they want to play or that play is starting now. They can then conjure up all kinds of 'plays' from landing on the moon to what would happen if Cinderella had big feet to cooking dinner. It's a major achievement but, as we shall see, society encourages it to be a transient one. At the time of writing the first edition, I don't think I realised what this achievement might mean. In the light of current concern, the evidence that children learn to pretend and can predict what other children might be thinking suggests that it is between the ages of 3 and 4 that most children begin to understand that other creatures have other minds.

Most 4 year olds have started to understand the differences between thinking, believing and hoping. They can anticipate what someone else will do. The evidence suggests a profound change in children's abilities between the ages of 3 and 4. Sceptics claim that it is not enough to show that children can achieve certain tasks younger than Piaget predicted. Smith (1984) argues for tougher criteria. Young children must be able to make conscious why they made certain judgements. Mere performance is not enough. Smith's criteria make it impossible for children to have a theory of mind and it is worth asking just how conscious adult theories of other minds ever are. Many will be surprised by how central play studies have turned out to be.

Piaget noted, and approved of the fact, that as children got older their games became more realistic, more adapted to the real world. That is a Calvinist position if ever there was one. I will ask later on why children stop playing and what might be done, in a changing world, to make adults play so that they don't lose all these skills they built up so cleverly – and naturally – in their infancy.

6   Playful people?

Are psychologists bothered by studying play? I have suggested that this may not be such an outrageous idea because of the picture that psychologists have about themselves and their work. Psychologists tend to see themselves as serious, scientific students of human behaviour. Throughout their training, they are taught that their task is to unearth laws of human behaviour. Theories differ widely, of course, but they share a common attitude. The soft psychoanalyst who has never deigned to carry out an experiment and the hard experimentalist who believes the only proper 'insight' would be a brand of perfume share the faith that their work is serious. There are not many jokes either in the *Quarterly Journal of Experimental Psychology* or in *The Psychoanalytic Quarterly*. The study of play may well feel wrong. Should intelligent adults devote so much time to observing and analysing how children mess about?

Play is also, I suggested earlier, the one area of developmental psychology where women predominate. There are obvious reasons for this including the one that perhaps men don't feel it's an area that deserves them.

These attitudes have affected the way longitudinal studies of the development of children have been carried out. A number of psychologists like Piaget, C.W. Valentine and Chukovsky have monitored the development of their own children. But these psychologists have nearly always concentrated on what might be labelled the proper, weighty matters of how the child learns to think and to become socially and emotionally mature. Play is tangential. The bulk of Piaget's one book to centre on play, *Play, Dreams and Imitation in Childhood*, devotes 95 out of 296 pages to play. Even Valentine who is happy to report 'sheer tomfoolery' focuses mainly on social and emotional development. It is telling, incidentally, that few female psychologists seem ever to have written up the development of their own baby. Another example of role conflict, perhaps? If you are a mother, does that involve you too much for you to be able to maintain scientific distance?

Most of this chapter centres on my own observations of my two children, Nicholas and Reuben. The observations formed the main part of my PhD thesis on the development of laughter and I have taken those parts that seemed specially relevant to the development of play. I have left this chapter virtually unaltered from the first and second editions and I apologise to my sons, 25 years on, for still citing them as 'data'. Detailed naturalistic observations of children's play in the family are, however, rare. So . . . and please remember, this was mainly fun!

Not all laughter occurs as part of play. There are some very isolated 'laughs'. Second, not all forms of playing lead to laughter. There are also some problems with the laughter literature which do not occur with play. It has been the tradition, for instance, for psychologists to try to use their own jokes to see what will make children laugh and to isolate the one 'risible stimuli'. Play research has not used this kind of paradigm at all. Despite these points, I believe that many of my observations of the development of laughter and play in Nicholas and Reuben make a useful contribution to the study of play. The observations show the way parents and children play together, the way children use games with family life, the way Nicholas 'taught' Reuben how to play some games and how, in the context of play, Nicholas in particular handled some tricky feelings of power and conflict.

The chapter is organised into the following sections:

*   Reuben's earliest games
*   The Mummy with dummy game
*   Peekaboo
*   Nicholas 'teaching' Reuben to play
*   Parents 'teaching' their children to play
*   Using games to deflect criticism and get away with naughtiness
*   Using games to coax children along
*   Obscenity in play
*   Pretending and sequences of play.

I do not claim that this is a complete account of all important aspects of the development of play. However, the headings raise a number of issues that have been neglected in the play literature and deserve study. I then look at the current thinking on the pretending of very young children and what that tells us. There is an interesting question of whether the fact that some 3-year-old children understand pretence actually means they grasp that we can think one thing and act another – and this is very much an ongoing area of research (Berguno and Bowler 2004). The chapter ends with a discussion of whether certain kinds of parents try to raise their children to be 'playful' and whether such a strategy is healthy and can succeed.

Origins

I first began to describe the laughter of Nicholas when he was 3:6. We were spending the summer and autumn in Greece and Aileen was pregnant with Reuben. Reuben was born in January 1975 and I recorded his laughter from birth on. For some time, there was both audio and video equipment in our house so that we kept long tapes of games of the children. Nicholas certainly became aware of the fact that I was studying play and laughter and that, at times, we carried out totally informal 'experiments' to see whether certain things might make the children laugh. But I don't think there was so much pressure of this sort – the study continued over four years – that it skewed the kind of laughter and games the children produced. Throughout the period I had video equipment but I still mainly relied on jotting down what was going on as it happened because paper and pencil notes still made it possible to get the most rounded view of the context in which play or laughter occurred. Video recordings, given the technology available in the 1970s and 1980s, tended, unless they were highly professional, to focus on just one subject and often to lose much of the overall sound. In studies of laughter and play the images caught on screen may be those of a peak of arousal (say, when a child laughs) but fail to catch either the build up to that event or other crucial elements of the situation.

Observing one's own children has many potential pitfalls. The observer is far from detached and is likely to bring his or her own assumptions to the work. Children may latch on to what is happening and play, or laugh, in an unnatural way. You may, if you have definite theoretical ideas at the start, simply end up confirming what you wanted to confirm. My counterpoints are that I did not start with any set of preconceptions other than that it was important to do such long-term studies and that I balanced the project by also doing research in a local playgroup with a fellow observer. We did not do a traditional inter-observer reliability test but each wrote up our observations of the same two-hour periods. We found that one had scored 340 instances of laughter while the other one had 314 instances of laughter. Often, the laughter was at the same event and our descriptions matched closely. In the home, the games and jokes were often more complex and more personal at a younger age. There were other influences. But the use of a second observer suggested strongly that what I was seeing in the home was not that strange because often similar situations led to laughter and play in both settings.

Reuben's earliest games

From the age of 4 months, Reuben could be made to laugh by being tickled. He was not then playing a game but his brother (aged 4:2) and his parents were, in tickling him, playing a game with him.

The difficulty in judging when Reuben's first games occurred lies in judging when Reuben first intended to play and became an active agent. By the time he started to play peekaboo at 9 months, he had moved to being able to do this. As we have seen, Bruner (1983) has described the way in which the child learns to play peekaboo first by being a passive player. Reuben also began in other games as a passive player. By 7 months Reuben often laughed in 'games' where Aileen was bouncing him up and down, swinging him between her knees and jiggling him up in the air to catch him just in the nick of time. Nicholas was too small to take the initiative in such physical games but he did do his share of tickling. Between 7 months and 11 months, tickling Reuben was an excellent way of getting him to laugh and Nicholas often did it while both children were eating.

The earliest instance of Reuben taking any initiative other than in peekaboo was at 9 months. He laughed, unexpectedly, when Nicholas stamped his feet on the seat of the chair. This was quite different from the laughter that Nicholas deliberately provoked either by tickling or by charging Reuben's playpen or by banging Reuben's feet together. Nicholas, responding to the laughter, stamped on the chair again; Reuben laughed again. Nicholas then slid down the back of the armchair, nearly hitting Reuben and making him laugh in the process. It would be premature to say that Reuben meant to start a game but, instead of his responding to Nicholas (something that happened often), here was an instance of Reuben leading the action.

The Mummy with dummy game

According to Fein (1975), parents do not play pretend games with children. When I was carrying out this research, I had never read Fein's dictum so what follows was not designed to contradict her. Reuben had a dummy from when he was 6 months old and became extremely attached to it. Aileen and I were ambivalent about whether the dummy was good for him and, at times, tried to discourage its use. Other times we gave him the dummy. By the age of 9 months, Reuben was very used to having the dummy and saw it as his own thing.

It was against this background that Aileen first started to play a game with him. In the game, Aileen would take the dummy and put it in her own mouth. When Reuben was 10 months old, he laughed when Aileen put the dummy in her mouth and said 'Yuck'. At that stage, Reuben was not yet laughing at rude noises. By the age of 12 months, the dummy game had become a routine. Reuben would be very amused and smile or laugh when Aileen or I put the dummy in our mouths. This game could make him laugh even at times when he seemed ready to cry. Reuben appeared to 'realise' – the verb needs quotation marks because it does seem risky to claim such awareness so young

– that the Mummy and dummy game might cheer him up. He was in a very miserable mood and held out the dummy for Aileen to take. Then, he inserted the dummy in her mouth and started to laugh. By 1:3, also, Aileen no longer needed to embellish the placing the dummy into her mouth with a noise in order to make Reuben laugh.

When Reuben was 13 months old, the dummy game seemed hugely successful. One evening I tried the trick with him six times. Every time I put the dummy in my mouth, and added an expressive 'Yuck', Reuben laughed hugely. Both as a psychologist and a parent, this encouraged me to repeat the performance. Without the 'Yuck', Reuben still laughed but much less. By the age of 1:5, he would laugh at the dummy in one of his parent's mouths without any noise.

The Mummy with dummy game follows the same pattern as peekaboo. At first, the parent has to start it; then, the child learns he can take the initiative and in unexpected ways, too. Sroufe and Wunsch (1972), in a study of the laughter of babies up to 12 months, discovered that one of the things that babies laughed at was seeing their mother crawl on the floor. This could start as early as 5 months and, typically, increased in the month after the baby had first started to crawl. Sroufe and Wunsch did not analyse this rather remarkable finding much but I also found that Reuben first laughed at role incongruities when these were associated with the parent taking on the child's role. The baby ought to crawl and the baby should have the dummy in its mouth. By way of testing whether any parental silliness would evoke a laugh, I put a fruit basket on my head when Reuben was 9 months old. It evoked not even a smile till I smiled repeatedly at him. This pleasure in games of role reversal also showed itself when Reuben was 1:3. Nicholas sat himself at my typewriter and began to ping the keys energetically. Reuben pointed to Nicholas doing this and laughed. He was used to seeing me there and having Nicholas in my place made him laugh.

The dummy game continued till Reuben was 2 years old. It became elaborated. When Reuben was 1:11, for example, he walked into the bathroom where Aileen was having a bath with Nicholas, who was then 5:9. Reuben had two dummies in his hand. He gave one of the dummies to Aileen and smiled. The fact that he did so sent Nicholas into transports of hysterical laughter. This made Reuben look worried. Aileen, to keep it playful, then gave the dummy to Nicholas. Then, she wailed that she wanted her dummy back. Nicholas laughed, then wailed that he wanted his dummy back. He got it and sucked it but that didn't amuse him so much. Throughout, Reuben stayed watching the game he had set up. A few nights later, Aileen seized the rubber duck which made both Reuben and Nicholas laugh uncontrollably. All these are instances, it seems, of adults doing things which they ought not be doing as they are activities reserved for children.

The Mummy with dummy game seems to be the earliest instance of the child seeing the parent doing something which is appropriate to the child but not appropriate to the adult. Technically, it is a role incongruity. What is interesting is that from 1:1, Reuben liked to play this game and to set it up. Equally, as parents, we knew it was a way of making him feel good even if he was feeling bad. Were we teaching him that laughter and playing was a good way of fending off feeling down? I don't think we consciously set out to do so but, nevertheless, we were doing it.

Peekaboo

Reuben's learning of peekaboo reflects many of the stages that Bruner identified. It also seems reasonable to argue, however, that children are not just learning about the rules of social playing but the fact that they can control their own appearance and disappearance. Duval and Wicklund (1972) studied how children reacted to seeing themselves in mirrors and found that they became quite self-conscious. Oakley (1985) has reviewed the literature on animals looking at themselves in mirrors and suggests that those species that do (chimpanzees and baboons) have a self-concept. The peekaboo game may also be a way of the very young infant playing with his own growing sense of identity, of where his 'I' begins and ends and of the possibilities and limits of that 'I'.

By the age of 9 months, Reuben was well practised in reacting to peekaboo. One morning, Aileen tried three ways of playing it. First, she hid her face in the pillow, turned it towards him and said 'Peekaboo'. Reuben laughed even though he could see most of her body. Second, Aileen just said 'Peekaboo', which made Reuben laugh a little. In her third method, Aileen bothered to hide her face even less. She just buried her face down against her shoulder, then turned it towards him saying 'Peekaboo'. This, too, evoked a laugh.

By the time he was 1:4, Reuben began to initiate games of peekaboo. The first time he did it with me, he grabbed a copy of a magazine out of my hand and used it to cover my face. We also played peekaboo with different parts of his body. Aileen covered and uncovered his toes.

In his analysis of peekaboo, Bruner covers the period up to 2 years of age and then suggests that interest in the game fades away. Long-term observation made it possible to see that the children continued to play the game for a surprisingly long time. When Reuben was 2:6, he still enjoyed it. One evening, I hid behind a door and came out saying 'Peekaboo'. Reuben then followed me out of the room, laughed, said 'Boo' and laughed again. He also played the game with a friend of his, John, who was also 2:6. Each of them hid in a curtain and then stepped out or just let his face be seen. Each revealing of the face made them both laugh but the game was less formal and less patterned than with an adult. At times, both children seemed to let their attention wander so they were too distracted to play it 'properly'.

Nicholas still enjoyed a form of peekaboo at 5:5. When Reuben was 1:7 and Nicholas 5:5, they faced each other at the kitchen table. Nicholas then ducked down underneath it; Reuben laughed. Reuben then imitated him and tried to poke his head under the table which made Nicholas laugh. The appearing and disappearing of the face was an important element here.

A month later, Nicholas still could enjoy peekaboo. In the middle of a boisterous game with balloons – the balloons were natives of Saturn but more of that later – Aileen tried to get the children to calm down. For Nicholas that was impossible and he shattered the quiet by hiding behind my chair and playing peekaboo with Reuben who laughed.

Even at 6:4, Nicholas liked games where he hid (often in blankets) and then appeared. One morning, he did this twice, wriggling around, covered from head to toe, till he burst out with a laugh. This happened on his bed. Reuben laughed and began to jump up and down on his bed. The boys then transferred this game to our bed where Reuben (aged 2:8) hid himself, peeked out and laughed as he appeared. I tried to start an ordinary game of peekaboo with Reuben but he wanted to play his game, not mine. Within two minutes, he had embellished the performance by singing 'Catch the Pigeon', as he surfaced. 'Catch the Pigeon' was the theme song of a then popular TV cartoon.

The power of games in which children make themselves appear and disappear became very evident when I took Reuben and some fifteen children from his playgroup to the Institute of Education television studio. In one sequence, the children watched film of themselves. At first, this film was played back to them without any tricky effects. Very often, the particular child who appeared on screen laughed when they saw themselves. In a second condition, I made the children appear and disappear quite suddenly off the screen. This led to contortions of laughter. A very similar reaction occurred in our home when Nicholas saw himself go on, and off, the television screen attached to the video. Unfortunately, the tapes on which the children saw themselves were subsequently stolen from a laboratory at the University of London so it couldn't be made available for more analysis but the effect was very powerful and reminiscent of what happens in peekaboo. Without wishing to make too grand claims, both in playing peekaboo and taking part in such games, the child may be doing more than learning the kinds of rules Bruner identifies. The child may also be toying with their own body image, an image important in establishing identity. The uses of immaturity may be to train us not only for society but also for self-consciousness. It is surely telling that children first play games in which they appear and disappear and then go on to play games in which they take a variety of roles. For it to be safe for Reuben to be Batman, does he need first to be sure that he is Reuben and will remain Reuben whatever cape he throws over his shoulder? The observation of games in the home can't answer that question but it seems worth raising it.

Nicholas 'teaching' Reuben to play

At the start of Chapter 4, I gave a description of some of the games that Nicholas taught Reuben. Reuben's earliest games, also, seemed often to be played with his brother. The relationships between siblings differ a great deal and since Freud, psychology has placed much stress on sibling rivalry. No brother loves his brother quite like a brother. Nevertheless, as suggested earlier, there is evidence that older brothers and sisters do teach their younger ones some rules and tricks of playing – if the experience of Nicholas and Reuben is remotely typical.

The observations of how Nicholas and Reuben played together suggest that Reuben learned a great deal both from watching Nicholas and also from joining in as best he could given his age. Perhaps, more interestingly, they also suggest that Nicholas used Reuben in three ways as a game partner. At times, Nicholas did teach Reuben how to play games either directly or indirectly by letting him join in. Second, Reuben did often provide Nicholas with a source of amusement. There were many times when he commented on, or imitated, the funny actions of a funny infant. These may have been ways of expressing some sibling rivalry but there were times when, frankly, Nicholas just found Reuben funny as in parts of the Flying Cucumber game. Finally, the presence of a younger brother gave Nicholas the chance to regress in games with him.

Earlier on, I gave some instances of where Nicholas had been playing around Reuben. He often played around Reuben's playpen pretending to be an elephant or a bird. Sometimes, he charged around, teasing that Reuben was going to charge. Usually, Reuben paid close attention to these demonstrations which repeatedly let him see the point that exaggerated grimaces of the face and a 'play face' were signals from his brother that what was going on wasn't real. There were few instances when Reuben mistook Nicholas's mock aggression for real aggression. I have also described the way that Nicholas allowed Reuben to take part in his bedtime Action Show, first being close to the bed, then on the bed, then leaping around as well. The frequent occasions on which Nicholas 'led' play and Reuben's gradual ability to initiate more kinds of play suggest that he was learning specific skills from his brother.

When Nicholas was 4:5, Reuben was 7 months old and there were two instances of Nicholas just being amused by Reuben. Nicholas looked at

Reuben crawling under a chair and laughed that Reuben was driving a giraffe. Would any psychoanalyst like to give an interpretation? Two months later, Nicholas laughs when he either gets entangled with Reuben's baby things or might be mistaken for a baby. One morning when both children are in our bed, Nicholas laughs because Reuben has put his dummy in Nicholas's ear. Two months later, Nicholas (4:9) starts a fantasy in which Reuben ought to play the baby Jesus in his school's nativity play, a fantasy which he toys with at some length. When Nicholas is 5:5, he watches Reuben play with the pepper pot and pepper his cake. Nicholas can hardly contain himself.

To suggest that Nicholas uses play only to tease and put down Reuben would be wrong: often, he is amused but affectionate. Again, there is evidence that, in the home, the themes of games recur. When Nicholas was 4:8 and Reuben 10 months old, Nicholas had another fantasy about his brother. He told us that he was going to tell a joke. His joke is a one-liner that has no resolution. 'What would happen if Reuben went to see a pop star naked?' Nicholas says and waits for a laugh. I comment that this isn't a joke and ask, waiting for a punchline, what would happen if Reuben did go naked to see a pop star. An adult teller of a joke would feel compelled to provide some punchline, however daft, but Nicholas just perseveres and repeats the question. 'What would happen if Reuben went to see a pop star naked?' And then adds, 'And got on stage naked?' Two weeks later, Nicholas produces a similar fantasy about Reuben. 'Listen to this joke', he starts. 'Reuben was sitting up on a motor cycle . . .' Again, there is no resolution. But the point is that Reuben was, for Nicholas, a source of amusement for his older brother. As we shall see in dealing with aggressive and obscene games, Reuben also allowed Nicholas the chance to act the baby.

Parents 'teaching' their children to play

When I began to observe my own children, I didn't think that parents taught their children much about playing. What I remembered of my own childhood didn't suggest that was the case. It was rare for my father to kick a football with me; it was equally rare for my mother to play with me. Taking me to have strudels in a smart restaurant was fun but little boys were on parade. Yet, parents are likely play partners.

Studies of laughter going back to Washburn (1929) have shown that parents play a lot of physical games with their children. They jostle them around and, at times, even toss them up in the air. Sroufe and Wunsch (1972) found that 6-month-old children were most likely to laugh when their mothers played physically with them. During these actions, parents usually smile or laugh or put on a very deliberate 'play face' with its characteristic elongations. The child needs some such signal to know that it is not under threat or at risk.

By the age of 7 months, Reuben was the passive partner in a number of vigorous games that Aileen and I played with him. He was bounced up and down on our knees. Aileen developed a variant in which he was allowed to swing back and forth between her knees so that he risked losing support and might fall to the ground but she always caught him in time. Reuben laughed hugely during these games as he laughed when I would toss him up a foot or so in front of me and catch him. The swinging, incidentally, was itself a variation of a game that Aileen and I played with Nicholas till he was 5. One of us took his right arm, the other his left arm and, running a little, we swung him to his great pleasure. By the age of 12 months, Reuben loved a game in which Aileen picked him up and slung him above her shoulder. Then, she eased him down her back so that his head was near her bottom. Then, she slid Reuben gently up and down her back. I also played this game with him which always made him laugh tremendously. At the same time, Reuben's first part in Action Show was being held by Aileen while he jumped up and down on the bed.

Such physical games are, clearly, not teaching the children in anything specific but it could be argued that Reuben was learning some key elements of play – that it usually starts with some signal which is quite physical and that it is safe. The physical games led, around 10 months, to games in which Aileen initially did baby-like things such as putting Reuben's dummy in her mouth. As I've tried to show in analysing the Mummy with dummy game, this game was played often and with interesting variations such as Reuben starting it or both Aileen and Nicholas taking the dummy. Aileen didn't consciously decide that it would be good for the development of her son to let him see her act the baby but it flowed out of quite normal activities. In one of the longer episodes I analyse later, Aileen played both a baby and a Mummy producing a baby.

My observations of how children learn to make jokes suggest some adult influence. Children first go through a stage of making jokes which have no resolution, and they may well learn some ways of producing funny resolutions from adults. Two examples may also illustrate the way in which verbal games involve a good deal of parents' teaching.

The psychologist Chukovsky (1963) noted her own pleasure when she found that her daughter discovered 'the imagination'. Chukovsky dated this to the moment when his daughter, knowing full well the facts of animal life, said that dogs miaow. When Reuben was 2:6, I thought I would try to see what happened if we explored this notion. On being told that dogs miaow, Reuben points out that dogs go woof-woof. I try to develop the game by saying that dogs go moo-moo. Reuben will have none of it. I change tack and tell him that if he has just said moo-moo, he must be a cow:

REUBEN: No I aren't.

ME: But cows say moo and you just said moo-moo so you must be a cow.

REUBEN: No.

ME: Look, cows say moo-moo. You just said moo-moo. Moo-moo so you must be a cow.

REUBEN: You say moo-moo.

ME: Moo-moo.

REUBEN: You're a cow.

At this, Reuben laughs and seems to relish a certain sense of triumph.

A far more prolonged game of turning into something else happened when we were living in Greece. Nicholas was 3:6. I had missed Nicholas and Aileen and gone to look for them. When I returned to the house we were renting, Aileen said they were wondering if I had turned into a tree. Nicholas picked up the idea and turned it his own way: 'I decided you had turned into an orange.' He laughed. That evening, he came back to this question: 'I decided you turned into a dog.' He laughed at this and added: 'I decided you turned into a brick.' Another laugh and he summed it all up globally: 'I decided you turned into everything.'

A few evenings later, a game started again by Aileen was developed by Nicholas. She had said that she thought I was a prune. It wasn't an acid domestic comment. Nicholas thought that we could both be watermelons. Aileen insisted that she wanted to be something different from me:

NICHOLAS: David can be a lump.

ME: (*protesting*) A lump.

NICHOLAS: David can be light. (*laughs*)

ME: That's better.

NICHOLAS: David can be a pie. (*laughs*) You can be a lump of light (*laughs*) and a light. (*laughs*)

Both in the moo-cow game and, later, in the turning games, it seems clear that the children picked up both a playful atmosphere and the actual structure of the games from something that Aileen and I started.

As Nicholas got older, the question of what was proper behaviour in a game could be discussed. When he was 5:6, he often took to imitating pop singers on the television. He made parodied, exaggerated movements and laughed at himself. But there were complex ideas behind his ironic movements. The following dialogue suggests quite strongly how Nicholas wanted to be in control of the phases of the game. After he had been dancing funnily a while, I laughed:

NICHOLAS: It's meant to be funny because it's a crying dance.
ME: Is crying funny?
NICHOLAS: Yes – that sort of dance is.

At this point, Nicholas, for some reason, stopped wanting to make me laugh. He became quite stern:

NICHOLAS: Don't laugh.
ME: What can I do if it's funny but laugh?
NICHOLAS: It's over now. Don't laugh.

I stopped laughing, ceding control.

The observations record almost no instances of either Aileen or I joining in, or modelling, some of the children's games. We didn't play Batman or Cowboys and Indians apart from very occasionally firing a shot by going 'Bang Bang'. Nevertheless, the observations suggest that both of us did a good deal to teach our children something of the structure both of games and of jokes and that these activities were fun. The examples I have given show Aileen leading the way into various games in which parents become all manner of things. For the child, these role plays may be important because they offer him, or her, some chance of controlling all-powerful parents. The fact that I was doing research in the area may have meant we played these games a bit more often than usual but I don't think we created them for the purpose of research. One clear effect of playing them, however, was that the children also learned a hallowed lesson – that they could get away with some naughtiness by turning it into a game. If you 'played' at being a brat, you were less likely to be punished for it.

Using games to deflect criticism and get away with naughtiness

Many observations showed that occasions of laughter that the children created for themselves were based on denying. Just saying 'No' to something could produce laughter in Reuben when he was 1:2. This developed into a technique used both by Reuben and by Nicholas (often expertly by the latter) in which he got away with naughtiness by turning it either into a joke or into a game.

Again, there seems to be the evolution of a familiar pattern. Before he is 2, Reuben does not seem to produce any contradictions of his own although he can respond to Aileen or me or Nicholas saying 'No'. At 1:4, Reuben is drinking water out of my bath in a yellow boat. I say 'No'. He laughs and it seems to me to be a naughty laugh. A few days later, Reuben bangs the coffee table up and down while I say 'No'. Reuben laughs on each 'No'. Three months later, Reuben takes a drink of someone's Tizer and when I say, 'It's not yours', he laughs.

By 2:2, Reuben can laugh when he contradicts. Aileen tells him not to be silly. He laughs and says, 'I'm not silly'. Between 2:3 and 2:6, Reuben enjoyed weaving contradictions into other games. In the game where Reuben and Nicholas played at being each other's mummies we saw that every time Nicholas refused to say something, Reuben laughed. By the age of 3:6, Nicholas was used to laughing either as I said 'No' or as he said 'No'.

From simply laughing when they said 'No', the children moved to using laughter in order to get away either with refusing to do something or with being rude. When he was 2:2, for example, Reuben went to the supermarket and trumpeted on a number of occasions: 'I don't like that lady.' Often, the poor disliked woman was an old age pensioner who looked dismayed at that verdict. Aileen once said: 'That's rude.' Reuben knew quite well that was naughty, laughed and repeated: 'I'm rude.' That evening, he grinned: 'I'm very rude.'

Being rude to parents is, of course, part of children asserting themselves. By 2:5, Reuben liked to create opportunities to be rude to me. By 2:6, he tried to turn his clumsiness into part of a game. One morning, he clambered into bed with Aileen and me. He had Ribena in his bottle and it was dripping all over me. I told him to stop it and that it wasn't funny. Reuben laughed and added, with a grin, that it 'is a bit funny'.

Observations of Nicholas started when he was 3:6. By that time, he was skilled both at contradicting, denial and the conjuring up of humour to deflect criticism. At 3:9, Nicholas knew it was time to go to bed. 'I won't,' he laughed at me. We went into his room where he put his pyjama top on the wrong way round, back to front. Having made it into a game, he gave a very flat laugh. Then, he put his trousers on and could not do up his top button. He then started to turn round and round like a top, punctuating that performance with this flat, mean laugh. 'Stop it,' I said. 'It's funny,' Nicholas said. 'It's not funny,' I said. But he understood that turning things into games opened up possibilities of getting away with bad behaviour.

During the same period, there is a running battle to stop Nicholas licking coins or putting them in his mouth. Five seconds after I have told Nicholas he mustn't lick, he puts a coin in his mouth and gives a very loud 'hahahahha' laugh. I stare at Nicholas and refuse to be drawn into any kind of game or laughter about it – which disconcerts him.

A few months later, when Reuben is 8 months old, Nicholas begins to involve him in defiant action against parents. I am bathing both children. Nicholas is being obnoxious and I threaten to smack him unless he brushes his teeth. While doing that, I'm holding Reuben, Nicholas picks up the toothbrush and pretends to brush his teeth, keeping the brush an inch away from his mouth. Then, he puts the brush near Reuben's toes, announcing: 'I'm going to brush his toes.' Nicholas laughs and I laugh too. Then, he elaborates: 'No, I'm going to brush his feet.'

Between 4:9 and 5:0, Nicholas produces a lot of bratty laughter and often gives his games a certain edge. Round the age of 5:0, he is very concerned with 'tricking' and the notion of being tricked bothers him. To be the one who is doing the tricking makes for pleasure. One weekend, when Nicholas is 5:2, he announced five times that he had tricked me.

In games, Nicholas does at times use power. At 5:9, Aileen wants Nicholas to give her a cuddle. Very deliberately, he gives his Batman doll a cuddle and teases Aileen, saying, 'This is a cuddle' when all he is doing is waving his arms. He laughs as he does so though, finally, he relents and gives her a cuddle. In situations with relative strangers, Nicholas also becomes aware of the fact that by making things into a game, he might get his way. At 5:11, we are visiting our neighbours. Nicholas makes a bad pun and, then, when it is time to go home, he whimpers. Jimmy, the man next door, says: 'If you don't go I shall kick you out.' Nicholas laughs at Jimmy and begins a mock fight. Giggling, he is led to the door where he collects himself and says a relatively calm and polite goodbye.

Again, Reuben provides Nicholas with a source of amusement. When Nicholas is 6:3, Aileen tells the story of how she took his little brother to see Nicholas's headmistress. The headmistress cooed at Reuben: 'Isn't he a darling?' To which Reuben replied: 'Shut up.' Nicholas laughs. Aileen added that the headmistress hadn't understood Reuben, who had gone on to say: 'I don't like that lady.' Again, Nicholas laughed. This was, of course, a conversation rather than a game but the same principle seemed to be operating. Through Reuben, Nicholas could express aggression and naughtiness that he was generally too old to get away with.

Using games to coax children along

At first, Reuben had been a passive victim of Nicholas's aggressive games. Nicholas had either charged round the playpen or when Reuben toddled energetically towards him, turned it into a game by saying 'Reuben is coming' and hiding. Nicholas made allowances for Reuben when he was even smaller (7 months) and tried to pull Nicholas's hair. At that, Nicholas had laughed.

By the time he was 12 months old, Reuben showed the first sign of starting chasing games. He once came at Nicholas under the table and Nicholas laughed: 'Here's Reuben storming the castle.' From 1:0 to 1:4, these chasing games were frequent. By the time Reuben was 1:7, the chasing games could be quite long and often wove in other 'themes'. One started when Nicholas laughed as Reuben peed outside his potty. Nicholas then encouraged Reuben to draw in the pee. Then, for no apparent reason, Nicholas decided to convert it into a chase. Calling 'Buff', Nicholas hides. Reuben rises from his potty and half gives chase. Aileen tries to stop them but, through the next ten minutes, the chasing game reasserts itself with Nicholas often teasing Reuben. Does Reuben want his food cooked in his bath? Then, why does Reuben only get sweets? Why is Reuben 'not having Cola?' These digs are peppered in through the chase. Aileen manages to stop the chase only by taking Reuben on her lap. Nicholas then stands between my legs swaying, using my thighs as pillars. He chants and laughs intermittently as he sways.

By 1:7 Reuben has a clear idea of mock fighting. One evening, I decided to 'test' the hypothesis of whether parents crawling made toddlers laugh. Being on the floor, I said, 'I'm a dog' and barked. Nicholas joined in, barking too. Reuben laughed. Nicholas (then 5:5) said: 'You really scare me.' There is a pause and I slowly rise up saying, 'I am Tyrannosaurus Rex.' Nicholas is interested in dinosaurs and knows Tyrannosaurus is the fiercest of all. He laughs, chases after me and says: 'Lower your head so that we can have a Tyrannosaurus Rex fight.' We tangle and Reuben laughs and joins in by smacking me on the bottom.

By 1:9, the children often pretend to shoot each other while chasing. By 1:11, Reuben is quite used to taking the initiative in chasing Nicholas. Once, he pinions his older brother on the floor and holds his hand close to Nicholas's mouth. Nicholas takes it and pretends that he might eat Reuben's hand. Reuben laughs long and then sticks his tongue out at Nicholas, a gesture he knows to be rude.

By the age of 2:0, Reuben likes to embellish chasing games by being either Batman or Superman. He appears to know quite well that he is pretending. He grins as he says (at 2:2) 'Superman . . . I fly' and runs around the living room. Part of his learning to play these pretend games does involve him in playing with Aileen or with me. When Reuben is 2:5, Aileen dons a blanket which she says makes her into Batman. She lunges both at Nicholas and at Reuben, which makes Reuben laugh as she swoops. In the same month, Reuben can laugh when I also make threatening lunges at him, saying: 'I'm going to get you.'

These mock aggressive games are relatively gentle with Reuben up to 2:5, with Nicholas by the age of 3:6, they could be quite rough. At 3:11, I tell Nicholas we'll play horse. He sits on me facing me. Then he turns round looking at my feet and tells me to put my knees up. He tugs at my flies and laughs. We tumble about quite roughly till Nicholas falls off. At 4:7, Nicholas laughs as he prods Aileen with a finger round the neck. On each prod, he laughs. Aileen starts to punch him back playfully and, again, Nicholas laughs.

At 4:11, Nicholas decides to have a mock battle with a friend of ours called Doug. Every time he hits Doug or Doug hits him, Nicholas laughs. The moment of contact produces the laughter. This pattern of play fights with parents, and with Reuben, continues. At 5:11, Nicholas plays a game in which he tries to pull Aileen's toe off and he can hardly restrain himself when he laughs so much. At 6:4, Nicholas has been pretending to be a baby when Aileen comes in wearing the cape that makes her Batman. Nicholas stops this baby pretence at once and enjoys a game in which Aileen attacks him.

These play battles with parents happen quite often. Perhaps more expected, given the literature on sibling rivalry, are play fights between the children. When Reuben was 9 months old, Nicholas was 4:7 and he often held Reuben by the neck. One day, Reuben was sitting in his high chair and dropped his bottle.

Nicholas said: 'I'm making him go mad with his bottle.' This produced a very nasty hissy laugh from Nicholas.

The next day, Nicholas laughed as he prodded Reuben with his finger. Another day soon after, the boys were in the living room and Nicholas was using his Lego to tease Reuben by putting it on his head.

ME: Nicholas don't torment him by putting your Lego on his head. (*Nicholas laughed and continued to torment him.*)
ME: Come on enough. (*Nicholas laughed.*) Take it away. (*Nicholas laughed.*) Play with your Lego on the table.
NICHOLAS: (*loudly*) Bababab. (*He laughed and then turned towards Reuben.*) Bubububu. Is that funny, Dubie?

Reuben didn't laugh, even when I tried to tickle him. Nicholas then began to chase me even though I told him to stop. He became hysterical with laughter and insisted on chasing me.

Nicholas seemed to use chasing and teasing games, then, both to teach Reuben and to tease him, to express hostility in a manner that was socially more acceptable. It is also worth noting that, with two young children in the house, Aileen and I felt free to muck about at being Batman and at play fighting ourselves. The notion that we become too old to play such games seems wrong. Even teenagers can play them. During this period, we had neighbours with an 11-year-old daughter, Helen. Although she would be slightly self-conscious when she joined in, Helen appeared to like playing chasing games with the two children, too, being afforded the chance to 'regress'.

Obscenity in play

We have already seen that Nicholas once encouraged Reuben to draw in his pee. Reuben was toilet-trained very easily but at 2:4, when he was already quite 'clean', he began to incorporate a new sort of character into his Batman games. Batman became Aaahman. At 2:6, Reuben can incorporate an obscene element into a game without the game becoming dominated by it. Reuben is about to take a bath and pretends he can see a man in the bath. 'Him a Dada,' Reuben laughs. 'I see a man, a Nanny man,' Reuben laughs. (Nanny is his name for Nicholas.) 'I see a man,' Reuben goes on and laughs, 'I saw a man in the potty.' Reuben peers in the potty, which is at the side of the bath. He laughs again. 'You saw a man in the potty?' I ask. 'I did,' says Reuben who waves at his imagined creation. By the age of 2:6, just saying a dirty word isn't funny for Reuben. He has to either incorporate it into a game or distort it.

From 3:7 to 4:8, Nicholas produced very few dirty jokes or games. But the birth of Reuben seemed to provoke a whole new interest in the subject. At 4:8, Nicholas laughs when Reuben loses his pyjama pants and his nappy. At 4:11, Nicholas laughs when I find him sitting on the oven door. I ask if he's toasting his bottom. He laughs: 'Yum yum toasted bum.' Then he picks at his bottom and offers us, with a laugh, a 'slice of bottom'. At 5:2, I'm reading Nicholas a book when we get to the letter P (which the book illustrates properly with policemen, paintings, pink and pyjamas), Nicholas laughs and says he is doing pee pee on himself. At 5:4, Nicholas laughs when Reuben is sitting on his potty playing with a little piece of silver paper. At 6:0, Nicholas sees a spot of wet on my filthy blue jeans and laughs: 'I peed on you. I peed on you mistakenly.' He adds a sly laugh and then picks up a piece of blue paper which he puts on Reuben's head. 'That blue spot is where I peed on Reuben,' Nicholas says, laughing. Again, some elements of the pattern are familiar. Reuben initially finds just saying a dirty word like 'Aaah' funny. Then that is embellished. Nicholas finds in Reuben an excuse to regress and, also, in some games like the one with the blue paper, expresses a certain hostility towards his tiny brother.

Pretending and sequences of play

Most literature on the growth of pretending tends to suggest that children play very literal games. In the home, we saw some of these but also many quite esoteric ones. From 3:6, N often became involved in games in which we pretended to take on each other's roles. I acted the child; he acted the parent. There are structural similarities with the Mummy with dummy game though, with Nicholas, the games were more elaborate. Again, in the home, it seemed that play occurred with people and in, and about, social situations far more than with objects. In looking at the development of Reuben's pretences, it seems clear that he pretended we were what we weren't (babies with dummies) long before he pretended to play using blocks or toys. These role plays also seem to me important in showing that the young infant has a certain self-awareness and even, the intention to amuse.

Reuben seems to display such self-awareness on two of the first occasions when he does something to make himself laugh, creating rather than reacting to a situation.

At 7 months, Reuben looks in the mirror with Aileen. She is clapping her hands to interest him. Clumsily, he begins to try and clap his hands, often missing, but sometimes succeeding. Reuben graces each clap attempt with a laugh. Four months later (he is 11 months), Reuben again plays a game which involves a measure of self-awareness. He sees Nicholas use the tube of a packet of foil. Nicholas uses this as a telescope. Reuben wants to do the same and, as I look at Reuben through the other end of the foil telescope, he laughs. This becomes a game with him laughing each time I or Nicholas puts his eye there. Reuben usually then puts his eye to the other end of the telescope. It could be claimed, with some caution, that he knows it's a game that involves looking at him in a strange way. For him, part of the game is to be seen in this odd way at the end of the tube. I became alert to the differences in the sounds of laugher and detected some differences between when he just looked down the telescope and when he looked – and was looked at – in return.

Reuben often repeated this game and its basic pattern. He laughs when you look at him through the telescope; he laughs when he puts his eye to the other end and looks at you. There is less laughter when he just looks down it.

Even if he remains just on the fringes of games, Reuben likes them. At 10 months, he laughs as he watches Aileen and Nicholas roll a ball to each other. At 1:3, Reuben appreciates complicated imitations. After both boys watch *Laurel and Hardy* on TV, Nicholas often imitates Hardy by puffing himself out and saying sternly: 'A fine mess you've got me into.' Nicholas then nods as Hardy does and the whole routine makes Reuben laugh.

Bower's (1977) work on imitation has suggested that newborns can imitate such movements as sticking out the tongue. Kaye (1982) has warned against inflating the abilities of babies but perhaps it is not too controversial to suggest that by 1:10, Reuben not only can imitate in games but also seems to know he's doing so. This seems especially clear with arm gestures. At 1:10, Reuben is out shopping with me. He is complaining and waving his arms in a kind of agitated flapping. I face him and begin to imitate the way he is flapping. Reuben laughs. He realises I am imitating him.

At 1:10 and 1:11, Reuben is obsessed by Batman. He often laughs when he just yells 'Batman', and it is one of the few laughs that seem to be of pure excitement or glee.

But it is not the pure glee that Spencer (1860) discussed, for Reuben is, in some way, acting out Batman. The fantasy fuels his laughter. At 1:10, Reuben says 'Batman' or 'Superman' but he does not seem aware of the fact that he is acting, pretending to be, Batman (if indeed that is what he is doing).

By 2:0, however Reuben has learned to act out the characters in the Batman myth. He laughs as he says: 'I fly.' He claims that he is Superman or Aquaman or other heroes. He often rushes around the room which is his form of flying. Over the next six months, this is a very frequent form of play. This basic sequence of flying and pretending to be Superman, say, is often woven into games of greater complexity and, at times, violence.

The swopping of identity which is evident in the dummy game occurs in a game that Reuben at 2:5 plays with Nicholas. They are playing at being each other's mummies. It amuses them both very much. Nicholas smiles. Reuben says: 'I give you a kiss' – a properly maternal act. But Reuben's maternal kiss turns out to be rather fierce. He grips Nicholas round the neck. Nicholas laughs: 'Strangling and kissing are a different matter.' But they continue the game.

At 2:6, Reuben has also started to play games in which his gender identity is brought into question. From 2:0, he has been very fond of 'Snow White and the Seven Dwarfs'. At 2:5, we have just been listening to the record. Reuben looks happy. I ask him if he is Cheerful (one of the dwarfs). 'No,' he smiles. Is he Dopey? 'No,' he smiles. Is he Sneezy? 'No,' he smiles. Is he Snow White? 'No,' Reuben now bursts out laughing. He goes on laughing as he says that Mummy – Aileen is indeed in a white dress – is Snow White.

At 2:6, Reuben also plays a game with Nicholas in which each of them is supposed to have a vagina. They cross their legs – Nicholas especially – and, from time to time, laugh a little. This is another instance where they create a game in which sexual roles are involved.

By the time I started to observe Nicholas, he was already 3:6 and well versed in pretending. At 3:7, in Greece, we employed an old man to do the garden. He tweaks Nicholas's nose and calls him Nikolaski. One evening, Nicholas says: 'Pretend I'm the gardener and (*to Aileen*) that you're Nicky and (*to me*) that you're Nicky's Mummy'.

Nicholas says: 'Nikolaski' – and laughs. Nicholas repeats it: 'Nikolaski' – and laughs again. Aileen giggles in the embarrassed way that Nicholas giggles when the old gardener pulls his nose. Nicholas laughs to see it. Nicholas then tells me to pretend that I am the gardener now. I put on a heavy accent imitating the old man. I grunt, I make faces in the way that he does in order to try and make his Greek understood. I say 'Nikolaski'. Each of these actions produces bellows of laughter from Nicholas.

At 3:7 Nicholas can use games in which he pretends in order to express what he is interested in. We play at dinner. I say: 'Pretend you're a puppy.' Nicholas: 'Ruff, Ruff' and he puts on a very shaggy look. I say: 'Now get a bone.' Nicholas rushes to a cushion. He brings it over, laughing at his cushion-bone. He then says: 'It isn't a bone, it's a dinosaur.' Dinosaurs fascinate him.

By 4:7 Nicholas can analyse the logic of some of these games that depend on a reversal of identities. At breakfast, Aileen asks what he wants to drink. Nicholas says: 'Coffee'. He doesn't mean it, for whenever he has sipped coffee he really dislikes it. Aileen says:

> Yes, we're going to give Nicholas coffee, David's coffee. In fact, Nicholas can be David. David can go to the nursery school and Nicholas can have coffee and go to work. David can have blackcurrant and nursery school. David can sleep in Nicholas's bed and Nicholas in David's bed.

Nicholas laughs on nearly all of the specifics of the reversals. But he does not laugh wildly. After a few instances, Nicholas declares: 'In this joke, we are pretending that David does everything that I do and we are pretending that I do everything that David does.'

As well as pretending to be an adult, Nicholas can pretend to be a baby. The curious thing is that his imitation of a baby is much less convincing than his adult impersonations. From when Reuben is about 6 months, Nicholas imitates him. When Reuben is 10 months and Nicholas 4:8, there is a host of these imitations. Nicholas often pretends to be Reuben and 'to cry' and laughs through this baby crying routine of his. The key feature of Nicholas's imitation is the voice. He makes his voice baby-like. He believes he can do this by slurring the sounds so that they become less distinct, by slowing his speech and by giving his voice a certain rhythmic lilt as if babies spoke in sing song. Nicholas also fixes on certain phrases as being the epitome of babyhood. One such phrase is 'Gaga'. These 'performances' as a baby are unconvincing. If Nicholas really wanted to regress and be a baby, one would imagine he would do it far more thoroughly. It clearly is play and it makes Nicholas laugh often while he pretends to 'cry'. Not until Reuben is 2:0 is there any indication that he realises Nicholas is imitating him.

At 4:10, Nicholas also appreciates imitation of him imitating. He is very much into warlike and aggressive games bred from his fantasy. He plays in the garden at being a knight. He lunges with a twig which is his sword and makes ferocious faces. I imitate these faces by grunting and pulling even more ludicrous ones. Nicholas laughs.

Nicholas continues to imitate Reuben. At 6:0, Nicholas is very keen to pretend to be a baby at times. At 6:3, he plays again at being the baby. Nicholas is sitting in Adele's lap (Adele is his aunt) and giggles at the flow of baby talk he produces – a flow no real baby would ever produce. Nicholas puts his thumb in his mouth and makes noises which include his old stand-by 'Gaga'. At a certain point, Nicholas gets up from the rug and jumps jerkily up and down, up and down, laughing as he does so. He appears to be imitating the unsure movements of a baby.

Nicholas's 'performance' is interrupted for a while by Aileen, who wears a cape and says that she is Batman. After a few aggressive swoops, arms outstretched, at both Nicholas and Reuben – swoops which produce laughter – Nicholas resumes playing the baby. Finally, Aileen gets impatient and says: 'I can only stand so much of your being two.'

Nicholas laughs at that. It's interesting that she's taken it to be a performance of a 2 year old!

Nicholas stops being the baby then. But between 6:0 and 6:3, there are often evenings at bathtimes when for two or three minutes, he adopts this babyish game, laughing as he does it. He says he doesn't 'wanna' brush teeth. He grabs his pyjamas out of my hand, twirls them and adds: 'I don't wanna jammas.' And laughs.

By the time Nicholas is 4:8 it is interesting to see how there are quite long sequences of laughter in some games. One sequence I timed lasted 18 minutes. In such sequences, all the kinds of laughter I have pointed out occur and, sometimes, there are very rapid shifts and combinations of different instances of laughter. In the two sequences I now intend to detail Nicholas was 4:8 and Reuben 11 months. Both sequences are recorded on audio-tape.

The first of these sequences began as Aileen was trying to cheer up Reuben, who was very tired:

AILEEN (*to Reuben*): Look at Nicky's hat.
NICHOLAS: I'm a cowboy.
AILEEN (*to Reuben*): Hat, hat, hat, hat.
(*Nicholas bursts into laughter at her teaching of Reuben.*)
AILEEN : Don't frighten him.
(*I then get the hat off Nicholas. He stamps and laughs.*)
NICHOLAS (to *me*): You look funny.
ME: Why does the hat make me look funny?
(*Nicholas bursts again into laughter. I cover my face with the hat.*)
ME: The hat is now my head.
(*Aileen takes the hat.*)
NICHOLAS: I want it to be a cowboy hat.

Nicholas and Aileen fight over who is to have the hat and, also, a balloon that is floating around the kitchen as it is Christmas time. Aileen and Nicholas laugh as they tussle for the hat. Nicholas gets the hat and hides it. Aileen suggests that the hat might be hidden by Nicholas in the freezer. I say: 'Frozen hat'. Nicholas laughs hysterically at that.

Aileen develops this idea by suggesting that the hat is in the mustard jar. Nicholas laughs. Or cooking in the oven. Nicholas laughs. Or that there will be hat for dinner. Nicholas laughs. But for all these guesses, we still don't know where the hat is for Nicholas is still hiding it.

Aileen now threatens Nicholas to 'cut out the crap, where's the hat?' Reuben joins in with a high pitched laugh. Aileen 'finds' the balloon and tries to run away with it. Nicholas shoots her – making shooting noises as he does so – and laughs.

AILEEN (*under the table*): I'm in my hide out.
NICHOLAS: Sit down. (*He laughs.*) Who gets it?

Aileen now lets go the balloon. Something happens and she warns Nicholas to be careful. He calms down at once, coming out of the game.

ME: Nicky just caught it.

As Nicholas catches the balloon, he laughs. But then, we get bored with the game. Nicholas collects both hat and balloon. He swaggers like a cowboy, says 'OK man' and laughs. Then, Nicholas begins to dance round Reuben and to chase him, which makes him laugh.

This sequence of a game has lasted roughly five minutes. We have seen during it, in succession, laughter that seems to be brought on by the following 'causes'. There is incongruity as in the idea of 'frozen hat' which is elaborated into the hat being in the oven and in the mustard. There is laughter at something both incongruous and a bit disgusting, the idea that there should be hat for dinner. There is a sort of peekaboo as Nicholas laughs when I cover my face with the hat. There is aggressive laughter as Aileen and Nicholas tussle over the hat. This highly aroused aggressive laughter does not stem from but leads into the incongruous jokes about the frozen hat. There is no simple progress – or regress – from conceptual jokes to more excited laughter. After the jokes about the hat, there is a small chase as Nicholas shoots Aileen, who hides under the table. Then, the hat ceases to be the origin of the laughter. The balloon becomes that and Nicholas laughs as it is released, as he tries to catch it and when he does catch it. Then, though Aileen and I get bored with the game and declare the hat game to be over, Nicholas still wants to laugh. A slightly similar event occurs in another game where, as the game seems to be at an end, Nicholas manifestly wants it to continue. So Nicholas first swaggers, imitating a cowboy which was one of the starting points of the whole game and then he chases Reuben. Often the tape of the whole sequence reveals the laughter as high pitched and excited but it is far from consistently so.

A longer game took place some days later. It started with our having two balloons left over from a Christmas party. The game began with pretending to pop the balloons. Both children (Reuben was now 11 months) laughed at the sound of the 'pop'. Aileen repeated the popping and Nicholas said: 'It scares me'. Having pretended to pop the balloon, Aileen now pretends it has really disappeared. Nicholas laughs. He knows quite well the balloon is still around. There is then a pause in the development of the game. We talk about what happened at Christmas. Then Nicholas asks Aileen if she will use the balloon which she does, to make herself look pregnant. She sprouts a giant belly. Aileen asks Nicholas what it looks like. Through asking Aileen to use the balloon, clearly a request to play, Nicholas has started a whole scenario:

AILEEN: What does it look like?
NICHOLAS: Big.
AILEEN: It's a baby, a very little baby.
NICHOLAS: I want to see what baby looks like.
AILEEN: My baby's coming out.

Nicholas laughs as the balloon appears from under Aileen's sweater. As she sees her baby is a balloon, Aileen recoils in mock horror. Nicholas laughs.

ME: A green baby. Oh dear.
(*Hysterical laughter from Nicholas.*)
AILEEN: It's a green baby . . . a flying baby. (*The balloon flies.*) A flying green baby.
(*Nicholas laughs hysterically again; Reuben joins in.*)
AILEEN: Don't operate on my baby. (*Nicholas laughs.*) You can't operate on a balloon. (*Nicholas laughs.*)

There is a short pause then Nicholas laughs again. Aileen then pushes the balloon. On each push, she utters 'Oah'. Another push, another 'Oah'.

ME: It might help if you didn't beat the baby up into the air. (*Nicholas laughs twice.*)
AILEEN: This baby has to be very specially handled. Hey, don't knock him down.

Aileen says that to Reuben but her stricture makes Nicholas laugh again. Aileen comforts her balloon. 'Poor child,' she says. Nicholas laughs.

NICHOLAS: Baby. (*Nicholas laughs.*) Baby.
AILEEN: Oah. (*Nicholas laughs.*) Oah. (*Nicholas laughs.*)
(*Again each 'Oah' comes on a push of the balloon.*)
NICHOLAS: Baby, baby, baby, baby, he's a balloon baby. (*Nicholas laughs.*)

There is an interlude, as it were, in which we talk of hot water.

AILEEN: Kiss him.
NICHOLAS: He says he wants to have a little rest. (*Nicholas laughs.*) My baby.
    My baby. He started to scream. (*Nicholas laughs.*) Didn't he, my baby?
(*Nicholas laughs.*)

This time, Nicholas's laugh is very like a scream he is so excited. The balloon is now flying around. Nicholas tries to catch it. Reuben waves his arms at it. There is a pitch of excitement.

AILEEN: I think he's a flying green hedgehog.

Nicholas repeats this assertion. Aileen then repeats it. Nicholas laughs.

NICHOLAS: No, nice baby . . . I caught it.
AILEEN: Oah . . .
NICHOLAS: Let's do the beginning again.

Now that the balloon is caught, it is time to have a replay. Interestingly, Reuben's laughter now becomes more marked and more individual. Up to here, he has very much laughed in the footsteps of Nicholas or, simply, as the balloon was being chased. Now, Reuben laughs as Nicholas says, 'Let's do it again'.

NICHOLAS (to *Aileen*): Can I see what your baby looks like?
(*On the birth of the balloon, Reuben laughs hugely.*)
AILEEN: It's about to come out. (*Nicholas laughs.*)
ME: It's dropped on the floor.
(*Nicholas laughs four times in a very excited burst.*)
NICHOLAS: It's a balloon baby.
ME: Maybe it's name is Jupiter.
NICHOLAS: Saturn. (*Nicholas likes Saturn.*) Noah of Noah and the Ark.

At this point, Aileen appears to have a second balloon concealed as a baby in her sweater. It appears.

AILEEN: Twins!
(*Nicholas laughs.*)
NICHOLAS: Can I see your twins?
(*Both Nicholas and Reuben laugh as the second of the balloons appears.*)
NICHOLAS: Let's call them Saturn and Jupiter . . . oohoh . . .
(*Saturn bursts.*)
ME: Someone sat on Saturn.
NICHOLAS (*repeating*): *Sat* on Saturn.
AILEEN: Saturn burst. (*chasing*) Mars.
NICHOLAS: Mars . . . I hope Mars doesn't die for a long time.
AILEEN: Easy come, easy go with these balloons.
NICHOLAS: Mars doesn't scream and he wants to have a sleep.
AILEEN: Which planet do you come from?
NICHOLAS: Saturn.
AILEEN: Oh you have a blue nose.
NICHOLAS: No. (*Nicholas laughs.*) They have red necks.
AILEEN: No, that's from Saturn.

Aileen attributes to the Saturn-dwellers green belly buttons and purple teeth. This gets no laughter. Nicholas adds that they have silver chins. Aileen gives gold ears. None of these evokes a laugh.

NICHOLAS: Yes and Dubi fare booms (*which is incomprehensible but seems to be a dig at Reuben*). All we do in Saturn is walk around in our Saturn trains.

There is now some talk of trains, sleeping in trains, not having houses, living in trains and staying on the same trains. None of this yields any laughs.

NICHOLAS: I'm in my Saturn train, sleeping. I can see things the wrong way round. (*To Aileen*) Come on my train. You can go into space.

Aileen is now pretending to be on Saturn. She says: 'Look at all these trains . . . how very peculiar.'
    Aileen now shows a number of implements from the kitchen to Nicholas. Each implement is given a wrong use.

AILEEN: That's to make soup with. (*Nicholas laughs.*)
NICHOLAS: He sits in a toy train.
AILEEN: Why is Saturn so full of trains? (*Nicholas laughs.*)

(*Nicholas explains that the houses were too big so they took to trains.*)
NICHOLAS: Let's go back shall we?
AILEEN: Can I sit on the cactus? (*Nicholas laughs.*) Funny cactus, it's
    attacking me . . . (*Nicholas laughs.*)
NICHOLAS: It's a stroking cactus.

At this point, the tape ran out and, also, the game wound down.

The long sequence reveals again a jumble of reasons for play and laughter. Three times, Nicholas starts the game. He asks Aileen to use the balloon, asks her to replay the birth of the balloon and says he wants to leave Saturn. If he had not asked her to repeat the birth, it is likely the game would have petered out as Aileen seemed quite bored with it.

The transcript shows a variety of types of laughter and play brought together. The most frequent laughter is at chasing the flying balloon. That is funnier because of the incongruity that the balloon is a baby. A green balloon baby is a pretty incongruous mix. There is also elaboration for at one point the flying baby becomes a flying hedgehog. If these are all intellectual variations, it is important to see that some of the themes are far more emotive. Nicholas says the balloon baby needs a rest. Aileen, the good mother, says it needs special handling – a double joke but also a valid point – and Nicholas kisses this baby who might stand for a rival.

The game allows both the children and the parents to express aggression. The actual birth of the baby is very funny but this highlight is crowned when, on the second birth, the balloon drops to the floor. Surely, this permits the expression of some hostility. One should not drop babies on the floor, let alone bounce them. Within the game, Aileen and Nicholas vent some general hostility to babies.

And yet the game feels like fun. Speaking from inside it, I experienced it as a delight. What happens after Saturn bursts is, also, interesting. Though the children are now very aroused, Nicholas reacts to the pun that I make by repeating it. 'Sat on Saturn,' he echoes. Then, the nature of the game changes very quickly from one that depends on physical activity to a very odd fantasy about life on Saturn, planet of the trains. All the initial incongruities thrown up by Aileen get little laughter. And, though Nicholas produces many incongruities about life in the trains, again, he does not laugh much at them though he is motivated as he goes on producing more and more oddities.

The return to laughter is marked by something very simple – Aileen using the 'wrong' implement for soup. Then, there are renewed laughs as Aileen asks Nicholas why Saturn is so full of trains. Now, he laughs at this question. Then, Nicholas laughs as Aileen sits on an aggressive cactus. Many of the events on Saturn are fantastic, incongruous and – even – have a resolution of sorts since Nicholas explains why they live on trains and the consequences. But little of this, though enjoyed by Nicholas, evokes his laughter.

At the time when the observations were made, I was not familiar with the arguments concerning goal-directed action (Harré and Von Cranach 1982). It seems possible to interpret Nicholas's restarting of the game as expressing an intention to get more laughter. He achieves his end after he has called for the birth of the balloon baby. But then the intention does not seem to peter out. Nicholas keeps throwing up more incongruities about Saturn but laughter dies away. Nicholas only laughs again at an unexpected action of Aileen's when she uses the wrong implement for soup. Aileen meant to provoke laughter but Nicholas seems to react uncontrollably. He 'can't help laughing'. Traditionally, studies of laughter have seen children always as responsive, not creative. This switch in Nicholas may be at a critical point between the two kinds of laughter.

Two other points are worth noting. First, Reuben does often start laughing with Nicholas. The second time the balloon is born, his own laughter is more confident and he does not seem to have to wait for Nicholas to laugh. The tape, unfortunately, reveals little more of what he did during the Saturn episode.

Second, any analytical view would highlight not the transitions between being responsive and creative in laughter but the nature of the material the game is about. What could be more anxiety-provoking than the birth of another child, another rival? Throughout the game, it is also interesting to note the way that Aileen and I, while being as silly as the children, also make informative asides about this not being the way to handle babies or the state of fantasy on Saturn.

Such observations suggest that there is much to be gained by detailed naturalistic observation of the ways children play with their parents. More rigorous observations may well miss an important kind of laughter – that which comes and goes during the course of long games. A variety of causes and motives surfaces in the game described above including perceptual incongruity, sheer fantasy, elaboration of fantastic themes, emotional relief, loud noises, balloons doing unexpected things and peekaboo. The capacity to play such complex games seems to develop as the child develops a number of play and laughter skills. But these comic and imaginative feats do depend on the child grasping, as Reuben seemed to by 12 months, that a play face or expression mean, 'This is not real'. Observations of Reuben suggested strongly that by 2:6 he had become able to act out being other people, to know he was doing that, to plan such episodes and to make himself laugh in the process. Valentine (1942) claimed that by the age of 4 he had seen all possible causes of laughter in his children including the ability to laugh at themselves. Few play researchers examine the importance of this. One curious finding is that after children have made a mistake such as falling over, some do it again deliberately and laugh at themselves.

These observations suggest that, by the age of 2, children not only create play situations deliberately but also are capable of intending to do so. Reuben donning a cape to be Batman was a conscious intentional agent. The evidence also suggests that parents play an important part in shaping their children's play and laughter. The transcripts of the long sequences would seem to support that, even though Aileen and I had no specific programme for using play and our playing remained 'fun'. But should parents be more deliberate about the play they encourage?

Pretending and other minds

The reason this issue has become a heated one is it has implications for the question of when children start to get a sense of other minds. Can children pretend if they don't understand that other people have other minds with other thoughts? This is a question that has fascinated philosophers for half-a-century if not more – and I will allow myself the boast that when I was an undergraduate at Oxford I had the terrifying privilege of giving a paper on that which the legendary Gilbert Ryle replied to; he was very gentle in demolishing my 20-year-old pretensions.

Many psychologists now argue that children start to pretend when they understand the false belief task because both such skills are based on a very similar skills. You can not pretend if you do not understand what it is – meta-representational. I questioned this in terms of Reuben and the Flying Cucumber. But there are some who argue that pretending is necessarily meta-representational. Leslie (1987) claimed this.

Nielsen and Dissanayake (2000) have suggested that many aspects of pretend play depend on such meta-representations. They observed forty children playing with their parents. They was a correlation between how well children did on the false belief task and 'pretend play acts of role assignment and object substitution'. But the results did not show any correlation between how well children did on the false belief task and role play, imaginary play and attribution of pretend properties. These are precisely the skills and the kinds of play you would expect to depend on some understanding of what is going on in the mind.

Lilliard (1993, 1994) has suggested that early pretend play is not meta-representation. She claims children who are younger than 6 see pretend as 'being as if'. Berguno and Bowler (2004) found that 3 year olds who under-stood enough about pretending to play pretending games did not have much understanding of pretence 'in a mentalistic fashion'. They claim the first signs of that come at 4. Lilliard compares – and it's a nice comparison

– understanding pretending with understanding what is read to us. We don't expect the child who enjoys a story to have any sense of the mental state of the author. As millions read Harry Potter, I doubt many spend an instant thinking of what is going on in J.K. Rowling's mind. (The more I think about Lilliard's point the dafter psychology seems.) Except when one has to write essays about them, does any reader ponder as follows: 'Excellent this description of Oliver Twist – I think Charles Dickens was thinking this when he wrote it.' What is essential is that the child just gets on with pretending and realises that this is not real.

I suspect that some of this research betrays what Gilbert Ryle would have called a category confusion. The really interesting question that the young child's ability to pretend throws up is that when you play pretend games you have to be able to understand that other people have other minds – and may lie to you. Children show they know this by the way they perform in games. Understanding how the mind is made up is very different.

Creating the creative child?

Today, everything aspires to be creative. Ads for managers and even civil servants seek the creative, we have not just the creative artist but also the creative cook, the creative architect, the creative engineer, the creative accountant, even the creative psychologist. But what might make a child more creative remains a mystery.

There have been many studies of gifted artists that have tried to isolate what made them creative geniuses. As Howard Gardner (1983) has pointed out in *Art, Brain and the Mind*, it is all too easy to generalise about the makings of the artistic mind. If you want the recipe for turning your child into a genius, it is no good asking psychologists what games you ought to play in your family or, even, if you ought to play any games at all. Some of the greatest innovators, like Isaac Newton, appear to have had rather isolated childhoods. It is even harder to know, as Liam Hudson (1967) pointed out in *Contrary Imaginations*, whether children who are good at solving logical puzzles are more likely to be truly creative than those who are fluent in their thinking. Our stereotype of the imaginative person is of an arty-type whose thinking flows from one point to the next to make unexpected, new connections. Some of the children who do this best, avoid the stereotype and have rather narrow, focused minds.

Developmental psychologists have sometimes concentrated on rather more modest questions such as if there are individual differences in the playfulness of children and what effect that might have. Jerome Singer (1973) reported on a series of studies of the fantasy and imaginative play of children that he had carried out over the years. He noted that girls were beginning to take part in more active, aggressive games, especially after Wonderwoman became the star of a television cartoon. The sexes were beginning to resemble each other in their play more than before because, while boys still spurned girls' games as being for sissies, girls had learned that they might be heroic too like Wonderwoman. New role models now allowed girls to swagger. Fantasy can help change sex roles, Singer (1973) suggested.

The many benefits of imaginative play were catalogued by Tower and Singer (1980) in an extensive review of imagination, interest and joy in childhood. They divided the benefits into cognitive and social ones. The imaginative child would learn to integrate experience, work out what was inner and outer, learn to organise information better, become more reflective, elaborate perceptions and cognitions, recognise mistakes quicker and develop better concentration. These were just the cognitive uses, too. The 'social benefits of imagery' included becoming more sensitive to others, increased empathy, poise, acculturation, self-entertainment reducing fear and anxiety, improved emotional well-being and self-control. In general, Tower and Singer conclude the more a child imagines, the happier he or she is. They give, in one section, a minor rhapsody on the value of playing with parents. It is worth quoting in full:

> When a child engages in imaginative play with a parent, a very special phenomenon is taking place: the child is generating and executing ideas based on its own experience in a context of mutual respect, interest and absence of criticism. Parent and child are free to experience each other in terms of possibilities. Constraints inherent in the usual roles they play in relation to each other may be temporarily put aside. They give and take of laughter and of shared 'dangers' and 'rescues' may enhance a positive sense of communion. Parents often have lost touch with their own childhood joys in fantasy play and can regain some of that excitement through play.
>
> (Tower and Singer 1980: 36)

I would agree whole-heartedly with this vision. Unfortunately, Tower and Singer (1980) are able to quote only a few studies that offer any advice on how to create the kind of situation in which parents and children are likely to play together. Even advice on how to rear an imaginative child is rare. Tower and Singer suggested that the 'child's natural responses of interest, curiosity and joy must be respected'. The child must have freedom to play and some privacy. Older siblings should not be allowed to interfere too much, they recommend. One study in South Africa (Udwin and Shmukler 1981) suggests there may be cultural differences in the need for privacy. In general, though, researchers find it hard to be specific. Love your child. Respect his or her imagination. Freeman (2004) suggests ways in which parents may nurture the talent of their children and playing with them is high on her list of must-do.

But will the respected and accepted child play more? Or does it depend on the personality of the child? One of the curious aspects of the play literature is the way it plumps for stages. There are almost no longitudinal studies that aim to tease out individual differences in playfulness between different children. The closest study is one by McGhee on the development of humour. McGhee (1980) reported that children who were more developed in their humour tended to be more talkative than their peers, to use language more expressively and to have a bigger vocabulary. The children tended to be more assertive too. Well before they went to school, McGhee found that his humorous children had had very protective relationships with their mothers who babied them a good deal. The mothers also approved of them. McGhee speculated that these children started to used humour when they were 3 in order to keep their aggressive impulses in check and to maintain control.

> By consistently clowning or joking, the individual can remain in charge of the flow of conversation or other interaction. By initiating a joke, anecdote or other comic behaviour, the humorist puts others in a situation where they are obliged to react in some way.
>
> (McGhee 1980: 233)

Usually, the audience like it too and, so, do not resent the control. A gloomier picture emerges from the study of professional humorists by Fisher and Fisher (1982). Their subjects tended to remember their childhoods as wretched and claimed they had become funny persons because their fates were so awful.

McGhee's humorist dominates; the deft role player perhaps infiltrates. Flavell (1962) and Kohlberg (1969) both argued that it was in the home that the child gets the earliest opportunities to learn how to play different parts. Light (1979) reviewed a series of modest experimental studies in the previous ten years and found that the best evidence was negative. Children who were in trouble, like juvenile delinquents, tended to have poor role-playing skills. Unfortunately, much of this literature did not look at how children played with each other but at skills such as being able to imagine what a picture would look like from a different perspective. Light used this kind of design and gave sixty children different role-playing tasks. The children who were good role takers when they were 3 were described as being friendly to strangers, more willing to be left in the care of others and more eager to explore novel surroundings. They could amuse themselves better and tended to be less bored. But there were problems too. Good role takers tended to whine and fuss more, to have more temper tantrums and to wet themselves! Light (1979) claimed that interviews with mothers suggested they were more 'personal' with their children. They interfered less, gave more emotional support and made more concessions to what the children wanted. The mother whose child was the best role taker was apt to give her child time to do something she had been told to do. Modest though his study was, Light did reveal some possibly interesting personality differences between good and bad role takers and their mothers' attitudes.

Unfortunately, we don't have studies equivalent to McGhee's of playful versus less playful children. Playing with parents does seem to build many bonds but it is far from certain that it benefits all children. The research has little say on how, and if, parents should coax children into play. A description of ultra orthodox Jewish children in New York states they hop all over the street 'like rabbits' (*New Yorker*, 23 September 1985, Liz Harris). But if your children don't do this should you try to get them to? And how? By hopping yourself? By reading rabbit stories? By playing games in which Daddy is Big Rabbit? There aren't the answers yet, even though it feels hard to argue with Singer's view that playing with parents must be good.

Children do gain a great deal from playing with parents. And parents do too. I shall argue in Chapter 8 that adults need to play far more – not just with their children. But, first, I want to look at what happens when playing stops being free expression and becomes part of a cure for a child who is diagnosed sick.

7   Play therapy or the pathology of play?

At the start of 2005, the British police were appalled by 'happy slapping', a new trend in juvenile delinquency. Gangs would beat people up and film themselves doing so on the new mobile phone cameras. In one case a gang who raped a girl filmed it. Throughout this book I have suggested that play can be an on-edge phenomenon – and this contrasts with much orthodox theory. We have seen that play can help cognitive and social development. In this chapter we will examine play therapy – the disturbed child can be helped to deal with his or her conflicts by play, the autistic child can be helped by learning pretend play – but we will also examine how play can scare societies.

In 1991, I was making a film called *Acceptable Risks* which tried to assess how well allegations of child abuse were being investigated in the United Kingdom. Later that year, I made a film on children who sexually abuse other children. *The Last Taboo* also covered ways in which agencies use play and play therapy techniques. Then in 1999 I made a film, *What Children Remember*, based on the work of Stephen Ceci (1999) of Cornell University, who has done much work on children's memory – especially in the context of child abuse investigations. Ceci has collected some gripping video material of how police and social workers use play techniques in order to get children to remember as accurately as possible what happened to them.

Another important debate that involves play stems from research on autism which argues that autistic children are unable to engage in pretend play. This is a very significant finding (Baron-Cohen 1988; Frith 1989). The last section of this chapter deals with new and quite detailed work on how children with autism play. The whole subject has entered popular culture with the success of Mark Haddon's (2003) book *The Curious Incident of the Dog in the Night-Time*, which is a diary kept by an apparently autistic boy who tries to solve the murder of a neighbour's dog. It is a tour de force of getting inside the skin and skull of a child who is disabled.

What is interesting about both these topics is the underlying assumption that play is good. We have seen throughout this book that play can be edgy.

At what point does larking about start to seem threatening? The research for all three of my films covered the work of the police, social workers and various specialist charities. As far as this book is concerned, what is relevant is what various workers assumed they could learn either by observing or manipulating the play of vulnerable children.

For my 1991 films I observed the work of a specialist police unit, a young person's psychiatric clinic which dealt with young abusers, three social services departments, a special unit run by the probation service for dealing with young abusers, two specialist charity schemes and, in addition, I talked to thirty-six perpetrators and victims. Most agencies that investigate abuse use some form of play therapy techniques. I do not pretend I was doing anything other than in-depth journalistic research but this is an area where academic research tends to concentrate on surveying the extent of abuse and the background and personality of the victims and perpetrators (see reviews by National Children's Home 1991; Wyre 1991; Becker 1991). Ceci (2000) has written extensively on these issues. Pellegrini (1995) deals with the future of play theory and therapy. Despite the limits of journalistic research, my observations do reveal useful facts about the use of play and play therapy techniques in this highly contentious area.

I observed the work of a specialist squad in West Yorkshire which deals with child abuse. The policemen and women in charge of the squad were not trained play therapists but they had absorbed many related ideas. One room in their station looked like a playroom. It had toys, dolls and doll's houses. In fact, of course, it wasn't a real playroom. The objects children use in play were being used to help children to talk, to get beneath the surface. Some of the dolls were ordinary enough but many were anatomical dolls with genitalia ready to flop out. I observed a number of sessions where children were being questioned. The dolls were used in two ways. First, the officers and social workers used them to try to create a relaxed atmosphere. In theory, the relaxed child would be less intimidated and find it easier to speak. Second, the dolls were there to help the child describe in accurate detail the nature of any abuse. This is a favourite use of play therapy techniques and the workers I saw tended not to see the problems involved. Even if officers and social workers are enormously scrupulous and self-aware, there is a risk of suggestion. Ceci emphasises the need to use open questions. Many officers and social workers were not aware of such risks and were just eager to get the child to 'confess' abuse had been going on. I use the word 'confess' because some of the interviews were much like police interrogations of suspects I have also observed. Police and social workers want to protect children but that makes it all the more important for them to realise what play therapy techniques can and cannot achieve.

Some researchers who have studied abused children claim their play is distorted. Only in very extreme cases does the experience of abuse obliterate totally the child's ability to play. I think it useful here to dig a little into history. Since the early 1920s, psychoanalysts and psychologists who were sympathetic to analytic ideas saw that play – its pattern and its pathologies – might offer interesting clues to inner conflicts. Children might act out what they could not say either because they were afraid or because they lacked the emotional vocabulary. Play could voice the inarticulate.

Even though Freud wrote rather little about play – the index to the *Collected Works* (Freud 1967) shows only twelve short references – the psychoanalytic thinking has contributed a great deal to play work. Freud's longest observation on childhood play concerned a small boy who used to pull a long rope repeatedly and made a sound like 'O' which sounded joyful. Freud interpreted the game as a means of coping with fear of separation from the mother. Freud's (1905) book on jokes deals largely with adult jokes. So psychoanalysts became interested in childhood play despite a relative lack of attention from the Master. A number of distinguished analysts, notably Susan Isaacs, Melanie Klein, D.W. Winnicott and Erik Erikson, have written on aspects of play.

Interestingly, just as in the Piagetian tradition, there has been increasing specialisation. This is not surprising but it has meant that play has been seen increasingly as a means of healing, and less and less in the round. It was seen by Susan Isaacs, for example, in the round: in her *Social Relationships* (1933), she was keen to see play as a total expression of personality. Isaacs had a very ambivalent attitude to Piaget, who had published two books by then. On the one hand, she acknowledged the merit of his observation; on the other, she sniped that the cognitive behaviour of the child is 'after all very much like our own'. Do not exaggerate egocentricity! There is a great distance between Isaacs' practical observations and work such as Silverman's (1982). He starts by claiming he is about to reveal 'a symbol when it is in fresh, pristine state', then reports the case of Johnny, who was 9 years old and liked playing with the telephone. He liked speaking on it too. Was this practising his motor skills or pre-exercising the adult phone call? No, because Silverman argues the telephone was a genital symbol and a bisexual one at that. 'On a phallic Oedipal level, telephoning was well suited as a symbol for masturbation.' Does this explain why one so often gets wrong numbers?

There have been developments since the 1980s but Silverman's article illustrates the trend of much analytic thinking about play. Play is a form of masturbation. In her rounded view, Isaacs tended to emphasise the emotional problems that surfaced in play more than the cognitive ones but she did not isolate these two aspects of play. Since then, analytic writers have tended to separate them even though they make occasional references to cognition. Erik Erikson conceded that the play observed in play therapy had to be abnormal. In a famous passage in *Childhood and Society*, Erikson (1981) described Ben whirling his arms around and revving himself up into being a paddle steamer. That passage, Erikson revealed, came from Mark Twain's *Huckleberry Finn* and was a nice example of normal play. In therapy, Erikson conceded, the child enters a 'thoroughly difficult situation'. He does not feel sick yet he is treated as if something is wrong.

Play therapy involves very particular forms of play. It is not a good basis on which to build general theories of play or its development. Yet, the fact that they are observing abnormal play with a distant adult has not prevented many theorists from writing as if the play they witnessed in the consulting room was real play. In this chapter, I do not claim to offer a systematic history of play therapy or an assessment of its current situation, but I do want to suggest that the psychoanalytic tradition has failed to look at normal play in sufficient depth. Melanie Klein, notes Mitchell (1986), saw 'the play technique as the complete equivalent of free association'. Klein (1955) wrote, 'it was by approaching the play of a child in a way similar to Freud's interpretation of dreams that I could get access to the child's subconscious'. She describes how in 1923 she soon stopped seeing the child at home and using his toys. That was too problematic. Play therapy reveals more about therapy than about play. The rather interesting observations of Isaacs, Winnicott and Erikson have not led to an integrated account of play in the normal child. And, just like the experimentalists, analytic workers have preferred to see the children on their own terms in the clinic rather than at home. As a result, we know about the stages of 'emotional' play in abnormal children far more than we do about the normal child.

Susan Isaacs reported observations in her playschool in non-disturbed children. She focused very much on the way children used play to express their conflicts and fears but also kept an eye on what they learned through play. She acknowledged the influence of John Dewey, the American philosopher and educationalist who believed that children learned by doing. She claimed Piaget had actually uncovered fantasies using his 'clinical method', a point that seems very true. She also argued that some 'phenomena' or skills that Piaget attributed to the child maturing were more likely to be the result of direct learning from experience. Far more than later analysts, Isaacs tried to forge links between the work of Piaget and that of her own school. She tried redefining egocentricity in emotional terms. Where Piaget stressed that children could not play together because they could not really communicate, Isaacs suggested that, at times, their play was deformed. The egocentric young child was likely arbitrarily to 'fix another person's part in the play with minimum regard either to the other person's wishes or to external reality'. Such a child was also likely to claim leadership, refuse to take turns at good and bad parts and make egocentric threats, bribes and appeals to maintain his, or her, leadership. This was a prospectus for developing bridges between Piaget and Freud but no one wanted to be the bridge maker.

One little boy, Frank, was apt to be very demanding. On 30 January 1925, he made everyone go to sleep while he went to be Father Christmas; on 26 February 1925 he refused to pull older boys on a trolley when he had had his turn. Equally petulant was Priscilla, who on 5 February 1926 when Dan would not join in a family game because he preferred to read Eeyore books snarled 'All right, I shan't marry you!' In much of their play, Isaacs detected a need that children had to show themselves to be powerful. On 11 March 1926, when there was a hubbub, Isaacs told the children 'everyone seems to want everything'. At that, they laughed heartily and became more amicable about sharing toys. This is an interesting instance of young children being able to laugh at themselves, a point often missed in the burgeoning literature on the development of humour.

But, despite this focus on the emotional sides of play, Isaacs remained alert to its cognitive side. Sometimes, she conceded play was 'purely repetitive, without progression and without thought'. At other times, though, a fantasy could become intellectual for 'make believe may at any moment slip over into genuine inquiry'. For Isaacs play was 'a bridge', both in the child's emotional development and in his or her intellectual development. She was more interested in one side than the other but she made some effort to notice both. Hamilton (1982) returned to this enterprise of marrying Piaget and Freud, one which had been largely neglected over the years partly because both great men purported to find nothing of merit in the other's work. Certainly, Freud never seems to have mentioned Piaget. And Piaget noted that he had only once witnessed in a child any behaviour that could be called Freudian. Not surprisingly, Isaacs accepted the view common both to Piaget and to Freud that children grow out of playing. Adults have more serious tasks.

Isaacs never coined the term play therapy. As her work opened up many possibilities, this is perhaps not surprising. But the direction in which her work was taken by psychoanalysts emphasised the emotional, conflicted aspects of play rather than a holistic approach. By the early 1930s, as well as Isaacs's pioneering observations, Melanie Klein and Anna Freud developed rather different approaches. Anna Freud was trying to extend the ordinary techniques of psychoanalysis to work with children. Play was a useful tool to that end. Initially, it was believed that you could compare the free play of the child with the free association of the adult client. Later, as we shall see, Freud came to doubt this view.

Melanie Klein began working in Hungary and moved to London in 1926: she is credited perhaps generously as being the founder of play therapy. Klein argued that the baby, even at 3 weeks, begins to distinguish emotionally good objects from bad objects. Play could be used from virtually the first weeks of birth as a means of understanding the child's traumas and, perhaps, resolving them. Klein argued that very young children could not be expected to be fluent verbally but they did play. Where the adult in analysis had his verbal communications interpreted, the child could have his, or her, play interpreted. The way the child played could be used the way the adult talked. Interestingly, Klein kept control of the toys that children could use just as developmentalists like Belsky and Most take their hampers of toys along into people's homes. Klein equipped a playroom in Hampstead with small, simple non-mechanical toys. There were men, women, children, animals, cars, trains, aeroplanes, small houses, as well as material to cut out and paint with. Klein argued that such equipment would give the child the chance to enact lots of games playing mother, father and others. The toys would stand for important people in the child's life. As Piaget observed, the doll would feel all the repercussions of the child's daily life. But as Winnicott sniped, Klein was not interested in play itself but in using play to get at the child's complexes and, perhaps, heal them. Tellingly, Mitchell (1986) calls these neutral toys the child's 'own set', but the experts provided them.

A recognised classic in this tradition was *Understanding Children's Play* by Hartley, Frank and Goldenson. Written in 1952, it was able to offer particular play remedies for particular ills. The book opened with a trumpet blast to liberation: 'We must learn to free the child, while he is still a child, from his conflicts, his terrors, his rages.' The authors observed 180 children in playschools and concluded that play was a form of compensation and that some forms of it, such as dramatic play, could be 'a good reducer of tensions in the group'. Dramatic play, Hartley et al. (1952) claimed, encouraged changes in attitude and allowed the child to experiment with possible solutions to his, or her, problems. They give the example of Donnie, who was aged 4. He did not have a father and his mother had a lodger. Teachers described Donnie as quiet and scared. His mother said he was stubborn, allergic, unclean and that he might suffer from 'a possible nudge towards femininity' since he used a bobby pin to pin his hair back. Donnie learned, through play, to be less timid and more manly.

Another boy, Perry, was not sufficiently assertive. Hartley et al. (1952) trace four episodes in which he learns, through play, to assert himself. In episode one, Perry suggests 'let's play house' to two little girls. Having had the idea for the game, Perry 'sits on the ladder and watches', only contributing that Jane is 'the mamma pussy cat'. In episode two, Perry is putting dolls to bed with the girls and then 'begins to occupy himself with trucks and trains, a more characteristically masculine interest'. But then Perry picks up some wooden blocks and uses them to build a house, returning to this less masculine play. Two months later, the authors approve, Perry has undergone 'a dramatic change' and 'the role he takes is a more aggressive one and he is beginning to express in fantasy some of the impulses which must have preoccupied him earlier when he seemed timid and inhibited'. In a game based on *Bambi*, Perry takes the initiative and follows through telling the girls to call him Flower, sitting down so that he and Bambi can hide in the snow and, finally, hopping into a hole. The authors make something of the fact that Perry is still timid enough that he needs to hide in the hole. In the fourth episode, Perry is play-ing with boys, not girls, and at airplanes. He has a mock aerial battle and, then, after he has fixed something on to his plane, he declares: 'A crash at the airport happened. Three million dead.' Perry then invites the girls to admire his plane which is a hospital plane which has helped rescue people. 'He seems well on his way to achieving the masculine role,' Hartley et al. (1952) note, with pleasure.

As well as providing such case histories, Hartley et al. (1952) indicate what specific methods of play can bring to the child. Sections are headed 'The Benefits of Water Play' and 'What Clay Can do for the Child'. What is telling is that these materials which would, to a non-analyst, seem to be ideal for developing practical skills become tools just for emotional exploration. Mucking about with water gives children a sense of mastery over their urine and an outlet for aggression. The child who 'gets stuck in water play and uses it repetitively' is reckoned to need 'special help' (Hartley et al. 1952: 116). Clay offers an outlet for aggressive impulses so the authors urge that teachers should 'regard the clay period not just as busywork or an activity to keep the child from getting into mischief but as a legitimate channel for exploration, expression and self-assertion' (p. 217). Painting offers release from anxiety while finger-painting 'has been found effective for both children and adults in overcoming certain inhibitions, in evoking a free flow of fantasy life among disturbed people and in exploring such aspects of personality as expansiveness and sensitivity to sensory impressions' (p. 219).

Despite their infectious enthusiasm for all kinds of play, Hartley and his co-authors leave a depressing impression. Play cannot really exist in its own right. It is there to be used to guide the child out of his or her traumas. The authors do not seem to have asked in any systematic way whether the improvements they noted in the playschool were mirrored in the home. Where Isaacs (1933) had been interested in seeing play in the round, Hartley et al. (1952) saw it very much as a therapeutic tool.

In a series of discussions towards the end of her life, Anna Freud seemed very sensitive to these risks. *The Technique of Child Psychoanalysis* (Sandler et al. 1983) was based on discussions she had with Joseph Sandler, Hansi Kennedy and Rober L. Tyson. In classical child analysis, play was a tool. It was an 'in-between stage falling between enacting without control and putting into words as a precondition for controlling thoughts' (p. 121). The analyst could use what the child brought in play as a bridge to verbalising problems.

Anna Freud warned against too much faith being placed either in toys or in play, especially as the kinds of toys available might well influence the kind of play that emerged. It seems worth reproducing in full the text which indicates the way she developed this train of thought because she was, after all, in an excellent position to judge how child psychoanalysis had developed:

ANNA FREUD: The emphasis on toys neglects one very important consideration. Child analysts all know that certain toys serve the production of fantasy better than others. But this ignores the division between those children who are able to produce their material displaced onto toys and those children who are not and who can use only their actual circumstances – either their own body or their analyst's body or real things – to act out their hidden impulses. Analysts know that it can be a progressive move if the child dismembers a doll instead of being aggressive towards the analyst. Providing sand and water, however, is also often a seduction to regression, and there is usually enough repression to be dealt with anyway. Historically in child analysis the initial idea was to choose toys for the child to make a so-called little world, in which almost everything in the real world was present in miniature form. No variation was allowed in the toys that were chosen and with which the child began treatment. These toys were part of the treatment setting, and they could be used by the child to express his fantasies. Quite apart from their use in this way, toys are used in quite different ways. They may express ideas of value, feelings of exclusiveness, or rivalry with others. They may, for instance, serve as missiles. The role of the toy as an instrument for analysis is greatly overrated. Whatever is provided is really only an adjunct to the treatment situation, and what is really important is what the patient and analyst say and how they relate to each other, what the child reveals, and so on. There is a point regarding play as an analytic tool which has always led to confusion. It concerns the difference between learning about the child by observing his behavior and then translating that behavior into its unconscious roots, and gathering analytic material which is produced relatively easily because it is disguised in free associations, in dreams, in fantasy, and in fantasy play. This difference has to be kept in mind with respect to play. Although it is perfectly true that one learns much by playing chess or by watching other activities, these cannot be equated with free association. I can also learn a great deal by watching a child at mealtimes or when he is undergoing a psychological test. The analyst as behaviorist can use pieces of behavior to extract unconscious meaning from them, for example to infer how the child deals with anxiety or with frustration. But this is quite different from free association or from the expression of a fantasy which results from an upsurge from the depths of the mind toward the surface because different conditions facilitate the emergence of the unconscious material.

(Sandler 1983: 125)

Freud accepted that psychoanalysis was not especially interested in the study of play except in so far as this shed light on the child's traumas.

Psychoanalytic child therapy turned into a form of investigation. By 1981, Anna Freud was worried about this development. Others had worried about some aspects of such directive psychoanalysis long before. In 1940, the American psychotherapist Carl Rogers introduced client-centred therapy. Instead of sitting supine and powerless on the couch, the client now faced the therapist. The client also determined far more of the agenda of the session. Rogers believed you should give every client warm regard, showing that you cared about them. Virginia Axline applied these basic principles to child therapy and wrote both a textbook of *Play Therapy* and *Dibs: In Search of Self*, a moving account of how an almost autistic, rigid, frightened child was cured through play. *Dibs: In Search of Self* is a wonderful document but the way Axline used play with her young client was far from simply letting him play. (As it happens Rogers spent ten years working with children in Rochester but he was sceptical about play therapy as I have argued: Cohen 1997.)

At the start of the book, Axline meets Dibs, who is 5 years old. His nursery school is very worried about him because he refuses to join in many activities and often spends hours underneath the table. If the children try to get him to join in games, he often hisses at them. Sometimes, he attacks them. If the teachers try to get him to co-operate, he screams and sometimes bites. Some of the teachers believe Dibs is mentally retarded. Axline spent one session in his school observing him. He insisted on staying under a table and wouldn't participate in the activities. Yet when Axline describes what followed, Dibs behaved remarkably:

> Dibs stood by the door. I went over and asked him if he would come down the hall to the little playroom with me for a while. I held out my hand to him. He hesitated for a moment, then took my hand without a word and walked to the playroom with me.
> (Axline 1971: 21)

Axline took him there and noticed: 'He was tense. But, surprisingly enough, willing to go' (p. 21).

In that first session, Axline saw him name a number of objects he held. She had already begun to suspect that he was not mentally retarded at all. Dibs named dolls, trucks, cows and other toys competently but monosyllabically until he sat down on the floor facing the doll's house. Axline refused to prod him because all too often adults had taken the lead in developing the relationship with him as with other children. After a while, Dibs clasped his hands tightly against his chest and repeated:

> 'No lock doors. No lock doors. No lock doors.' His voice took on a note of desperate urgency. 'Dibs no like locked door,' he said. There was a sob in his voice.
> I said to him, 'You don't like doors to be locked.'
> Dibs seemed to crumple. His voice became a husky whisper. 'Dibs no like closed doors. No like closed and locked doors. Dibs no like walls around him.'
> (Axline 1971: 23–4)

'Obviously, he had had some unhappy experiences with closed and locked doors,' Axline said in a masterpiece of the deadpan. This outburst was the initial key to her work with Dibs. He had somehow trusted her and the situation enough to allow his feelings to burst out. Axline was always careful not to create pressure for her child clients. They knew they had an hour to spend with her. 'There was no urgency to get anything done. To play or not to play. To talk, or to be silent. In here, it would make no difference' (p. 22).

In the subsequent sessions, Axline kept to this very relaxed programme. Dibs was allowed to flood the playroom, to suck on a bottle and, at times, he showed a precocious interest in the way Axline was making notes about his behaviour. Once, he told her to put down that 'Dibs came. He found the sand interesting today. Dibs played with the house and the fighting men for the last time' (p. 57).

The atmosphere certainly allowed Dibs to express himself with growing confidence. After some months, he arrived at 'the magic room where I do whatever it is I have to do' with clear plans (p. 132). He first picked up the mother and father dolls from the house and put them down again. Then, sighing deeply, he looked out of the window and admired the fact that there were so many kinds of people. He added philosophically, with no toy to hand:

> 'Sometimes I am afraid of people.'
> 'Sometimes, you are afraid of people?' I said, hoping he would be encouraged to go on.
> 'But sometimes I'm not afraid of people,' he added. 'I'm not afraid of you.'
> 'You don't feel afraid when you're with me?' I commented.
> 'No,' he said. He sighed. 'I'm not afraid now when I'm with you.'
> (Axline 1971: 132)

Axline relates how Dibs then went over to the sandbox and threatened that someone might get buried there. Then, he picked up some crayons.

> 'I am a boy,' he said slowly, 'I have a father, a mother, a sister. But I do have a grandmother and she loves me. Grandmother has always loved me. But not Papa. Papa has not always loved me.'

> (Axline 1971: 133)

Axline managed to get Dibs to pursue talking about this painful subject though he scurried away at times into intellectual defences by discussing what he could see under his microscope. But, then, he returned to the main theme and told a story about a father telling off a child. He held the father doll while he told it but, at the climax, the bad father ended up setting fire to the house with the smoke from his pipe. The emotional power of the tale is striking and Dibs felt tearful. None of this is play as we normally understand it. Sensitively Axline created an atmosphere in which the child was able to take the initiative. Play was part of it and play sometimes helped focus what needed to be discussed. But play was just part of the process and, at times, not such a large part.

Axline did offer in *Dibs: In Search of Self* a detailed case history and, very successfully, showed how her treatment did not just affect Dibs emotionally but also intellectually. It is worth noting, however, that much of the play therapy was taken up with getting Dibs to talk about his problems and discussing his feelings. Axline even suggested solutions forcefully such as when she urged that Dibs might try to understand what his father was feeling, too. I am not in any way trying to belittle Axline's achievement but one must not be seduced by the label play therapy. Much of her methods consisted of getting the child to talk by allowing him to play. Play was less of an analytic tool than a simple way of relaxing him and building up trust. And no play explains that odd, magical start when Dibs just went with her trustingly, a lovely quirk Axline doesn't seem to reflect on enough.

Two other psychoanalysts have attempted a slightly more integrated approach to play. These are D.W. Winnicott and Erik Erikson. I have already reported some of Winnicott's ideas in Chapter 6. Both Winnicott and Erikson, though they owed much to Virginia Axline, saw that it was wrong to focus on abnormal play even though, as clinicians, most of the evidence they gathered was from children who came to them for treatment.

Winnicott summed up his ideas in a short essay 'Why Children Play' (1949) and in *Playing and Reality* (1971). He started by attacking the crude notion that children play just for fun. 'Most people would say that children play because they like doing so and this is undeniable.' But it is also superficial. Children also played to work off hostility and aggression. Aggressive play allows the child to express such troubling feelings 'in a known environment, without the return of hate and violence from the environment to the child'. The child by expressing aggression in play rather than in rage made a 'social contribution'. Adults should not ignore it. Winnicott also believed that anxiety was a major factor in child's play and attacked the psychoanalytic belief that play was a form of masturbation.

Winnicott was keenly aware of the problems of erecting a theory of play on the basis of abnormal children seen in treatment. In *Playing and Reality*, he noted that in so far as Melanie Klein was concerned with play at all, she 'was concerned almost entirely with the use of play' while he went on to quibble that psychoanalysts have 'been too busy using play content to look at the playing child'. Winnicott applied two of his theoretical concepts to play – that of 'transitional object' and that of a 'potential space' between the mother and baby. Transitional objects are basically fetish objects used by babies. Piaget's J seemed to have one in her blanket; the cartoon character Peanuts has his blanket, too. These objects, with which the child does many things, are at the root of all normal play. Through them, the baby evolves shared play, first, with parents, then with peers. Second, Winnicott postulated a potential space between mother and baby. He defined this space through negatives. It was neither inner space like the baby's body. Nor was it external reality.

The potential space required the mother of mother-figure to be 'in a "to and fro" between that which the baby has a capacity to find and (alternatively) being herself waiting to be found' (p. 55). This would give the child a sense not just of confidence but of 'magical control'. 'Confidence in the mother makes an intermediate playground here where the idea of magic originates since the baby does to some extent experience omnipotence.' In this potential space, created by the mother's ability to give the baby confidence, 'the child gathers objects of phenomena from external reality and uses these in the service of some sample derived from inner or personal reality'. Winnicott argued that, without hallucinating, the child 'puts out a sample of dream potential'. The potential space also allowed the child to experience 'the precariousness of interplay of personal psychic reality and the experience' and if he had an effective mother, to experience a reliable relationship. Winnicott argued, against most psychoanalysts, that playing is essentially satisfying even though it involves much anxiety. Experiencing the anxiety was part of the learning process. Winnicott wrote:

> Whereas it is easy to see that children play for pleasure, it is much more difficult for people to see that children play to master anxiety or to master ideas and impulses that lead to anxiety if they are not in control.
>
> (Winnicott 1964: 144)

Play touches deep material even though Winnicott insisted 'play is health'.

Though Winnicott always stressed that playing is crucial to the normal development of normal children, the illustrations in his writings tended to be of abnormal children like Edmund who stammered and gave up talking because the stammer frightened him and Diana whose mother came seeking help because her brother was mentally defective and had a heart deformity. Winnicott performed a useful service in harping on the normality of play, in likening psychoanalysis to a kind of play and in advising that: 'Grown ups can contribute here by recognising the big place it has, and by teaching traditional games, yet without cramping or corrupting the child's own inventiveness.' Potential space, Winnicott's key idea, is an apt metaphor for some of the interplay between mothers and babies. It reinforces the idea that playing starts at home, certainly. Winnicott also outlined the obvious fact that there must be links between childhood play and adult creativity though, like all other writers, he failed to be very specific about how these might operate.

Compared to the psychoanalytic tradition which used play as a diagnostic tool and which claimed that play was a phase, the child had to work through to become a qualified adult, Winnicott's ideas are enlightened. They were, indeed, greeted as such. But his theory of play is, at best, a number of useful insights into some aspects of play grouped round the driving theme of potential space. Winnicott hinted that one ought to be able to integrate research on child play and research on adult play but he provided little direct evidence of that. And in a memoir of doing adult therapy with Winnicott, Little (1985) suggests that that experience was serious, gruelling and, though rewarding, nothing like play even though Winnicott suggested one should view analysis as 'a highly specialised form of playing in the service of communication with oneself and others' (p. 48).

The other psychoanalyst who has done much to promote the idea of playing is Erik Erikson, who claimed long ago that we pass through a series of developmental stages in which a person's basic orientation to the world is formed. He developed his ideas on play in *Play and Development* (1972), *Toys and Reasons* (1977) and *Childhood and Society* (1981). Erikson took a fairly conservative view for an analyst of play in childhood. He spent a long time developing his ideas of how boys and girls used building blocks differently. Boys tended to make thrusting phallic structures while girls tended to make inclusive womb-like ones. In *Play and Development*, Erikson reported a series of studies in which children were invited out of their play-schools to use a set of toys for about 20 minutes. A black boy built an elaborate edifice and put a black human doll at the top. He was, it turned out, worried because he felt he was stupid and could not hold his own intellectually in class though he was good at physical sports. Like classic analysts, Erikson believed that this showed the child's 'capacity to project a relevant personal theme on the microcosm of play'.

Where Erikson differed from writers like Klein and Freud was that he did not see play as a phase that children worked their way out of. He believed that encouraging children to play helped them to integrate social and emotional capacities. It also helped to bolster their creativity: when he was 3, Einstein could not speak but 'preferred communing with building blocks and jigsaw pieces'. While Erikson believed in the value of adult play, he drew attention to the fact that, when children play, there are limits. If necessary, adults set limits to stop a play fight turning into a real fight. But the limits of adult play were much more problematic.

Erikson wrote *Play and Development* in 1972 when he was influenced by the students' protests of the 1960s. He drew attention both to sexual play and to political play. Rather than choose a movement like the Campaign for Nuclear Disarmament, Erikson chose the slightly sinister Black Panthers as an example of youth at play. Society allowed teenagers to try out various roles. Teenage romance was a prelude to real marriage. If you made a mistake in your partner, it did not matter. But in the 1960s, youthful play came to border on the dangerous, a sign of collapse in values. Erikson noted that the Panthers devised new sets of roles for themselves, new insignia and, in fact, a new sense of identity. Erikson suggested that 'youth and revolution both play with that theatre of action where personal conversion and radical rejuvenation confirm each other'. Sometimes, history proves them right; but sometimes the play gets out of hand.

Erikson concluded his essay by accepting that there are problems adults face when they try to be helpful.

> Must he do something in which he feels he were again playing as if he were a playing child, or a youth in a game? Must he step outside of his most serious and fateful concerns? Or must he transcend his everyday condition and be 'beside himself' in fantasy, ecstasy or 'togetherness'.
>
> (Erikson 1972)

Erikson could only advise that the adult must 'remain playful in the centre of his concerns and concerned with opportunities to renew the leeway and scope of his and his fellow man's activities'. But the way you played as an adult had to reflect the stages you had gone through.

Both Winnicott and Erikson transcended the failure of most psychoanalysts to see the importance of ordinary play. They did more than use play to reveal personality conflicts or to attempt to heal them. They saw that play was linked to creativity and 'the search for self'. This marked a major step forward for, as I have tried to argue in this chapter, psychoanalysts used play much as empirical psychologists did as a means of measuring children's faults and progress rather than observing and treasuring it. Winnicott and Erikson tried to go beyond this but though they usefully showed the importance of early play in the home, many of their ideas remained a little vague.

Neither of these eminent therapists foresaw that in the mid to late 1980s, play therapy techniques would become crucial in social work. Physical abuse of children became acknowledged in the late 1960s and 1970s. In Britain, the crucial tragedy was the death of 7-year-old Maria Colwell in 1973. Two eminent directors of social work who sat on inquiries into physical abuse in the 1970s both told me they now realised they had been presented with evidence of sexual abuse but did not recognise it for what it was. They were ignorant and, perhaps, they confessed, did not want to see. That all changed. In the 1980s, child sexual abuse became an important issue. Estimates of the number of victims range from one in one hundred to one in ten.

After the discrediting of the medical evidence in the Cleveland Inquiry, it is now agreed that sexual abuse usually leaves no physical traces. The best evidence is what a child says or how a child behaves and, especially, how she or he plays.

Can play therapy really help in identifying and coping with child abuse?

So far, there has been little systematic study of what play therapy techniques can really offer either as a tool to help children speak or as a healing device. Many social workers and therapists have faith in such techniques without proper scientific evidence to support them. Getting reliable evidence of abuse from young children is hard. It has been claimed good evidence for abuse is either

- if a child shows far too many sexual signs of play. Where would the knowledge come from if adults had not taught them?
- or if a child betrays too great signs of fear and embarrassment and, therefore, represses sexuality in their play.

The problem with the two criteria is that they would appear to be contradictory. Moreover, there is evidence that doctors, police and social workers are often all too eager to find evidence. The following is a transcript of a conversation in a playroom which shows how play therapy techniques can be misapplied:

> A kind and caring policewoman took a 3-year-old girl into the playroom. The child went into a corner. The WPC picked her up and brought her into the middle and sat her on her knee.

WPC: My, you're a big lump for 3. (*Pause.*)

WPC: Can you not tell us what this little white secret is with Uncle Sam?
I'm sure you can tell and we'll see what a big girl you really are and
I bet nothing will happen.

The little girl gets off the policewoman's knee and buries herself in her
mother's skirt. The child can't really play in this play setting. Two
minutes later, the WPC is also crawling on the floor offering toys, and
yet also putting intense questions about the secret – a secret she is sure
is sexual.

WPC: Why did Uncle Sam tell you it was a secret? (*Again the child shies
away.*)

WPC: You're getting tired. If you're tired and want to go home, home to
Grandma, can you not tell me the secret?

GIRL: It's mine.

The play setting was quite at odds with what was going on. Another policewoman demonstrated all the sexual parts of the dolls to the child and asked
what she called various parts.

The Orkney Inquiry was also critical about the use of play therapy
techniques in the questioning of young children who were removed from
their homes.

By far the most convincing example I found of play therapy techniques was
in the context of a playschool in Greenwich run by the charity, Dr Barnardo's.
The playschool knew, given its deprived local clientele, that abuse was a
risk. The following manifestations by a child would make them particularly
suspicious. Too much sexual language, a great readiness to throw off clothes,
aggressive play which involved a sexual element and, paradoxically, with-
drawal. The playschool stressed the need to consider the child's behaviour
in context and, of course, they had the chance to observe children day in, day
out. They tended to call in social services and the police when they had
reasonable grounds for suspicion. One remark would probably not be enough
to trigger anything other than a chat with a parent. This playschool's attitude
seemed very sensible especially given how hard it is for play therapy
techniques to give unambiguous information. Police and social workers are
under great pressure in child abuse cases but it is now clear that the process
of investigating allegations itself often damages the child. This should not
be embarked upon lightly.

A much more rigorous examination of play in distressed children is to be
found in the work of Leslie (1987), Frith (1989), Van Fleet (2001) and Baron-
Cohen et al. (1985) on autism.

Many of the pioneers of play therapy like Anna Freud and Virginia Axline are figures of historical importance, charismatic healers one might suggest. As play therapy has become part of the psychology-psychiatry industry, many therapists have been rather more ordinary personalities. And while some authors like Van Fleet (2001) claim play therapy has proved itself, there are contrary opinions such as Campbell's (1992). Campbell is especially angry that the American Psychological Association produced a First Book for children on play therapy, a publication that gives the impression play therapy is a valid and validated technique. Campbell writes:

> First Book promotes play therapy so convincingly that it qualifies as a marketing dream. It indicates that the difficult problems which burden children often leave them severely distressed (thus arousing a sense of need for a particular service). First Book then informs its audience about the expertise of play therapists who assist youngsters to overcome their difficulties (thus promoting a service that supposedly aids the previously cited need).
>
> First Book evokes images of increasingly secure children triumphing over troublesome feelings, and then sharing a final hug with their therapist who will not forget them. In turn, one can readily imagine parents smiling gratefully out of appreciation for the good works of perceptive therapists who relate to their children with such warmth and understanding. If produced as a TV-commercial with appropriately scored background music, these scenes could provoke misty-eyed smiles from millions of deeply-touched viewers.
>
> Despite its shortcomings, APA seems sufficiently pleased with First Book to vigorously publicize it. Advertisements touting it as an 'invaluable resource' have appeared in the *American Psychologist, APA Monitor, Clinical Psychology Review, Journal of Consulting and Clinical Psychology, Professional Psychology,* and *Psychotherapy.* One can only assume that APA's publication office sees considerable sales potential in First Book. Perhaps its sentimental impact will prompt sequels titled Second Book, Third Book, etc. that are as inspirationally moving as their predecessor.
>
> (Campbell 1992)

Outcome research in play therapy

Campbell backs up his attack on a number of empirical fronts. He shows that two reviews of the effectiveness of psychotherapy for children rather ignore play therapy. Kazdin (1991) suggested that outcome research must identify: 'What treatment, by whom, is most effective for this individual with that specific problem under which set of circumstances?' (p. 111). Interventions such as problem-solving skills training, parent management training, and functional family therapy did help but Kazdin made no reference to play therapy. Kendall and Morris (1991) also seemed less than impressed with play therapy techniques. They quoted Davids' (1975) observation that the era of blind faith in the activities of play therapy rooms has ended.

Campbell also looked at detailed reviews. He claims that play therapy does not appear to increase academic and intellectual achievement (Clement and Milne 1967; Clement et al. 1970; Elliot and Pumphrey 1972). Play also does little to improve the communicative and social behaviours of schizophrenic children (Ney et al. 1971). Worse, play therapy does not improve the interpersonal adjustment of children who participate in it (McBrien and Nelson 1972).

But for those who believe in play therapy, these negative results don't seem to matter. In his summary of research that often reported non-significant outcomes and some equivocal results, Phillips (1985) lamented:

> This is a disheartening state of affairs for those who feel strongly about play therapy. The data lead to a puzzling paradox — Why is it that clinical wisdom regarding the value of play therapy is unsubstantiated by the empirical results? Is a clinical activity being utilized whose value is at least suspect?
>
> (Phillips 1985: 757)

But Phillips is a believer and suggested more sophisticated methodologies would prove the value of play therapy. 'If the facts do not agree with the theory, so much the worse for the facts,' the great philosopher Hegel sniped and Campbell uses the sentence to damn the arrogance of play therapists.

Campbell (1992) argued this arrogance led to three errors.

> (1) Play therapists appoint themselves to positions of undeserved importance in their clients' lives. (2) Play therapy indulges in irrelevant procedures that disregard the clients' needs. (3) Play therapy neglects its clients' relationships with other people in their lives who are important to them.
>
> (Campbell 1992)

Play therapists act as if only their skills can help children. Parents cannot get too involved. The key relationship is between the child and the play therapist – a relationship that has to stay confidential just as in adult therapy (Nemiroff and Annunziata 1990). So the true to his or her plasticine play therapist explains to parents:

What a child actually does in his therapy must be between him and me. Only then will he feel free to bring to me those things that he has secreted in little grubby hideaway holes in his mind or that he has interred for fear that they will frighten or destroy.

(Baruch 1952: 15)

Any such therapist is likely to distance parents from their children, Campbell claims, and disempowering the parents oils the therapist's own ego. The therapist tells himself that he is better with – and better for – the child than the pesky parents.

Yet research clearly shows children get greater benefit from treatment when both of their parents actively participate in it (Gurman and Kniskern 1981; Wolman and Stricker 1994). Sexually abused children recover better from their trauma when parents are involved (Myers et al. 1989). For children of divorce, any therapy that shuts out one of their parents often creates more problems than it solves (Campbell 1992).

Campbell's point is obvious. However good it is for children to enjoy a sense of security with a therapist, it is surely better for them to enjoy that sense of security with their parents. Too many play therapists seek to make the child feel safest with them. Campbell (1992) describes how play therapists often hug and hold children to cement this 'love'. One play therapist described how she physically held a 7-year-old boy:

He came to the playroom each time and climbed straight into my lap. No dubiousness. No hesitance. This was what he wanted. Contact with me *as though I were his mother*. To be held by me quite simply.

(Baruch 1952: 14, italics added)

But the therapist was not his mother, as she did recognise, yet she did nothing to promote a more affectionate relationship between mother and child. While hugging and holding this boy, the therapist tried to give him the warmth and affection that his parents allegedly could not.

When play therapists act as if they are better at meeting the needs of children than are their parents, they undermine their clients' psychological welfare. Play therapy can lead its practitioners into competing with a child's parents (Coppolillo 1987). Campbell even suggests that play therapists who hug children should be regarded as abusive. They are abusing the normal bonds of affection between parent and child.

Campbell's attack reminds one that in therapy much depends on the personality of the therapist.

I want now to deal with the increasingly important subject of autism. Some research suggests that we have underestimated the number of autistic children in the population.

Autism and play

Baron-Cohen et al. (1985) argued autistic children hardly ever engage in pretend play, a finding that has proved robust. Not pretending could be due to a lack of intelligence, to a general fear of getting involved with other children and/or adults or to a general avoidance of play. Autistic children, however, do play by themselves and with objects. Many are not passive. Frith (1989) suggests it is a myth that autistic children do not like getting physically close to other people. Baron-Cohen found that Down syndrome children, whose IQ is generally lower than that of autistic children, pretend perfectly well. The reasons why autistic children don't pretend are more subtle.

Baron-Cohen's later work argues that the failure of autistic children to pretend is associated with their failure to develop a theory of other minds. They cannot perceive what another person might think. In one experiment Baron-Cohen, Leslie and Frith (1985) used dolls called Sally and Anne. Sally hides a marble in a basket and then leaves. Anne finds the marble and puts it in a nearby box. Sally then returns. When normal children aged 4 and older are asked where Sally would look for her marble, they say she would look in the basket. That's where she left it: it's where she has every reason to believe it would still be. Autistic children do not do that: they say Sally would look where Anne had left it. Baron-Cohen and his colleagues theorise that autistic children just cannot get into someone else's mind. Is this failure a result of not pretending or the cause of it? Teasing out whether this is cause or effect is hard.

Leslie (1987) has suggested that pretend play requires the ability to 'decouple' primary representations – i.e. what we perceive – and meta-representations. He has put forward an information-processing model (see Figure 7.1) which envisages some sort of decoupling device which 'grows' (there is really no other word for it) as the child engages in pretend play and gets used to manipulating real and unreal symbols.

Research in this area has developed and one criterion for autism now, according to the DSM-IV (American Psychiatric Association 1994), is a lack of spontaneous make-believe play. Baron-Cohen (2003) has developed the Checklist for Autism in Toddlers (CHAT). The authors of CHAT assume that children who do not show signs of starting to pretend play by the age of 18 months could end up diagnosed as autistic. The current literature contains all too many examples of children with autism not playing or not playing properly. Most research has concentrated on pretence, especially symbolic play.

It seems that even when young children with autism do play, they tend towards more sensori-motor play than is appropriate for their mental age. And even then they are likely to use toys and objects in an inflexible way. For

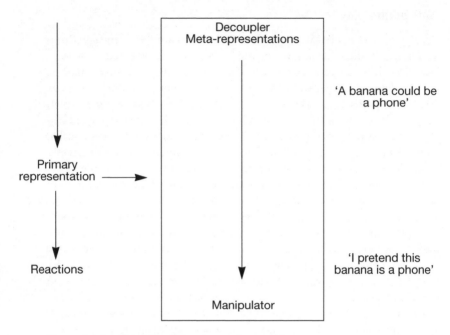

Figure 7.1 Leslie's information-processing model

example, a child with autism may focus on spinning the wheels on a toy car, rather than playing a racing or driving game. Roeyers and van Berckelaer-Onnes (1994) suggest that children with autism often are not as curious as other children and tend not to use play to explore. There are interesting parallels here with Berlyne's work on young rats who are too timid to explore (Berlyne 1960).

For children with autism, there is also the issue of isolation. Some children with autism do not give the impression that they want to play with other children, and if they do play, they prefer to play by themselves. This however is not always the case but one well-established problem children with autism have is that, if they do want to play with other children, they find it hard to communicate this wish.

The area is controversial, however, and it is only since the 1990s there have been serious studies of play and autism though the Nobel prize winner Niko Tinbergen told me in an interview back in the 1970s that he saw interesting parallels between animal behaviour and autism. He said to me

we found we could 'cash in' on our lifelong studies of social behaviour in animals and by careful study of the situations in which children showed, let us say, 'autisoid' behaviour, we arrived at . . . a dual hypothesis really: we concluded that many autists suffer from a severe emotional conflict in which fear blocked affiliation and socialisation and also exploratory learning.

(Cohen 1977: 328)

In these controversies, some researchers claim that children with autism may not be totally unable to engage in pretend play but if they are to do so the play has either to be very structured or to involve prompts which stimulate pretence (e.g. Jarrold et al. 1996). Jarrold et al. (1996) suggest that children with autism have problems in starting pretend play, rather than with the actual business of pretence itself. (Studies of how children with autism deal with peekaboo might be interesting in this context but I cannot find any because few 9 months old get a diagnosis of autism which is, I suspect, a good thing.)

Given the bad press television for children usually gets, it is interesting that television can help – to some extent, at least. Often, when symbolic play does appear to occur in the child with autism, it is copied from the television or something similar. For example, children act out time and again a clip from *Toy Story* (1995). That reveals how repetitive the play in children with autism can be. Wolfberg (1999) gives the case history of Freddy, who played the same chasing game everyday. At first, he would play the game only with his classmate Jared, but eventually Freddy mustered the confidence to initiate chasing games with other children. But Freddy could usually only do this with an adult there to prompt and guide.

Jarrold et al. (1996) also found that children with autism spend significantly less of their time compared with controls in functional play (like making a doll walk). Such play does not involve understanding how things look from the other's perspective or meta-representational analysis. So Jarrold et al. (1996) claim that if children with autism also play such 'games' less that is a problem for Leslie's meta-representational account (Leslie 1987) because functional play does not require meta-representational abilities.

The reason for all these difficulties may be that children with autism have a more rigid organisation of thought processes than normal as well as problems in communicating these thoughts to others. Sherratt and Peter (2002) suggest that teaching children with autism to play may make their mental processes more fluid and could help them reduce repetitive and rigid behavioural patterns.

But this is not the only theory of why children with autism do not play or play much less. Roeyers and van Berckelaer-Onnes (1994) offer three explanations. First, children with autism explore less and appear less curious, and so they have much less experience of simple but basic play such as stacking one object on top of another or even just waving. Instead they often engage in stereotyped, persistent behaviour and self-stimulation such as sucking and licking themselves. This fits Tinbergen's ideas rather well. Roeyers and van Berckelaer-Onnes (1994) also put forward Leslie's theory which, as we have seen, is not without problems in the light of the latest research.

The final suggestion is motivational. Children with autism can pretend play, but do not do so spontaneously, perhaps because they have often failed to get other children to play with them (Stahmer 1999).

Therapy has not helped much yet. Wolfberg (1999) reviewed the literature and found that there was little emphasis on play (particularly with peers) in the education and treatment of children with autism. Sherratt (2001) agreed. Both found that where there were interventions they were not comprehensive and often did not take account of how 'normal' children play naturally. So children with autism do not get the best help. A great pity, according to Sherratt, because helping/teaching children with autism to play can be useful therapy. Symbolic pretend play requires the manipulation of symbolic representations, which is something children with autism find particularly difficult. If one can manage to teach children with autism to play, Sherratt and Peter (2002) suggest, this may lead to learning and, even, to changes to the brain. The children's thinking may become more flexible. Learning to play with others also draws children into a social world – and fun, something such children often do not get much of.

Sherratt (2001) stresses the importance of the following three conditions for anyone who wants to teach children with autism how to play:

- *Structure*: this helps the child to understand the sequence of skills, activities or ideas that will help reach an agreed goal. The tale of Red Riding Hood, for example, has a clear structure with stereotyped characters, repetitive phrasing and an effective hook line – when we find out that Grandma is in fact a wolf.
- *Effect*: there needs to be an inherent pleasure in play or it ceases to be play. Children with autism may enjoy slapstick or programmes like Mr Bean.
- *Interests*: the child must have an interest in the manipulation of materials to make the play experience personally meaningful. Using a subject that has an inherent meaning for the child (such as a favourite video sequence) is more likely to help the child to start to pretend.

Different ways have been used to teach pretend play. One useful method is the use of photographs, video or digital camera photographs linked to a computer, the aim being to make pretend play explicit. For this to work best, the technique needs to be part of the work of speech and language therapists to help the child develop social scripts for pretend play sequences.

Stahmer (1999) looked at the use of pivotal response training (PRT). PRT is a training technique used to increase motivation. Techniques include giving clear instructions and questions, allowing the child to choose the toys it will pretend with, and reinforcement of 'good tries'. Stahmer suggests that types of play that can be taught include manipulative play, functional play, symbolic play and sociodramatic play. But Stahmer found it was still hard to get that much interaction during play with peers and that children still did not initiate much play.

As Jordan and Libby (1997) conclude, teaching spontaneous play skills to children with autism, or developing existing play skills, is not easy; if it were so, it would not be a recognised core problem of autism. Play, however, can and should be a valuable part of the school curriculum for pupils with autism, facilitating all aspects of development (Jordan and Libby 1997).

If young children who seem to be autistic are taught to pretend play, might that help? In addition, it is hard to be sure whether the failure of autistic children to play leads to or is the product of a deficient 'theory of mind', and this body of work again makes clear how very important the role of play is.

But as I suggested at the start of the chapter, play can sometimes seem just too much.

Don't play too much – it'll frighten the neighbours

A number of commentators like Panksepp worry that spontaneous rough and tumble play may be increasingly seen as a sign of pathology rather than as an ordinary childhood activity. In the United States, there seems to be a link between a growing intolerance of children playing and one of the more intriguing trends in the diagnosis of childhood psychological problems: the dramatic increase in the diagnosis of attention deficit hyperactivity disorders in the late twentieth century (Panksepp 1998). It has been estimated that 15 per cent of American children (about 8 million) were so diagnosed in 2000, up from 1 per cent at the beginning of the twentieth century and 5 per cent at the start of the 1990s. Panksepp thinks it unlikely that there really has been an increase of genuine neurological disorders in the United States and that it is far more likely that experts have redefined what we consider to be normal childhood behaviours. So boisterious physical play is sometimes labelled a form of pathology (Panksepp 1998).

The irony is that play may actually be therapeutic. There is evidence that genuine attention deficits in children are correlated with reduced frontal lobe size and activity, although brain-imaging data are obviously not a prerequisite for a diagnosis of ADHD. Animal research suggests that rough and tumble play not only reflects frontal lobe development but also promotes it. Energetic, spontaneous physical play may facilitate neurological development. If this is the case, stopping children playing either by punishing them or medicating them might actually contribute to developmental abnormalities. Indeed, while psychostimulant medications such as Ritalin are quite effective in focusing children's attention, another of their major effects is to reduce rough and tumble play (Panksepp 1998).

Teachers often complain that children who lark about in the classroom are disruptive but the irony, Panksepp (1998) maintains, is that, as is true of other appetites, the need for rough and tumble is a self-regulating process. You can be played out – and then quiet. There is evidence to suggest that if children are deprived of physical play, they will play with even greater vigour when given the opportunity to do so (Pellegrini 1995; Smith and Hagan 1980). Stopping children playing – and that does happen – could be truly bad. If rough and tumble play not only reflects but also promotes neurological maturity, then the last thing adults should do is to try to stop it.

But then adults have their own issues when it comes to play, as we shall see in the next chapter.

8 Adult games in a changing world

Sports and card games are, as Huizinga (1949) observed, very old. The Olympics began in 776 BC and the festival must have built on even older traditions of competitive races and throwing contests. The pack of cards we use now in the west dates back to medieval times. Koreans played card games before the Greeks and the Romans were addicted to all kinds of games. Did Cro-Magnon persons develop a form of *Monopoly* based on which cave was worth more than another? Probably. In a nice phrase, Sutton-Smith (1983) has written of a human instinct 'to game'.

Strangely, psychologists have not come to terms yet with the games that adults play. Some of the reasons are historical. When Piaget (1952) finished his book on play, he felt he had to explain the bizarre behaviour of grown men and women who indulged in football or canasta. He tried to make these seem a natural evolution of childhood games. As children grew older, they insisted on playing games that reflected reality accurately. Piaget was amazed by his son, who created an eighteenth-century world with loving research and care. Older children also preferred games with more formal rules. In his analysis of how children played marbles, Piaget found that, as they grew older, they understood and abided by ever more complicated rules. But the link that Piaget tried to draw between children's games and the behaviour of adults is flawed. When you play football or roulette, you certainly have to play according to the rules. Those rules create a world of their own but it is hard to see how this world 'reflects' reality. I finished *Play, Dreams and Imitation in Childhood* feeling that Piaget thought that sensible adults had better things to do than lark about on the football pitch or in the casino. Piaget worked in Geneva, the city that bred Calvinism, so he might be specially inclined to disapprove of such frivolity.

Psychologists have also been influenced, I suggest, because the word 'game' refers both to playing and to gambling. (In Britain that is also known as 'gaming'. There used to be a Gaming Board which controlled betting.) When studying gambling, psychologists have concentrated on compulsive gambling and that, of course, has been seen as some form of sickness. So adults shouldn't play because that's immature and if they do play, they're dysfunctional! So it's not surprising research on adult games comes with a bit of baggage.

Media games

The start of the twenty-first century has brought with it many paradoxes. In the well-fed, well-developed world, games are all the rage for children and adults too. The marketing of games often now pushes family appeal. *Nintendo®* is bought by adults for children and by adults for adults. Psychological theory has yet to catch up with such developments.

Language, however, reflects the fact we think that adults shouldn't play games. If I say that Alexandra plays games, I am not usually flattering her but warning you to steer clear of the little minx. Two of the most successful writers on adult games are Eric Berne and Stephen Potter (Potter 1977). In their different ways – Berne is a therapist, Potter a comic writer – both disapprove. The adult who plays games is doing something slightly disreputable. Potter describes and, even, recommends a series of ploys – discuss, if you like, the significance of the closeness between ply, ploy and play with particular reference to word games. Astute use of these ploys can make you triumph and others land in the soup or worse. But Potter makes the gamesman a conscious operator.

Berne (1973) describes a very different creature. In *Games People Play*, he suggests that we all carry within us a Child, a Parent and an Adult. These warring selves make different demands and often make us play games without knowing that's what we're doing. If you reject me and say that you don't want to make love, I may sulk like a 2 year old. I won't realise, however, I am doing that. I may sincerely believe that I am horribly hurt. The games people play are games forced upon them because they don't know themselves well enough and are not well enough adjusted. It could be said, exaggerating slightly, that Berne claims adults play games because they are sick while Potter suggests they do it because they are bad. Neither formulation makes it sound healthy.

In this chapter, I want to argue that psychological analysis has lagged far behind reality. The world knows that adults play and has known so for a long time. Back in the heady 1960s, sociologists wondered how we were going to cope with the 'problem' of leisure. It had to be a problem, of course, for sociologists to write about.

The vision in the 1960s was an optimistic one. Technology would free us from the drudgery of work. Benign robots would do the dirty jobs. Liberated from the nine to five grind, human beings would finally have the chance to be human, to explore, create, educate themselves. It is very hard to be sure of what the truth is about this. In the west many middle-class people complain they are starved of time and stressed at work and, now, there is even a journal called *Stress News*. On the other hand, we spend far more than ever before on leisure activities. Even the Japanese, who we think of as corporate-crazed workaholics, seem to love their hobbies. In 1985 in Harpers I reported (Cohen 1985) a survey by the Japanese Ministry of Industry back in 1983 which said that 18 per cent of Japanese wanted to become very rich, 9 per cent to live an honourable life, and a frivolous 38 per cent wanted only 'an easy life with their hobbies'. In 1960, only 11 per cent mentioned life with hobbies as a major goal.

Games have become big business. Sega and Nintendo, giants of the computer games, clock up sales of over $1000 million worldwide. Civilisation has indeed become game-playing as Huizinga (1949) observed long ago. A proper account of contemporary play has to explain why adults play games apparently more than we did previously. Is this some real need that was long suppressed or have the over-sixteens just been manipulated by clever marketing persons? Psychologists also need to explore why many of the games children play can also appeal to adults and how it is that children can enjoy games which seem to be steeped in quite complicated cultural references. These are all areas that Piaget never touched. In his days there were texts and media but no media studies. It is hard to see how we will get a proper explanation of these phenomena without some co-operation between psychology and media studies since many of the games adults play are media based.

The tensions surrounding all this – isn't it a bit silly, or childish, for adults to play? – can be seen not just in how adults go about playing but also in the way they study the subject. Sports and recreations have become an academic speciality all of their own. In a world where you can get an MA in Leisure Studies and a PhD in writing cookery books, one chapter can't hope to cover all aspects of adult play. It seems sensible to focus on four areas, therefore.

The four areas are the growth of sports and participation in sports and, especially, dangerous sports; computer and fantasy games like *Dungeons and Dragons*; the boom in adult computer toys; and what can be called 'therapy' games which include the games people play when they want to go beyond the games described by Eric Berne (1973). Psychology finds it hard to explain this general surge of playfulness. If the purpose of play is to prepare the child in various ways for adult life, what is the motive for adult play?

Sports

In 1969, the Greater London and South East Sports Council commissioned a survey of the sports facilities in its area and, along with it, a separate study of the likely demand. The council found that far more people wanted to take part in every sport than actually did so. Some sports, like pony trekking and gliding, were interesting because although no one took part in them at all, 5 per cent of those who answered the survey said they wanted to. The general conclusion of the 1969 survey was clear. Apart from swimming, few sports had more than 5 per cent of the population ever taking part. Golf was the next most popular together with tennis. But about 5 per cent to 10 per cent of the survey, depending on the sport, said they were very likely to take part if given the chance.

At the time when the survey was commissioned, the growth of leisure was considered nothing but good. By the 1980s, when there was much agonising about unemployment, it was clear that many people had leisure forced upon them. In its annual report for 1982–3, the Sports Council in Britain reported that far more people participated in sports than ten years previously. Some 600 swimming pools had been built since 1960 and over 190 indoor sports stadia. All of these were being used. The Sports Council believed, moreover, that it was important to target particular sections of the population to make them take up sport. Considerable success had been seen with campaigns aimed at disabled and unemployed people.

In the run up to the 2012 Olympics in London, the government wants the hoopla to get more of us – oldies, fatties, unfits – to sport and disport ourselves. Britain and even more, the United States, have recently seen a series of crazes for sports. People have taken up tennis and golf in more numbers than ever before. *Inner tennis* became, for a year or two, very popular, which is especially telling since it offered the chance to use meditation to improve your forehand. What could be more playful? Aerobics and running have become very popular.

This popularity had led to a host of magazines like *Road Runner, Running, Fitness, Marathon Runner, Mountain Bike, Water Sports.* All these regularly offer advice on what kind of sports will improve what part of your body. Then, as well as more people taking part in sports, more people are getting involved in what used to be called minor sports. Once, basketball and volleyball were games that were hardly played in Britain. Now, there are thriving teams and you can even play American football in London as well as Australian rules football and Siberian football. I made that last one up, I confess. And if you can't play with your body, you can become a 'sports quizzer'. Quizzers are people whose hobby it is to devise, organise and take part in quizzes about sports. A small industry of books churns out the latest statistics to allow such quizzes to flourish. Sometimes, publicity leads to a rise in participation. When four Scottish women won the curling champion- ship at the 2000 Winter Olympics, many people started playing this bizarre sport.

Perhaps the most interesting development is the growth of dangerous sports. In the past, there were always people attracted to dare-devil sports but they were few and, usually, rich. In 1977, the American magazine *Human Behaviour* ran a long study of lethal sports which was sparked off as a result of an increase in deaths of hang-gliders. Peter Greenberg (1977) looked at 'Escape Centres', scuba diving and fun aviation and came out with some interesting conclusions. There was indeed considerable growth in centres where people could take part in dangerous sports. Often, they had to waive all legal claims before being allowed in. Too bad if they crashed! Greenberg found no lack of customers because there was a growing number of release centres or areas where Americans in increasing numbers can put themselves to the test. The more dangerous the test is, the stronger is the siren call of such 'sports' as hang-gliding, motocross, hot dog skiing, night snowmobiling and fringe scuba diving. Customers went in with their eyes open to the risk but, Greenberg found, they said the risks were alluring. Greenberg inter- viewed David Klein, professor of social science at Michigan State University. Klein had studied 500 snowmobile accidents. He had found that most of those who went in for such sports were 'blue collar workers in dead end jobs'. Unlike middle-class sportsmen, they liked instant gratification and were not willing to spend a long time learning how to sail. Ads for snowmobiles pushed the message that anyone who drove a car could be a champion on the snowmobile. So there were accidents when inexperienced snowmobilists tried to execute daring feats. Klein believed that middle-class men were far more likely to have the patience to take part in sports that were as thrilling but less risky, such as sailing.

Since the early 1980s, evidence suggests that many middle-class people are becoming more interested in such risky sports. Doctors and dentists with routine practices seem especially susceptible to taking up hazardous sports. The number of accidents in snowmobiling, hang-gliding and scuba diving has risen constantly. In the United States, the National Safety Council and in Britain, the Sports Council has commented on these trends. Fairly con- sistently, the figures point to more injuries and deaths. Even bad publicity such as deaths due to hang-gliding does not seem to deter enthusiasts. Urban free jumping is the latest craze. As on TV, urban jumpers leap between high buildings. It started in France in 2002. The home of existentialism has become the home of Extreme Sports which has a TV channel devoted to it. Sartre must be extremely cross in his grave. The Extreme Sports Channel offers viewers a chance to gawp at activities like speed kayaking and 2004 has even seen the publication of a very glossy, artily designed magazine called *Adrenalin*. The title says it all.

The increase in the number of people taking part in such risky sports illustrates some of the paradoxes of adult play. It could be argued that, as general expectations rise, people are less willing to accept that life should be boring. If work can't give you thrills, seek them elsewhere! So many adults seek out a kind of play which has lost some of its relaxing characteristics. Usually play is safe, stress-free and can be casual. It isn't too competitive. But risky sports are not like that at all.

The results of the survey in *Human Behaviour* suggest that an article on 'The Americanization of Rock Climbing' was woefully accurate. Csikszentmihalyi (1964) noted that rock climbing developed out of mountaineering. But while mountaineers like Chris Bonnington write of their love of the mountains and the beauty of the mountains, rock climbers have become technical experts. Their interest is in climbing a rock face by the most direct, most efficient method. Most rock climbers in 1964 were theoretical physicists or mathematicians. There was an emphasis on using the best equipment and technology. A climber often spent hours 'obsessed with his gear' which clearly mattered more than the view. The article also lamented a new obsession with quantification. By 1962, American climbers had introduced a grading scale for faces which could range from F1 to F10 if they could be climbed free and from A1 to A5 if they needed artificial equipment. In Britain, there is a similar grading scale. Instead of climbing a rock for pleasure, it became a task, in which the climax wasn't getting to the top of the mountain but performing the most difficult move on the mountain. Csikszentmihalyi suggested that the changes in rock climbing reflected the general changes in society and moaned eloquently that: 'A game activity which until a generation ago was performed leisurely, within a complex logico-meaningful framework of experiences is now becoming a calculated, precise, expert enterprise within a much narrower framework of experiences.'

Some sports that have attracted a popular following have shown similar trends. Those of us who don't jog take secret delight, of course, in stories of enthusiasts who jog so relentlessly they make themselves ill. In extreme cases, they may even die. One marathon was spoilt by the fact that one competitor, a 28-year-old man, died. American research has pointed to a number of cases where 'athletes' push themselves to the point of heart attacks. It's even been said that compulsive jogging is the male equivalent of anorexia. It is easy to dwell on the macabre. In London, both the annual marathon and the *Sunday Times* 'fun run' attract over 20,000 starters. Both events are very jolly and give many runners a chance to play the fool as well as the athlete. Each marathon has its crop of runners in silly costumes, running as Mickey Mouse or wearing odd hats. But the way in which adults have come to play many sports has both its ironies and its dark side, enough to make one wonder if we don't play a little too seriously.

Dungeons, Dragons and other fantasy games

If sports have bred a whole host of fan-zines so have the fantasy games which developed from the late 1970s. There are such titles as *Imagine* and *White Dwarf*. I first heard of *Dungeons and Dragons* when a friend of mine in television suggested we base a screenplay round them. The market for adult games has evolved into a mega billion business. Hits over the last 20 years include *The Dungeons of Wrath*, *Car Wars*, *Truck Wars*, *The Land of Lankthmar*, the *Justice Machine*. I once spent hours in a Games Workshop. Each of these games had all kinds of associated literature available. Some of these were slim booklets with *Confidential* stamped on them. On a noticeboard, there were requests for people to join a variety of *Wargame* clubs including the Warwickshire Wargamers and the slightly less aggressive sounding Birmingham Role Players. London has seen a number of similar shops flourish, carrying even more stocks. They have allowed those who devised the games to make truly undreamt of fortunes. Some of the games and fantasy lands have to be played like traditional board games, others can be played on a computer, like *Adventureland* and *Pirateland*. It's an irony that the least technological of dons, J.R.R. Tolkien, should have, through his creation of Middle Earth, helped launch such an industry in the early twenty-first century. Sales of *Lord of the Rings* games based on the films released in 2002–4 have broken all records.

All this shows our modern 'need' for adult play. Though many fantasy gamers are young, there are reckoned to be some adults who play such games regularly – and provide the money. But, again, how really playful are such games?

Computer and role-playing games are fun but they can also lead to problems. There is increasing evidence that gazing too long at video screens causes perceptual difficulties, that it can occasionally trigger epileptic fits, that some children become addicted to video games and, oddest of all, that there are risks to interacting too avidly with your favourite home computer. When the home computer market boomed it was rumoured, with nice black irony, that university students who specialised in computers often came to believe that their computers had personality and spent hours chattering with them socially. Obsessed with the human–machine interface, these students' social skills suffered. Brod (1984) wrote of technostress in work due to the arrival of the computer. Since then we have seen increasing concern that children and some adults become addicted to computer games.

The user becomes so obsessed with the computer game as to lose perspective. My son Nicholas showed a few signs of this when we first acquired a Commodore in 1982 when he was 11 years old. He taught himself the basics of computing and often spent a whole weekend with a friend, who was always playing with his BBC Micro. Nicholas would go to the video arcade as often as he was allowed and became a regular at the local fish and chip shop not because of the food but because of the video machine he could play there. On weekend trips, we had to make detours so that he could get in the odd game. For three years, Christmas and birthday presents centred round computers and their accessories. It wasn't odd that Nicholas should react like this since much popular science fiction, from *Star Wars* on, turned computers and robots into romantic objects. But the slightly addicted quality of his behaviour was worrying especially when he started dreaming he was a robot! That was also to do with pressure of work at school but, still, it wasn't something he enjoyed. Then, gradually, he became far less obsessive about computer games.

The paradox with role-playing games is slightly different. They are sold on the basis that they give free rein to the imagination. In fact, they do no such thing. The authors have provided a very skilful set of building blocks – with enchanted forests, living corpses, relics of Tolkien, manacled monsters, etc. – which players can assemble in different ways. There is no way you can create a new set of characters within a game. You have to stick to certain rules. The games are only imaginative in a very limited sense, though players tend not to accept this. Aged 10, Reuben told me that he liked 'to form my own world' and then, when I asked about rules, set characters and the importance of chance, conceded that you couldn't really be that omnipotent within the game. Still, he battled back, you used your imagination much more than in reading a book.

Not that computer games and role-playing games are bad, just that they don't offer the creative freedom they pretend to. And, also, that some of those who play them appear to get sucked into a very obsessive (and not very playful) style of handling them. For adults, playing remains hard to do.

Adult toys

Marketing experts recognise that there is a kind of consumer who will always go for the latest gadgets in a particular field. Bring out a hi-fi which flashes different colours to go with different music and they will buy it! Bring out a food processor which also plays the latest hits and they will want to possess it. The US economist Thorstein Veblen argued in the 1920s that one of the ways in which the very rich showed the rest of us that they were very rich was by their conspicuous consumption. They flaunted their wealth by buying objects that were perfectly useless. In the developed west since the 1960s, a much larger class of people has had money to waste on things which are not necessities and they have become willing buyers of 'consumer toys'. From the point of view of play, what is interesting is how willing people are to buy knick-knacks of all sorts that are often described as adult toys. One London shop, Parrotts, specialises in such toys including presents for 'Those Who Have Everything'. New York has its equivalents and the smart *New Yorker*, in its pre-Christmas issues, often reviews the trivia and toys which can be bought 'On and Off the Avenue'.

There has been little research into why people buy such consumer toys but one only has to scan the papers to come away with a list of the most bizarre things that are now on the market. One weekend's survey of the quality papers available in London showed that the following were on offer: Farts and Burps, the cassette tape; The Porkscrew, which was a corkscrew fast as a greased pig; many mobiles; and, now, even soft toys for adults.

The interesting thing about such toys is that adults buy them but then rarely know how to play with them. Not surprisingly, there has been little academic research into the way consumers use the functionless knick-knacks you can buy from Parrotts or *Private Eye*. My totally unscientific, utterly anecdotal impression is that we don't use them for any purpose. They are not for play but for dis-play. (I wonder what Wittgenstein would have made of that; play is fun, dis-play is some sort of opposite.) I think, in particular, of the following adults toys I have, or have been given: there is a small pig in a rocking chair, a Dutch porcelain boot, a fine figure of a clown and an old pirate's box. All of these objects are on show in my living room but I don't use them. Does this mean that I have lost the knack of playing? Or just that the things that sell as toys for adults still reflect our unease about playing as grown-ups? Barthes (1973) assumed toys were for children, and that adults foisted on them a microcosm of the real, and, for him, denatured world. Adult toys seem to me far odder – not quite designed to be played with and hardly ever, in fact, played with. They are cute contradictions. It will be a landmark when we have Galt-like toys for adults to really muck about with.

Is personal growth a game?

Just as Parrotts offers you the latest consumer goodies, the classified ads in *Time Out* or the *Village Voice* offer the latest in encounter group-grope your way to your true self games. The 19 September 1985 issue of *Time Out* advertised therapeutic massage, body–mind integration, which included repatterning and experimental anatomy, holistic massage, firewalking which promised to 'turn fear into power, experience mind over matter, walk over hot coals without burning your feet, the latest technique for self-development', play world with the intriguing extra 'life after therapy', 'inner sound and voice workshops', 'gestalt group', 'Alexander Technique', 'Working with Dreams', 'The Life Training', which is 'an intensive two weekend adventure which will help you to see the truth about what really works for you', the Gurdieff Ouspensky Centre, 'Compulsive Food Addicts' group, hypnotherapy, 'women's shiatsu/healing self-esteem sessions', 'astrology-psychotherapy', 'assertiveness training', the lyrical-sounding 'Bach Flower remedies' where, I hope, you sniff roses while listening to the Brandenburgs, 'transcendental meditation', 'the Dervish way to expand consciousness' and the 'Vegetarian Singles Club'.

Nineteen years on, the 7 July 2004 edition of *Time Out* offers Metaphysical Counselling, Hot Stone Massage, speed dating, Sufi teaching, 57 Varieties of Quakerism, the Alexander Technique (again), London's Naturist Massage Centre, personal clairvoyant readings and – this is a sign that we have become more narcissistic than in the notorious Me decade – tooth whitening, and Genesis Unisex Health and Beauty, which includes head massage. Tooth whitening and head massage seem the greatest innovations.

City Limits, the other main listings weekly in London until it folded, offered some of these and, also, 'a self-forgiveness group', 'muscular manipulation', 'transactional analysis for professionals', which is clearly a cut above the same for amateurs, 'primal therapy' and 'co-liberation' which is 'co-counselling for personal and social liberation'; and the chance to 'cast off unwanted habits'. In Germany, *Psychologie Heute*, the monthly psychology magazine, has five to six pages of similar advertisements. The week I scanned the listings there was mention of some powerful therapies such as Rolfing, the Silva Method and 'aromatherapy', where the therapist massages you with sweet-smelling herbs and essential oils.

By the end of the 1970s, it was fashionable to talk of that decade as the 'Me decade'. In the 1960s, radicals had hoped to change the world; in the 1970s, they were content to change themselves in one group after another. A variety of books, like the sharp *Psychobabble* (Rosen 1977), examined the growth of these movements as did Clare and Thompson (1983) in *Let's Talk about Me*. Both books aimed to catalogue the main forms of encounter group available rather than to evaluate them but both left the reader with the feeling that what was on offer was very different from ordinary psychotherapy – and attracted many different customers. The 1990s saw the huge bestseller *Men are from Mars, Women are from Venus* (Gray 1992). Nowadays even the once sober London *Times* offers personal ads where a 'Zany blonde' seeks a 'Virgo'.

A rather interesting book could be written on the reasons for the growth of all these various therapies but it seems clear that two crucial figures were Fritz Perls and Abraham Maslow. Both were psychoanalysts who became convinced by the fact that the whole human race needed treatment. You did not have to be formally ill to benefit from therapy. In an introduction to *Gestalt*

Therapy, Perls (1969) wrote that children learn to walk, talk and 'to accept and reject. So the development continues and children realise some part of their potential for existence. Unfortunately, in our time, the average person uses only about 10 to 15 per cent of their potential; a person who uses 25 per cent is already called a genius'. Perls felt that the techniques he developed would enable everyone to realise their potential and to open their eyes and their ears. He added: 'But how do we open the ears and eyes of the world? I consider my work to be a small contribution to that problem which might contain the possibility of the survival of mankind.'

Abraham Maslow accepted the pessimistic view that most of us only realise a small part of our potential. Maslow (1967) argued we all needed to *self-actualise* ourselves, which is a technical way, perhaps, of saying that we needed to make the most of ourselves. To this end, he stressed the value of *peak experiences*, moments of great liberating joy. One of the aims of all kinds of groups listed in *Time Out* and other publications is to create either the peak experiences themselves or the freedom people need to find them. The search for this is often weird and wonderful. I was once taken to see a film of a particular brand of therapy where people went on a nude marathon encounter weekend where they could experience peaks they had never experienced before like being tied up naked against a totem pole! I'd love to add that some left in a fit of pique but everyone lapped up the weekend.

Many people go to such groups because they need help and have not been able to get much help from conventional medicine or therapy. But many groups appear to enjoy the experience, as a hobby almost. Groom your ego to perfection. Some of the rules of such groups resemble the rules of more prosaic games. For example, people usually choose to go to these groups in their own free time and pay fees to the organisers. Nobody is compelled to attend. Usually, there is a clear structure to the activities and, usually, a time limit. 'The Life Training' advertises weekend groups. Many encounter groups take place for two or three hours during the evening. Even marathon encounter groups have a time limit. Almost all the groups accept they operate outside real life. Members can do things which normally would be impossible, such as yell at one another, explore a range of feelings and, sometimes, do all this in the nude. When particular groups go too far there is often major controversy. There were complaints about some encounter groups in the late 1970s, alleging that participants became physically violent and were obliged to take part in sex. When some ex-members of EST complained that, during some marathons, they were not allowed to go to the lavatory, there was also an outcry. The game of groups has its own limits.

Very frequently, role playing is encouraged. In assertiveness training groups, for example, shy and diffident people are asked to role play situations they normally find difficult. Having seen them mutter under their breath rather than complain that the avocado they have just bought is bruised, the group leader will often get them to 'act out' making a loud complaint. One technique often encourages people to go over the top. If you can't be angry at all in real life, your task will be to fume, rage and foam vitriol in the 'safety' of the group. Once you have pretended major fury, the hope is that you will learn proper, appropriate anger. Not only assertiveness training involves such role playing. It is a major part of some encounter groups, of gestalt therapy where you often have to pretend to feel what your partner is feeling and, sometimes, even to feel what the sofa on which you both are sitting is feeling. The aim is to discover your own feelings. Groups see themselves as creative and that, often, involves role playing and improvisation. Such techniques are now even used by recruitment agencies.

The spread of role-playing techniques is, again, an illustration of the paradox – that we play more and, yet, we still don't feel too comfortable with it. Curiously, too, the origins of role playing are anything but amusing. In ancient Greece, games emerged out of religious rituals – healing led to play; for the psychiatrist Jacob Moreno, play led to healing. In the 1930s in New York, Moreno began to experiment with psychodrama. There was nothing in orthodox analysis to suggest that it would benefit patients to act out their problems. Such a notion went against Freud's restrained therapy. Moreno believed, however, that some patients could best be helped through being encouraged to act out some key scenes and relationships. If Hamlet had been his patient, he would have had him act out the bedroom scene. The technique, Moreno argued, brought to the surface the feelings that the patients did not want to deal with. He never recommended chaotic, undirected psychodrama but believed that under the control of a therapist/director, it had much to offer. Britain has never seen much work of this sort, though one centre in Devon specialises in it. A drug clinic in Birmingham has also experimented with Moreno's ideas. But psychodrama has remained a fringe rather than a mainstream form of therapy.

Moreno never became a very fashionable thinker and psychodrama always remained a minor form of therapy. But he focused attention on the possibilities of drama. A much more attentive observer, Erving Goffman, made the notion of role playing far more popular. Goffman (1959) was a sociologist whose book *The Presentation of Self in Everyday Life* suggested that we all play roles all the time. If you are a doctor, you have to fulfil certain expectations. You first listen to patients, then prescribe; you are slightly superior to nurses. If you are a patient, you have to fulfil the reverse of these roles. Goffman sketched out a world in which we were constantly taking on a variety of roles. In one day, I may act out the following: father at breakfast who nags children to do well at maths and remember their PE kit; commuter who complains about the rail service; aspiring executive who makes sharp decisions, is tough to his underlings and obsequious to superiors; flirt at lunch when I take out Miss Joanna, someone I should like to have an affair with; and so on till, in the evening, I resume the role as father and husband. Goffman popularised the idea that we could train ourselves to act various roles better. This promoted the growth of role playing both in encounter groups and in totally serious activities like job training.

Nowadays, we role play for fantasy, for fun (in some groups), for therapy (in other groups like assertiveness training) and to teach us to do jobs better. Concerned by the fact that many patients were complaining of the lack of rapport they were feeling with their doctors, the British Medical Association set up a role-playing course where doctors could drop their professional role and act being the patient. What did it feel like to be sitting there, in front of the man or woman with the prescribing pad, who ought to know whether the pain in your chest was serious or not? Many doctors scorned the idea but it caught enough attention for a film to be made about it. While researching the growth of Victim Support Schemes which aim to provide practical help and counselling to victims of crime, I sat in on a number of training sessions. Volunteers were asked to act out situations in which they went to help someone. What happened if the victim didn't want to let them in? How did they cope with the person who swamped them with need? The volunteers were divided into groups of three. One had to play the victim who had just been burgled or assaulted; the second one had to play the eager helper; the third person provided feedback, noticing what went on and, like a director in a play, giving advice on how to polish up the performances. If the victim clammed up, why not try for rapport by doing this rather than that? On the basis of this feedback, the volunteer would then have another go, trying to turn in superior sympathy.

At first, almost all the role players looked embarrassed. They had put themselves forward in order to help people in trouble, not to act charades. But, after 20 minutes, most of the trios were absorbed in the activity. There was a good deal of laughter as people were listening to what impression their performance had conveyed. Many industries and professions now regularly use role playing as a training technique. It teaches feeling and also happens to be a bit of fun. It's jollier than making notes out of textbooks – and can be more useful.

The growth of role playing illustrates how the Victorian distinctions between work and play no longer fit the developed western world. The stressed American executive will engage in many activities that are, super-ficially at least, playful. A story in the *New Yorker* illustrates the breakdown of these divisions nicely. The first concerns a small company that made home-made ice-cream. The executives of the company frequently dressed up in silly costumes, wrote advertising material that was deliberately frivolous and, once a year, engaged in a ceremony in which they hit ice-creams with sledgehammers. Selling ice-cream ought to be fun, they believed. They fought a major corporate battle during all this with an ice-cream giant and, as the *New Yorker* commented, their executive style was at complete odds with that of traditional business. But they were doing very well. A second story concerned two therapists who came to New York to buy toys for their clinic. The *New Yorker* followed them on a toy shopping spree which was, of course, work but which they also revelled in, especially when they had amassed five carts full of cuddly toys, mobiles and other frolics. Buying the right toys was work but, also, play. Of course, not everyone works in such a way. In many jobs, work is still grinding work. But it is no longer possible to demarcate work and play as totally as before. Furthermore, as sports, holidays, consumer toys and personal growth all suggest, adults are clamouring to play more.

Piaget studied children in a world before television. Television has not just had a cultural impact but a cognitive one. Exposure to the complex sequences of factual and fictional programming television offers in the west has certainly influenced what children think about and the themes around which they play. That much is obvious. It may be argued that television has also critically affected the ability of young children to tell fact from fiction. The average American child spends over 20 hours per week watching television. He or she will have seen over 1600 murders by the age of 6. Child viewers receive a mix of messages. Most children are familiar with video games by the age of 5. Views as to the age at which most children can distinguish the facts of news programmes from the fictions of war films differ but there is no doubt that children watching sequences begin to grasp the idea that some images they see are really happening while others are stories. For a good account of these controversies, see Kinder (1992).

The media child is not just a passive viewer absorbing material. Much research suggests that children incorporate what they have viewed on television and in video games into their everyday fantasies and games. The media child also appears to be precocious, and understands different levels of play. Helpful accounts of how children interact with television and the media can be found in Kinder (1992) and Applebee's (1979) *The Child's Concept of the Story*. Both have tried to assess the impact of television and video games on the intellectual development of children. Their most startling finding is that very young children are extremely adept from early on at picking up the curious mixture of narrative and comments on narrative which are a feature of much American programming. Kinder (1992) argues that children are introduced to the idea of narrative by television. Yet they don't see simple stories. They see stories which operate on a number of levels.

Kinder studied how her son watched a number of children's shows. She started observing him when he was 2. Kinder highlights one cartoon episode in the series *Garfield* called 'Eating Fellini'. In this episode Garfield, who loves lasagne, is discovered by an egomaniacal Italian film director called Federico Fettucine. The film is accompanied by music from the soundtrack of *8½* (1963), which was directed by Federico Fellini. Garfield wants to be the star but he has instead been cast as the stunt double. Garfield manages, however, to take over the film. He changes the film and usurps the role of the director and stars. In another episode, Garfield finds himself in the wrong end of the cathode ray tube. He is trapped inside the television and the television keeps on changing channels so that Garfield is successively caught in a Frankenstein movie, a football game, *Swan Lake*, a cowboy film and as a bargain in a used-pet emporium. Clearly, young children will not get some of the jokes. The most TV-literate child won't know that Fellini is a real and famous Italian film director. But children of 3 and upwards do get many of the basic jokes and they appear to understand the frames of reference that make it possible to parody ballet, cowboy movies, horror movies and other kinds of TV programming. Otherwise, *Garfield*'s rating in the United States would not be so high. That means children can grasp the changes of identity Garfield goes through in these episodes and the changes in his language that go with them.

Kinder's analysis of how her son viewed *Garfield* is the most detailed of a number of analyses of how he viewed shows. She also reports on how her son dealt with *Sesame Street* as well as less fashionable series like *The Flintstones*. Obviously, Kinder talked about television to her son – something which she could give more details about. There are also risks in studying one's own children as I know having done it. Yet, historically, it has also often been the case that important advances do come from such studies. Like many others before her, Kinder had to resort to in-depth observation, day in, day out, of a child to whom she had access in order to really get a sense of complicated cognitive development. There has now also been work on how children see *The Simpsons* and there are profound discussions on the meaning of Homer's Doh and, of course, the different levels of meaning of Doh.

Clearly, the present-day postmodern toddler grasps some of the ironies that television presents without too much effort. Characters insinuate themselves into different genres, swop identities, Dracula becomes a cowboy and children well under 5 follow at least some of it. The parallels with my observations of my own children seem interesting to me.

Useful as the observations that Kinder (1992) and Applebee (1979) describe are, they do not explain how very young children achieve such feats. Cognitive psychologists have plenty to do. But the results of Kinder, especially, do lend support to the trend identified by Wellman, Flavell and others. Only if young children between the ages of 3 and 5 are beginning to develop a quite sophisticated theory of other minds could they grasp the kind of identity swops and ironies Kinder (1992) describes. You have to know what Garfield expects in order to find it funny when his expectations are violated. Here again play studies seem to be at the centre of new developments in developmental psychology.

The questions about adults and games are perhaps less fundamental but still of great cultural interest. Initially, some psychologists argued that taking risks reflected the consumerist, get rich quick, culture of the 1990s. There is no sign, however, that the start of the twenty-first century has seen less interest in high-risk sports. In fact, Britain has witnessed a boom in often fatal base jumping where people leap illegally off tall buildings. Europe now has hundreds of enthusiasts for extreme skiing – it is no accident that the name parodies extreme unction. Extreme skiers go down pistes that do not exist taking risks that would seem to be insane. And as Grand Prix motor-racing has become safer, flying power boat-racing has come into its own as a death-defying activity. Hard economic times do not seem to make high-risk sports less attractive – and neither base jumping nor extreme skiing is a sport you have to be rich to play.

Just as the ability of children to play complicated games younger than was believed requires us to revise our ideas about the way children develop intellectually, the new love of games by many adults means psychologists will have to revise some theories. Cultures change and theories need to catch up with those changes.

These developments are healthy. In an earlier chapter, I suggested that we needed to play more, play more with our children, play more with our partners and lovers. The only paradox of the trends I have outlined in this chapter is that while we have learned to play more at work, some kinds of adult play are being 'worked at' too much. The American rock climber filled with pride in the latest technology of crampons, the snowmobilist with an eye on the rev counter, and the computer freak seem to be as much at work as at play. Adults may feel inhibited by the thought that they are doing something that only children do and, so, bring into their 'play' many of the stresses of real life. Americans tend to admire men and women who work *hard* and play *hard*. Perhaps we need to convince ourselves that it is more than possible to play soft, to play playfully or, even, to work playfully.

9 Endgames

Books follow rules too. As the writer, you come to the last chapter, where you sum up and announce your conclusions. Unlike all previous authors, poor misguided word processors that they were, I have solved the mystery of play.

And the answer is . . .

The difficulty is, when it comes to play, that some of the answers have been canvassed for a long time in a general sort of way. It has been known that children play to test their manipulative skills, to exercise their cognitive skills, to let off steam, to express their anxieties, to be naughty, to develop their imaginations and to learn how to do things together. Earlier, I offered a longer list of reasons why children play and, in most of them, there is some truth. The problem is that such general answers are not very useful when you attempt to explain why a particular child or a particular group of children are playing a particular game at a particular time. Psychologists have themselves made it harder to answer such questions by concentrating on establishing universal stages of the development of play. As I have argued, it is very artificial to look in isolation at the cognitive, social and emotional 'skills' children use, and learn, while playing. When Reuben was standing on a table, waving a stick around and calling it a Flying Cucumber to make his brother laugh, he was acting, socially and intellectually. The dissection of play into different skills has produced theories which are sophisticated but rather limited. These theories also tend to leave out the important questions of how conscious children are of what they are doing when they play. Threading one's way through the data, it seems possible to offer a less disjointed account of the development of play and to map out some key landmarks. These landmarks aren't separately cognitive, or social, or emotional, but, often, involve all three faculties especially because, in play, a child can transform a situation.

When babies play with the mobile in their crib, it seems safe to assume that they don't know that what they are doing is playing. There is no cognitive distinction in the baby's head between executing this act and executing the 'real' act of grasping for a bottle of milk. Yet, the child still plays with the mobile and still exercises or practises a variety of skills in doing so. Play starts off as being an activity that the infant is unconscious of. During this period, it seems likely that the child, when playing, has an attentive alert face rather than a play face. A hypothesis that requires longitudinal testing is when, and under what influences, the child starts to show the play face both in its minor form with the smile and in its major form where it is nearly a laugh and is usually recognised as a play signal.

Since it is not possible to interview 1 year olds about their thoughts and motives, research on the facial expressions used is important. It seems clear that a crucial landmark in the development of play is when the child can recognise that its mother, father and siblings are putting on a face that means 'this is not for real' and 'this is play'. Bateson (1956) argued that such signalling was crucial and was surprised to find young monkeys capable of it. Bruner (1975) in his meticulous work on peekaboo has found that children first recognise the signal that it's time to play the game and, then, learn to initiate the start of play signal. We know rather little though of how peekaboo fits with the other games that children play. With my son Reuben, it was far less important than the Mummy with the dummy game. It is not surprising, of course, that we know rather little about how children respond to the play signals of adults because psychologists like Piaget were keen to efface themselves on the whole. In reading *Play, Dreams and Imitation in Childhood* we notice the great psychologist surfacing only very occasionally as a person who larked about with Jacqueline, Lucienne and Laurent. But the turning point of when the child can recognise the 'exaggerated' adult's face as being an invitation to play is an important one which needs to be studied in the home.

The next crucial landmark is, it seems, when children can initiate play and are able to 'emit' a play signal. Until that point, children may well be playing and may well be exercising a repertoire of skills but they don't know they are doing so. As I have tried to show in analysing my observations of Nicholas and Reuben, Reuben by 18 months was able to initiate a variety of games and appeared from the age of 12 months to deliberately start certain episodes of playing. He was becoming a conscious agent. Research into the point where children can start games seems important not just because of what it might reveal about playing but also because it marks the point at which the child is, if you like, a conscious, intending agent who can have, and carry out, intentions.

In her still excellent longitudinal study, Nicolich (1977) rightly makes much of the point where children plan to play games. She puts this roughly between 18 months and 26 months. The question that merits more research, and especially more naturalistic research in the home, is the point at which infants begin to be able to start any form of play.

In starting play, individual differences may be important. My son Reuben had the benefit of a clever, energetic and affectionate brother who was nearly four years older. The observations I made showed that Reuben became very conscious of his ability to start playing between 12 months and 24 months. At 12 months, he could enjoy the Mummy with dummy game, which was usually started by Aileen. By 13 months, he often began the game by putting the dummy in her mouth. By 24 months, he could whizz around as Batman. By 26 months, he could select a cape which acted as a pivotal prop to start him playing Batman. By 27 months, he could announce that he was going to play Batman and engage his peer John in playing with him. Between 2 and 3, Reuben moved from just recognising a play signal to being able to initiate play and, even, to comment on his intention of doing so. He had become a conscious player.

In most western societies, children are initially brought up in the home. Between 2 and 5, they began to venture out to play with other children in nursery schools. The only major study of kibbutz children, Bettelheim's (1965) *Children of the Dream*, has little to say about the way these children played together. Bettelheim noted the babies crawled over each other without much bullying and that, later, they acted truck drivers a great deal, a job with much prestige on the kibbutz. Western culture dictates that children between 2 and 5 begin to cope outside the home. We know very little about the way in which young children transfer how they have learned to play with their parents and siblings at home to nursery school or playing with his peers. Yet, this is an important area. Both Reuben and Nicholas played at their nursery school in a rather more basic and less sophisticated way than they did at home. It is obviously dangerous to read too much into one study of two children but those observations do highlight the importance of early play in the home.

In playing with peers, the young child has, in some senses, to be a 'master' of play. There is no one older or more experienced to lay down the rules of a game or authoritatively to state that now we are playing. Fein's (1984) study of children in playschool, McCune-Nicolich and Fenson's (1984) work and my own observations (Cohen 1985) all show that by the age of 3–4, children not only unconsciously know the rules of the game but also can comment on them. The work of Flavell and his colleagues from the mid-1990s to the present has shown how true this is. It is worth perhaps contrasting these play skills with language skills. Chomsky (1957) has made much of the difference between competence and performance. By the age of 4, children can usually speak according to the rules of grammar – i.e. they perform competently – but they could not begin to articulate the rules of grammar that they are using. When it comes to play, observations in playschools from 3 onwards show that young children have a grasp of the grammar of play. They say a particular action isn't right for the game or that it's too silly to pretend a colander is a shoe. Many writers have been struck by this. As I have been stressing the issue of consciousness of play, we see that very young children become both conscious of certain very variable rules of games and, additionally, self-conscious about playing.

But why do children need to be so knowing about the rules of the game? If all they were learning was how to behave in certain situations, such self-awareness would be superfluous.

Bruner (1983) claimed that through peekaboo and other games children were taught the basics of all social exchanges. Knowing when to start an interaction, how to take, and how to yield, a 'turn', knowing how to end it, were all skills acquired through games. My emphasis on the extent to which young children become intentional, and conscious, players who know the rules of their playing suggests an additional knowledge they gain – knowledge of their own sense of identity. I don't mean to suggest that all 4 year olds are embryonic existential philosophers but the frequent skipping in, and out, of roles would seem to be a way of testing identity. I learn who I am through playing many roles; I test the boundaries of myself. It is, as Winnicott (1974) suggested, precarious. The more traditional view sees pretending games as just ways of learning about how to act certain roles and that view would need us to believe that when a 2 year old plays doctor, he or she is just learning about that profession. Goffman (1959) suggested that we present different aspects of ourselves in different situations. The roles maketh the man. It could be said that pretending games of children are the start of that process. One need not accept Goffman uncritically to accept that children are learning more than how to be a doctor. Perhaps it is because playing involves problematic and self-conscious 'knowledges' such as testing a growing sense of identity that children are aware of some of the rules of what they are doing.

When I first studied play in the 1980s, much of this seemed very speculative. But the link between pretend play and a sense of identity seems less so in the light of the research of Flavell, Wellman and others. Their research and the very persuasive work on autistic children – all combine to suggest that the process of pretending allows the young child to develop in some unsuspected ways. It is not just that play rehearses emotional and social skills that will be used later. The process of playing, of manipulating what behaviour is for real and what is not 'for real' is crucial to the very necessary human process of discovering that other people have ideas, hopes and beliefs – and that these can be influenced and manipulated. The evidence that points to some form of 'leap' in awareness of others between 3 and 4:6 is growing and the process of pretend play is clearly crucial.

There is a great deal of associated research to be done, especially in seeing whether children of 4 and 5 have very different ideas of how children and adults operate. Do children learn about other minds from playing with other children or from playing with adults?

I set out trying to prove that psychologists were perhaps too serious about play. In some ways, I still believe I am right. But it must be said that much of the research I have reported supports the irony that play is truly serious.

The *endgame* in a book often includes the author humbly solving the puzzle, having all the answers. I only claim to have some of the questions and the view that many traditional questions tend to ignore the complex mix of cognitive, social and emotional factors that are 'at work' in any play. We need a more rounded approach to the development of play and, in particular, one which includes the question of consciousness. The landmarks which seem critical in the development of play must include when the child plays without knowing he or she does so; when the child begins to recognise that parents and siblings are offering to play; when the child can begin to emit a play signal; when the child can string together a sequence of play acts; when the child can announce, either in words or actions, that it is starting to play. The meticulous research on transformations of objects outlined in Chapter 3 and the work on how groups of small children play together might be more meaningful if set in the context of such larger questions involving the child's ability to intend to act and to know what he or she is doing.

The question of consciousness of play seems especially important because the ways in which we play appear to be changing. Society is becoming more game-oriented. While some authors bewail the end of play, western society seems to have more and more time to play games. The standard texts on children's games have a dated feel. Piaget's (1933) *The Moral Judgment of the Child* is cited by Bruner et al. (1976) as the best description of games ever, yet Piaget did his research on how children played marbles in the 1920s. Iona and Peter Opie (1969) in their study of the street games of children evoke a rather nostalgic world far from the video games, television tie-ins, computer obsessions and teen culture of the early twenty-first century. As psychologists have assumed that the key questions about the development of play are working out its various 'stages', they have paid relatively little attention to cultural changes. We know more about the games of the Mexican Indian child in the desert than about the antics of children in British or American suburbia. For the record, in my observations of Reuben and Nicholas and of the Greenwich playgroup, I never saw them play marbles according to the rules of Piaget or hopscotch or Halma or mumbledypeg or any of the hundred or so games listed by the Opies or by Arnaud and Curry (1976) in his book which suggested traditional play offered a way of saving children from the influence of television. The study of play needs to examine contemporary children's culture far more. Once they are out of the nursery school, children interact with a changing world in which rules are being questioned more than in the past. For Piaget, children's play developed so that they adhered more and more to formal rules. That was undoubtedly true in his culture. It is probably less true now but studies rarely now look at formal games.

The other value of emphasising consciousness of play may be that it offers a way into the phenomenon of adult play. I have said, perhaps a little evangelically, that adults ought to play more and that we seem to have considerable inhibitions about doing so. Much health literature stresses relaxation and sports; the 'grow your own psyche' strand of advice for the perplexed pumps out the message that we need to play. Yet, we remain rather self-conscious about play. The traditional view that play is something children do cramps our style. I believe psychologists need both to study how adults play and to help expose the reasons for the kind of inhibitions I outlined in Chapter 8. Nothing is sadder, perhaps, than adults with time and leisure on their hands who can't quite make use of it. We ought to develop our play from womb to tomb. Psychologists ought to make a role for themselves in making that easier. There is no way of providing it but it is plausible, at least, that a world in which adults felt freer to play would be a happier and less dangerous one. Jaw jaw may be better than war war, as Churchill quipped long ago, and war games are better than war.

I argued in both the first and second editions for a more rounded view of play with more naturalistic longitudinal research. Some research since then has met this. The link between play and the development of the child's theory of mind is exciting and points to new areas of work. I never believed this book could solve the mystery of play but I hope it will help point research in new directions and assist further in the process of freeing the subject from certain traditional patterns and preconceptions. Some early twenty-first century 'guru-like' (ho ho) pronouncements to end the book. Adults ought to play more. And psychologists ought to play more with play and, paradoxically, that may lead to further deep findings. The rest of us need to play more with psychology.

Bibliography

Adams, R.E. and Passman, R.H. (1979) 'Effects of Visual and Auditory Aspects of Mothers and Strangers on the Play and Exploration of Children', *Developmental Psychology*, 15: 269–74.

American Psychiatric Association (APA) (1994) *Diagnostic and Statistical Manual of Mental Disorders*, 4th edn (DSM-IV), APA, Washington, DC.

Applebee, A. (1979) *The Child's Concept of the Story*, University of Chicago Press, Chicago, IL.

Apter, M. and Kerr, J.H. (1991) *Adult Play*, Swets and Zeitlinger, Amsterdam.

Ariel, S. (1991) 'Semiotic Analysis of Children's Play', *Merrill Palmer Quarterly*, 38(1): 119–38.

Ariès, P.A. (1962) *Centuries of Childhood*, Cape, London.

Aristotle (1996) *The Poetics*, Penguin, Harmondsworth.

Arnaud, S. and Curry, N.E. (1976) *Study Guide for Eight Films on Pittsburgh's Children's Spontaneous Play*, Arsenal Centre, Pittsburgh, PA.

Arnold, A. (1975) *Your Child's Play*, Pan, London.

Axline, V. (1947) *Play Therapy*, Houghton Mifflin, New York.

Axline, V. (1971 [1964]) *Dibs: In Search of Self*, Penguin, Harmondsworth.

Bakeman, R. and Brownlee, J.R. (1980) 'The Strategic Use of Parallel Play: A Sequential Analysis', *Child Development*, 51: 873–8.

Baron-Cohen, S. (1988) 'Social and Pragmatic Deficits in Autism: Cognitive or Affective?' *Journal of Autism and Developmental Disorders*, 18: 379–402.

Baron-Cohen, S. (2003) *The Essential Difference*, Allen Lane, London.

Baron-Cohen, S., Leslie, A.M. and Frith, U. (1985) 'Does the Autistic Child have a Theory of Mind?' *Cognition*, 21: 37–46.

Baron-Cohen, S., and Wheelwright, S. (2003) 'An investigation of adults with Aspergers Syndrome or High Functioning Autism, and normal sex differences', *Journal of Autism and Developmental Disorders*, 33: 509–17.

Barthes, R.R. (1973) *Toys in Mythologie*, Paladin, London.

Baruch, D.W. (1952). *One Little Boy*, Victor Gollancz, London.

Bates, J.E. and Bentley, P.M. (1973) 'Play Activity of Normal and Effeminate Boys', *Developmental Psychology*, 9: 20–7.

Bateson, G. (1955) 'Theory of Play and Fantasy', *Psychiatric Research Reports*, 2: 39–51.

Bateson, G. (1956) 'The Message "This is Play"', in B. Schaffner (ed.) *Group Processes*, Transactions of the Second Conference, Josiah Macy Foundation, New York.

Bateson, G. (1972) *Steps to an Ecology of Mind*, Paladin, London.

Becker, J. (1991) Contribution to 'The Last Taboo', *Dispatches*, Channel 4.

Belsky, J. and Most, R.K. (1981) 'From Exploration to Play', *Developmental Psychology*, 17: 630–9.

Belsky, J., Goode, M.K. and Most, R.K. (1980) 'Maternal Stimulation and Infant Exploratory Competence', *Child Development*, 51: 1163–78.

Berguno, G. and Bowler, D. (2004) 'Understanding Pretence and Understanding Action', *British Journal of Developmental Psychology*, 22(4): 531–44.

Berlyne, D.E. (1960) *Conflict, Arousal and Curiosity*, McGraw-Hill, New York.

Berlyne, D.E. (1969) 'Laughter, Humor and Play', in G. Lindzey and E. Aronson (eds) *The Handbook of Social Psychology: vol. 3*, Addison Wesley, Reading, MA.

Berne, E. (1973) *Games People Play*, Penguin, Harmondsworth.

Bertelson, J. (1943) *Adventure Playgrounds*, International Playground Association, London.

Bettelheim, B. (1965) *Children of the Dream*, Pan, London.

Bettelheim, B. (1975) 'Some Further Thoughts on the Doll Corner', *School Review*, 83, 363–8.

Bornstein, M.H. and Tamis-LeMonda, C.S. (1989) 'Maternal Responsiveness and Cognitive Development in Children', in M.H. Bernstein (ed.) *Maternal Responsiveness*, Jossey Bass, San Francisco.

Bower, T. (1977) *Infant Development*, W.H. Freeman, San Francisco, CA.

Bowlby, J. (1946) *44 Juvenile Thieves*, Bailliere Tindall, Edinburgh.

Bowlby, J. (1975) *Attachment and Loss*, Penguin, Harmondsworth.

Brod, C. (1984) *Technostress: The Human Cost of the Computer Revolution*, Addison Wesley, Reading, MA.

Bronson, G.W. (1972) 'Infants' Reactions to Unfamiliar Persons and Novel Objects', *Monographs of the Society for Research in Child Development*, 37, 3, serial no. 148.

Brown, G. and Desforges, C. (1979) *Piaget's Theory: A Psychological Critique*, Routledge, London.

Brown, N., Curry, N.E. and Tittnich, E. (1971) 'How Groups of Children Deal with Common Stress through Play', in G. Engstrom (ed.) *Play*, National Association for the Education of Young Children, Washington, DC.

Bruner, J. (1972) 'The Uses of Immaturity', *American Psychologist*, 27: 1–28.

Bruner, J. (1975) 'The Ontogenesis of Speech Acts', *Journal of Child Language*, 3: 255–87.

Bruner, J.S. (1983) *Child's Talk: Learning to Use Language*, W.W. Norton, New York.

Bruner, J.S., Jolly, H. and Sylva, K. (1976) *Play*, Penguin, Harmondsworth.

Burghardt, G. (1984) 'Animal Play', in P.K. Smith (ed.) *Play in Animals and Humans*, Blackwell, Oxford.

Burns, S.M. and Brainerd, C.J. (1979) 'Effects of Constructive and Dramatic Play on Perspective Taking Skills of Very Young Children', *Developmental Psychology*, 15: 512–21.

Burton, R. (1609) *Melancholia*, republished in Everyman Classics, Dent, London.

Campbell, T.W. (1992) 'Psychotherapy with Children of Divorce: The Pitfalls of Triangulated Relationships', *Psychotherapy*, 29: 646–52.

Ceci, S. (1999) *What Children Remember*, video produced by *Psychology News*, London.

Ceci, S. and Bruck, M. (1995) *Jeopardy in the Courtroom*, American Psychological Association, Washington, DC.

Chandler, M., Fritz, A.S. and Hala, S. (1989) 'Small Scale Deceit', *Child Development*, 60: 1263–77.

Chomsky, N. (1957) *Syntactic Structures*, Mouton, The Hague.

Chukovsky, K. (1963) *From Two to Five*, University of California Press, Berkeley, CA.

Claparède, E. (1913) *L'Association des idées*, Octave Dion, Paris.

Clare, A. and Thompson, S. (1983) *Let's Talk about Me*, Ariel Books, BBC, London.

Clarke Stewart, K.A. (1978) 'And Daddy Makes Three', *Child Development*, 49: 466–78.

Clement, P. and Milne, D. (1967) 'Group Play and Reinforcers', *Behaviour, Research and Therapy*, 5: 301–12.

Clement, P., Fazzione, R. and Goldstein, B. (1970) 'Tangible Reinforcers and Child Group Therapy', *Journal of the American Academy of Child Psychiatry*, 9: 409–27.

Cohen, D. (1977) *Psychologists on Psychology*, Routledge, London.

Cohen, D. (1983) *Piaget: Critique and Reassessment*, Croom Helm, London.

Cohen, D. (1985) 'The Development of Laughter', unpublished PhD dissertation, University of London.

Cohen, D. (1985) Slapdash Josh, Harpers, May 1985.

Cohen D (1997) *Carl Rogers*, Constable, London.

Cohen, D. (2004) *Psychologists on Psychology*, 3rd edn, Hodder, London.

Cohen, D. and MacKeith, S. (1990) *The Development of Imagination*, Routledge, London.

Cohen, N. and Tomlinson-Keasey, C. (1980) 'The Effects of Peers and Mothers on Toddlers' Play', *Child Development*, 51: 921–4.

Coppolillo, H.P. (1987) *Psychodynamic Psychotherapy of Children*, International Universities Press, Madison, WI.

Corrigan, R. (1982) 'The Control of Animate and Inanimate Companions in Pretend Play and Language', *Child Development*, 53: 1348–53.

Corter, C. (1976) 'The Nature of the Mother's Absence and the Infant's Response to Brief Separations', *Developmental Psychology*, 12: 428–34.

Crowe, B. (1982) *Play is a Feeling*, Souvenir Press, London.

Csikszentmihalyi, M. (1964) 'The Americanization of Rock Climbing', *The University of Chicago Magazine*, 61(6): 20–6.

Curry, N.E. (1974) 'Dramatic Play as a Curricular Tool', in D. Sponsellor (ed.) *Play as a Learning Medium*, National Association for the Education of Young Children, Washington, DC.

Curry, N.E. and Arnaud, S. (1984) 'Play in Preschool Settings', in T. Yawkey and A. Pellegrini (eds) *Child's Play, Developmental and Applied*, Lawrence Erlbaum, London.

Curtis, L. (1921) *Education through Play*, Scribners, New York.

Dale, N. (1982) 'Early Pretend Play in the Family', unpublished PhD thesis, Edinburgh.

Dansky, J.L. (1980) 'Make Believe Play', *Child Development*, 51: 576–9.

Dansky, J.L. and Silverman, I.W. (1973) 'Effects of Play on Associative Fluency in Preschool Children', *Developmental Psychology*, 9: 38–43.

Dansky, J.L. and Silverman, I. (1975) 'Play, A General Facilitator of Fluency', *Developmental Psychology*, 11: 104.

Darwin, C. (1872) *The Expression of the Emotions in Animals and Men*, John Murray, London.

Davids, A. (1975) 'Therapeutic Approaches to Children in Residential Treatment: Changes from the Mid-1950s to the Mid-1970s', *American Psychologist*, 30: 809–14.

Dickens, C. (1854) *Hard Times*, London.

Donaldson, M. (1979) *Children's Minds*, Fontana, London.

Doyle, A. and Doehring, P. (1992) 'Transitions in Children's Play', *Developmental Psychology*, 28(1): 137–44.

Dunham, R. and Dunham, F. (1991) 'The Nonreciprocating Robot', *Child Development*, 62: 1489–502.

Dunn, J. (1981) *Siblings*, Fontana, London.

Dunn, J. and Kendrick, C. (1982) *Siblings*, Grant Macintyre, London.

Dunn, J. and Wooding, C. (1977) 'Play in the Home and Implications for Learning', in B. Tizard and D. Harvey (eds) *The Biology of Play*, Lippincott, Philadelphia, PA.

Dunn, J. and Youngblade, L.M. (2003) 'Individual Differences in Children's Pretenal Play', *British Journal of Developmental Psychology*, 21: 43–58.

Duval, S. and Wicklund, R.A. (1972) *A Theory of Objective Self Awareness*, Academic Press, New York.

Eckerman, C.O., Whatley, J.L. and Kutz, S.I. (1975) 'Growth of Social Play with Peers during the Second Year of Life', *Developmental Psychology*, 11: 42–9.

Eifermann, R. (1973) 'Social Play in Childhood', in R. Herron and B. Sutton-Smith (eds) *Child's Play*, Wiley, New York.

Elder, J. and Pederson, R. (1978) 'Preschoolers' Use of Objects in Symbolic Play', *Child Development*, 49: 500–4.

Elliot, C.D. and Pumphrey, P.D. (1972) 'The Effects of Non-directive Play Therapy on Some Maladjusted Boys', *Educational Research*, 14: 157–63.

Ellis, M.J. (1973) *Why People Play*, Prentice Hall, Englewood Cliffs, NJ.

Empson, W. (1949) *Seven Types of Ambiguity*, Chatto and Windus, London.

Erasmus (1473) *In Praise of Folly*, Penguin, Harmondsworth.

Erikson, E. (1972) *Play and Development*, W.W. Norton, New York.

Erikson, E. (1977) *Toys and Reasons*, W.W. Norton, New York.

Erikson, E. (1981) *Childhood and Society*, Pan, London.

Fagen, R. (1981) *Animal Play Behaviour*, Oxford University Press, Oxford.

Farver, J. (1993) 'Cultural Differences in Scaffolding Pretend Play', in K. Macdonald (ed.) *Parent–Child Play: Descriptions and Implications*, State University of New York Press, Albany, NY.

Farver, J. and Wimbarti, S. (1995) 'Cultural Variations in Children's Play', *Child Development*, 66: 1493–503.

Fein, G. (1975) 'A Transformational Analysis of Pretending', *Developmental Psychology*, 11: 291–6.

Fein, G. (1981) 'Pretend Play in Childhood: An Integrative Review', *Child Development*, 52: 1095–118.

Fein, G. (1984) 'The Self Building Potential of Pretend Play', in T. Yawkey and A. Pellegrini (eds) *Child's Play, Developmental and Applied*, Lawrence Erlbaum, London.

Fein, G. and Apfel, N. (1979) 'The Development of Play: Style, Structure and Situation', *Genetic Psychology Monographs*, 99: 231–50.

Feitelson, D. and Ross, H.S. (1973) 'The Neglected Factor – Play', *Human Development*, 16: 202–23.

Fenson, L. and Ramsay, D. (1980) 'Decentration and Integration of Play in the Second Year of Life', *Child Development*, 51: 171–8.

Fenson, L. and Ramsay, D. (1981) 'The Effects of Modelling Action Sequences on the Play of 12, 15 and 19 Month Old Children', *Child Development*, 52: 1028–36.

Fischer, K.W. (1980) 'A Theory of Cognitive Development', *Psychological Reviews*, 67: 452–535.

Fisher, S. and Fisher, R.L. (1982) *Pretend the World is Funny and Forever*, Lawrence Erlbaum, London.

Flavell, J.H. (1962) *The Developmental Psychology of Jean Piaget*, Van Nostrand, Princeton, NJ.

Flavell, J.H. (2004) Contribution, in D. Cohen, *Psychologists on Psychology*, 3rd edn, Hodder, London.

Flavell, J.H., Domme, M. and Flavell, E.R. (1992a) 'Young Children's Reliance on Sensory Information', *Child Development*, 63, 960–77.

Flavell, J.H., Lindley, N.A., Green, F. and Flavell, E.R. (1992b) 'The Development of Children's Understanding of the Appearance Reality Distinction', *Merrill Palmer Quarterly*, 38: 513–25.

Freeman, J. (2004) 'Cultural Influences on Gifted Children', *High Ability Studies*, 15: 7–23.

Freud, A. (1984) *Ego and the Mechanisms of Defense*, International Universities Press, Guildford, CT.

Freud, S. (1905) *Jokes and their Relation to the Unconscious*, Penguin, Harmondsworth.

Freud, S. (1967) *The Collected Works Index*, Hogarth Press, London.

Frith, U. (1989) *Autism*, Blackwell, Oxford.

Froebel, F. (1887) *The Education of Man*, Appleton, New York.

Gardner, H. (1983) *Art, Brain and the Mind*, Basic Books, New York.

Garvey, C. (1977) *Play*, Harvard University Press, Cambridge, MA.

Gaskins, S. and Goncu, A. (1995) 'The Role of Pretense in the Development of Self', *Human Development*, 41: 200–204.

Gesell, A.L. (1929) *The Child from One to Five*, Yale University Press, New Haven, CT.

Goffman, E. (1959) *The Presentation of Self in Everyday Life*, Doubleday, New York.

Goffman, E. (1976) *Frames of Mind*, Penguin, Harmondsworth.

Golding, W. (1967 [1954]) *The Lord of the Flies*, London: Faber and Faber.

Golomb, C. (1977) 'The Role of Substitution in Pretence and Puzzle Games', *British Journal of Educational Psychology*, 47: 175–86.

Goncu, A. and Mosier, C. (1991) 'Cultural Variations in Toddler Play', paper presented at Society for Research into Child Development conference, Seattle, WA.

Gray, J. (1992) *Men are from Mars, Women are from Venus*, HarperCollins, New York.

Greenberg, P. (1977) 'The Thrill Seekers', *Human Behaviour*, 6: 16–21.

Groos, K. (1898 [1896]) *The Play of Animals*, Appleton, New York.

Groos, K. (1901) *The Play of Man*, Heinemann, London.

Gurman, A. and Kniskern, D. (1981) 'Family Therapy Outcome Research: Knowns and Unknowns', in A. Gurman and D. Kniskern (eds) *Handbook of Family Therapy*, Brunner/Mazel, New York.

Haddon, M. (2003) *The Curious Incident of the Dog in the Night-Time*, Cape, London.

Haight, W. and Miller, P. (1992) 'The Development of Everyday Pretend Play', *Merrill Palmer Quarterly*, 38(3): 331–49.

Haight, W., Parke, R.J. and Black, D.E. (1997) 'Mothers and Fathers Beliefs about and Participation in Toddlers Play', *Merrill Palmer Quarterly*, 43, 271-90.

Haight, W., Fung, H., Wang, X., Williams, K. and Mintz, J. (1999) 'Universal, Developmental and Variable Aspects of Young Children's Play: A Cross-cultural Comparison of Pretending at Home', *Child Development*, 70: 1477–88.

Hamilton, V. (1982) *Oedipus and Narcissus*, Routledge, London.

Harris, H.A. (1972) *Sports in Greece and Rome*, Thames and Hudson, London.

Harris, L. (1985) 'The Lubavitch', *New Yorker*, 23 September.

Harris, P., Brown, G., Marriott, C., Whittal, S. and Harner, S. (1991) 'Monsters, Ghosts and Witches: Testing the Limits of the Appearance Reality Distinction', *British Journal of Developmental Psychology*, 9: 105–25.

Hartley, R., Frank, L. and Goldenson, R.M. (1952) *Understanding Children's Play*, Routledge, London.

Henderson, B.B. (1981) 'Exploration by Preschool Children', *Merrill Palmer Quarterly*, 27: 241–55.

Henderson, B.B. (1984) 'The Social Context of Exploratory Play', in T. Yawkey and A. Pellegrini (eds) *Child's Play, Developmental and Applied*, Lawrence Erlbaum, London.

Henderson, B.B., Chalkesworth, W.R. and Gamradt, J. (1982) 'Children's Exploratory Behaviour in a Novel Field Setting', *Ethnology and Sociobiology*, 3: 93–9.

Hill, P.M. and McCune-Nicolich, L. (1981) 'Pretend Play and Patterns of Cognition in Down's Syndrome Children', *Child Development*, 52: 611–17.

Hobbes, T. (1652) *Leviathan*, London.

Howes, C. and Matheson, C. (1992) 'Play Sequences', *Developmental Psychology*, 28: 59–75.

Hudson, L. (1967) *Contrary Imaginations*, Penguin, Harmondsworth.

Hughes, M. (1975) 'Egocentrism in Preschool Children', PhD dissertation, University of Edinburgh.

Huizinga, L. (1949 [1944]) *Homo Ludens*, trans. R.F.C. Hull, Routledge, London.

Humphreys, A.and Smith, P.K. (1984) 'Rough and Tumble Play in Preschool and Playground' in P.K. Smith *Play in Animals and Humans*, Blackwells, Oxford.

Isaacs, S. (1926) *Intellectual Growth in Young Children*, Routledge, London.

Isaacs, S. (1933) *Social Development in Young Children*, Routledge, London.

Jackowitz, E.R. and Watson, M.W. (1980) 'The Development of Object Transformations in Early Pretend Play', *Developmental Psychology*, 16: 543–9.

Jarrold, C., Boucher, J. and Smith, P. (1996) 'Generativity Deficits in Pretend Play in Children with Autism', *British Journal of Developmental Psychology*, 14: 275–300.

Jeffree, D. and McConkey, R. (1976) 'An Observation Scheme for Recording Children's Imaginative Doll Play', *Journal of Child Psychology and Psychiatry*, 17: 189–97.

Jersild, A.T. (1943) *The Psychology of Adolescence*, McGraw-Hill, New York.

Johnson, C.N. and Wellman, H. (1980) 'Children's Developing Understanding of Mental Verbs', *Child Development*, 51: 1095–102.

Jordan, R. and Libby, S. (1997) 'Developing Play in the Curriculum', in S. Powell (ed.) *Autism and Learning*, David Fulton, London.

Kaye, K. (1982) *The Mental and Social Life of Babies*, University of Chicago Press, Chicago, IL.

Kaye, K. and Fogel, A. (1980) 'A Temporal Structure of Face to Face Communication between Mothers and Infants', *Developmental Psychology*, 16: 454–64.

Kazdin, A.E. (1991) 'Effectiveness of Psychotherapy with Children and Adolescents', *Journal of Consulting and Clinical Psychology*, 59: 785–98.

Kendall, P.C. and Morris, R.J. (1991) 'Child Therapy: Issues and Recommendations', *Journal of Consulting and Clinical Psychology*, 59: 777–84.

Kinder, M. (1992) *Playing with Power in Movies, Television, and Video Games*, University of California Press, Berkeley, CA.

Kingsley, C. (1863) *The Water Babies*, London.

Klein, M. (1955) 'The Psychoanalytic Play Technique', in M. Klein, P. Heimann and R.E. Money-Kyrle (eds) *New Directions in Psycho-Analysis*, Tavistock, London.

Kohlberg, L. (1969) 'Stage and Sequence: The Cognitive Developmental Approach to Socialisation', in D.A. Goslin (ed.) *Handbook of Socialisation Research*, Rand McNally, New York.

Kuhn, T. (1962) *The Structure of Scientific Revolutions*, University of Chicago Press, Chicago, IL.

Ladd, G.W. and Hart, C. (1992) 'Networking in the American Toddler', *Developmental Psychology*, 28(6): 1179–87.

Ladurie, L.R. (1981) *Carnival in Romans*, Penguin, Harmondsworth.

Laing, R.D. (1965) *Families of Schizophrenics*, Tavistock, London.

Lamb, M.E. (1976) 'Interactions – between Eight Month Old Children and their Mothers and Fathers', in M.E. Lamb (ed.) *The Role of the Father in Child Development*, Wiley, New York.

Lamb, M.E. (1977) 'Father Infant and Mother Infant Interactions in the First Year of Life', *Child Development*, 48: 167–81.

Langdon, G. (1948) 'A Study of the Use of Toys in Hospital', *Child Development*, 19: 197–213.

Lawick Goodall, J. (1968) 'Early Tool Using in Wild Chimpanzees', *Animal Behaviour Monographs, Vol. l, Part 3*, Bailliere, Tindall and Cassell, Edinburgh.

Leslie, A.M. (1987) 'Pretense and Representation: The Origins of Theory of Mind', *Psychological Review*, 94: 412–26.

Liebermann, N.J. (1977) *Playfulness*, Academic Press, New York.

Light, P. (1979) 'The social consequences of role-taking', in M.V. Cox (ed.) *Are Children Egocentric?* Blackwell, Oxford.

Lilliard, A.S. (1993) 'Pretend play skill sand the child's theory of mind', *Child Development*, 64: 348–71.

Lilliard, A.S. (1994) 'Makig sense of pretence', in C. Lewis and P. Mitchell (eds) *Children's Early Understanding of Mind*, Psychology Press, Hove.

Little, M.I. (1985) 'Winnicott Working in Areas where Psychotic Anxieties Predominate', *Free Associations*, 3: 73–80.

Locke, J. (1692) *Some Arguments Concerning Education*, Oxford University Press, Oxford.

Locke, J. (1972) *Correspondence*, Oxford University Press, Oxford.

Lowe, M. (1975) 'The Development of Representational Play in Children', *Journal of Child Psychology and Psychiatry*, 16: 33–47.

Lowenstein, M. (1953) *Children's Laughter*, The Free Press, Glencoe, NY.

McBrien, R.J. and Nelson, R.J. (1972) 'Experimental Group Strategies with Primary Grade Children', *Elementary School Guidance and Counseling*, 6: 170–4.

McCune-Nicolich, L. (1981a) 'Towards Symbolic Functioning', *Child Development*, 52, 785–97.

McCune-Nicolich, L. (1981b) 'Infants Don't Pretend Do They?', *Beginnings*, 4: 17–25.

McCune-Nicolich, L. and Fenson, L. (1984) 'Methodological Issues in Studying Child's Play', in T. Yawkey and A. Pellegrini (eds) *Child's Play, Developmental and Applied*, Lawrence Erlbaum, London.

MacDougall, W. (1919) *An Introduction to Social Psychology*, Dent, London.

McGhee, P. (1980) *Children's Humour*, Wiley, Chichester.

MacKeith, S. and Silvey, R. (1983) 'Paracosms', unpublished manuscript.

McLoyd, V.C. (1980) 'Sociodramatic Play: Verbally Expressed Modes of Transformation of Fantasy Play in Black Children', *Child Development*, 51: 1133–9.

McLoyd, V.C. (1982) 'Social Class Differences in Sociodramatic Play: A Critical Review', *Developmental Review*, 2: 1–30.

Marcuse, H. (1959) *Eros and Civilisation*, Beacon Press, Boston, MA.

Maretzski, T. and Maretzski, H. (1963) 'Taira: An Okinawan Village', in B. Whiting (ed.) *Six Cultures*, Wiley, New York.

Maslow, A. (1967) *The Farther Reaches of Human Nature*, Penguin, Harmondsworth.

Matthews, W.S. (1977) 'Modes of Transformation in the Initiation of Fantasy Play', *Developmental Psychology*, 13: 212–16.

Mead, G. (1934) *Mind, Self and Society*, University of Chicago Press, Chicago, IL.

Middleton, T.H. (1980) 'Boys and Girls Together', *Saturday Review of Literature*, May issue.

Mill, J.S. (1924) *Autobiography*, Columbia University Press, New York.

Mill, J.S. (1974) *On Liberty*, Penguin, Harmondsworth, original edition 1859.

Millar, S. (1968) *Play*, Penguin, Harmondsworth.

Mitchell, J. (ed.) (1986) *The Selected Melanie Klein*, Peregrine, London.

Montessori, M. (1910) *The Advanced Method*, Longmans, Harlow.

Moyles, J.R. (1989) *Just Playing? The Role and Status of Play in Early Childhood Education*, Milton Keynes, Open University Press.

Myers, J.E., Bays, J., Becker, J., Berliner, L., Corwin, D.L. and Saywitz, K.J. (1989) 'Expert Testimony in Child Sexual Abuse Litigation', *Nebraska Law Review*, 68: 1–145.

National Children's Home (1991) Contribution to 'The Last Taboo', *Dispatches*, Channel 4.

Nemiroff, M.A. and Annunziata, J. (1990) *A Child's First Book about Play Therapy*, American Psychological Association, Washington, DC.

Newson, J. and Newson, E. (1979) *Toys and Playthings in Development and Remediation*, Allen and Unwin, London.

Ney, P.G., Palvesky, A.E. and Markeley, J. (1971) 'Relative Effectiveness of Operant Conditioning and Play Therapy in Childhood Schizophrenia', *Journal of Autism and Childhood Schizophrenia*, 1: 337–49.

Nicolich, L. (1977) 'Beyond Sensorimotor Intelligence: Assessment of Symbolic Maturity through Analysis of Pretend Play', *Merrill Palmer Quarterly*, 23: 89–99.

Nielsen, M. and Dissanayake, C. (2000) 'An Investigation of Pretend Play', *British Journal of Developmental Psychology*, 18: 609–24.

Oakley, D. (ed.) (1985) *Brain and Mind*, Methuen, London.

O'Keefe, J. (1985) 'Is Consciousness the Gateway to the Hippocampal Cognitive Map', in D. Oakley (ed.) *Brain and Mind*, Methuen, London.

Opie, I. and Opie, P. (1969) *Children's Games in Street and Playground*, Clarendon Press, Oxford.

Paley, G. (1973) 'Is the Doll a Sexist Institution?', *School Review*, 81: 569–76.

Panksepp, J. (1993) 'Rough and Tumble Play', in K. MacDonald (ed.) *Parent-Child Play*, SUNY Press, Albany.

Panksepp, J. (1998) *Affective Neuroscience*, Oxford University Press; New York.

Panksepp, J. (2005) 'Beyond a Joke', *Science*, April 1st 2005, 5718: 62–3.

Panksepp, J., Normansell, L., Cox, J. and Siviy, S. (1995) 'Effects of Neonatal Decortication on the Social Play of Juvenile Rats', *Physiology and Behavior*, 56: 429-43.

Panksepp, J. and Burgdorf, J. (1997) 'Anticipation of Play', *Journal of Comparative Psychology*, 112: 65-73.

Panksepp, J., Normansell, L., Cox, J., Crepeau, L. and Sacks. (1998) 'Neural and Neurochemical Control of the Separation Distress Call' in J. Newman (ed.) *The Physiological Control of Mammalian Behaviour*, Plenum, New York.

Parker, G., Tupling, H. and Brown, L.B. (1980) 'A Parental Bonding Instrument', *British Journal of Medical Psychology*, 52: 1–10.

Passman, R.H. and Erck, T.W. (1978) 'Permitting Maternal Contact through Vision Alone', *Developmental Psychology*, 14: 512–16.

Passman, R.H. and Weisberg, P. (1975) 'Mothers and Blankets as Agents for

Promoting Play and Exploration by Young Children in a Novel Environment: The Effect of Social and Non Social Attachment Objects', *Developmental Psychology*, 11: 170–7.

Pellegrini, A.D. (1995) *The Future of Play Theory*, State University of New York Press, Albany, NY.

Pellegrini, A.D. and Smith, P.K. (1998) 'Physical Activity Play', *Child Development*, 69(3): 577–98.

Pellegrini, A.D., Huberty, P.D. and Jones, I. (1995) 'The Effects of Recess Timing on Children's Playground and Classroom Behaviors', *American Educational Research Journal*, 32(4): 845–64.

Pepler, D. and Ross, H.S. (1981) 'The Effects of Play on Convergent and Divergent Problem-Solving', *Child Development*, 52: 1202–10.

Perls, F. (1969) *Gestalt Therapy*, Souvenir Press, London.

Peskin, J. (1992) 'Puppets and Play', *Social Development*, 12: 496–507.

Phillips, R.D. (1985) 'Whistling in the Dark? A Review of Play Therapy Research', *Psychotherapy*, 22: 752–60.

Piaget, J. (1928) 'The First Year in the Life of the Child', *British Journal of Psychology*, 18: 276–301.

Piaget, J. (1933) *The Moral Judgment of the Child*, Routledge, London.

Piaget, J. (1952) *Play, Dreams and Imitation in Childhood*, Routledge, London.

Pitcher, E.G. (1957) 'An Interest in Persons as an Aspect of Sex Differences', *Genetic Psychology Monographs*, 55: 287–323.

Pitcher, E.G. and Schultz, L.H. (1983) *Boys and Girls at Play*, Praeger, New York.

Pollock, L. (1984) *Forgotten Children*, Cambridge University Press, Cambridge

Potter, S. (1977) *Theory and Practice of Gamesmanship*, Penguin, Harmondsworth.

Preyer, W. (1909) *The Mental Development of the Child*, Edward Arnold, London.

Queen's University of Belfast (1990) *Child Sexual Abuse in Northern Ireland*, The Research Team of Dept of Child Psychiatry Royal Belfast Hospital and Epidemiology and Public Health, Greystone Books, Belfast.

Reed, T. and Brown, M. (2000) 'The Expression of Care in the Rough and Tumble Play of Boys', *Journal of Research in Childhood Education*, 21: 331–6.

Roeyers, H. and van Berckelaer, I.A (1994) 'Play in Autistic Children', *Communication and Cognition*, 27: 349–60.

Rosen, R.D. (1977) *Psychobabble: Fast Talk and Quick Cure in the Era of Feeling*, Atheneum, New York.

Ross, H.S. and Goldman, B.D. (1977) 'Infants' Sociability towards Strangers', *Child Development*, 48: 638–42.

Rousseau, J.J. (1759) *Emile*, Penguin, Harmondsworth.

Rubin, K.H. (1982) 'Historical Theories of Play', in D.J. Pepler and K.H. Rubin (eds) *The Play of Children*, Karger, Basle.

Rubinstein, J. and Howes, C. (1976) 'The Effects of Peers on Toddler Interaction', *Child Development*, 47: 597–605.

Rubinstein, J.L., Pederson, F.A. and Yarrow, L.J. (1977) 'What Happens When Mother is Away', *Developmental Psychology*, 13: 529–30.

Ryle, G. (1947) *The Concept of Mind*, Hutchinson, London.

Sandler, J., Kennedy, H. and Tyson, R.L. (1983) *The Technique of Child Psychoanalysis*, Hogarth Press, London.

Sarason, I. and Sarason, B. (1983) *Abnormal Psychology*, Prentice Hall, Englewood Cliffs, NJ.

Savage Rumbaugh, S. (2001) *Apes, Language and the Human Mind*, Oxford University Press, Oxford.

Schiller, F. (1845) *The Aesthetic Letters, Essays and the Philosophical Letters*, Little, Brown, Boston, MA.

Schwartzman, H.B. (1978) *Transformations: The Anthropology of Children's Play*, Plenum, New York.

Schwartzman, H.B. (1984) 'Imaginative Play: Deficit or Difference', in T. Yawkey and A. Pellegrini (eds) *Child's Play, Developmental and Applied*, Lawrence Erlbaum, London.

Scott, E. and Panksepp, J. (2003) 'Rough and Tumble Play in Human Children', *Aggresive Behaviour*, 29: 539–51.

Shatz, M., Wellman, H. and Silber, S. (1983) 'The Acquisition of Mental Verbs', *Cognition*, 14: 301–21.

Sherratt, D. (2001) 'Play, Performance and Symbols', in S. Coates (ed.) *Autism*, Jessica Kingsley, London.

Sherratt, D. and Peter, M. (2002) *Developing Play and Drama in Children with Autistic Spectrum Disorders*, David Fulton, London.

Siegler, R.S. (1996) *Emerging Minds*, Oxford University Press, Oxford.

Silber, K. (1954) *Pestalozzi, the Man and his Music*, Routledge and Kegan Paul, London.

Silverman, M.A. (1982) 'A Nine Year Old's Use of the Telephone', *Psychoanalytic Quarterly*, 51: 598–612.

Silvey, R. and MacKeith, S. (1988) 'The Paracosm, a Special Form of Fantasy', in D.C. Morrison (ed.) *Organizing Early Experience*, Baywood, New York.

Simon, T. and Smith, P.K. (1983) 'The Study of Play and Problem Solving', *British Journal of Developmental Psychology*, 1: 289–97.

Singer, J.L. (1973) *The Child's World of Make Believe*, Academic Press, London.

Singer, J.L. and Singer, D. (1979) 'The Values of the Imagination', in B. Sutton-Smith (ed.) *Play and Learning*, Gardner Press, New York.

Singer, J.L. and Singer, D. (1990) *The House of Make Believe*, Harvard University Press, Cambridge, MA.

Sliosberg, S. (1953) 'On the Dynamics of Substitution in Play Situations', in K. Lewin (ed.) Investigations on the Psychology of Action XIX, *Psychologische Forschung*, 19: 122–81.

Smilansky, S. (1968) *The Effects of Sociodramatic Play on Disadvantaged Schoolchildren*, Wiley, New York.

Smiley, P. and Huttenlocher, J. (1987) 'Early Word Learning', *Cognitive Psychology*, 19: 67–89.

Smiley, P. and Huttenlocher, J. (1991) Young Children's Acquisition of Emotional Concepts, in P. Harris and C. Saarni (eds) *Children's Understanding of Emotion*, Cambridge University Press, Cambridge.

Smith, L. (1992) 'Judgement and Justification: Criteria for the Attribution of

Children's Knowledge in Piagetian Research', *British Journal of Developmental Psychology*, 10: 1–25.

Smith, P.K. (1978) 'Play and Non-Play in Tutoring in Pre-School Children', *British Journal of Educational Psychology*, 48: 315–25.

Smith, P.K. (ed.) (1984) *Play in Animals and Humans*, Blackwell, Oxford.

Smith, P.K. and Hagan, T. (1980) 'Effects of Deprivation of Exercise Play in Nursery School Children', *Animal Behaviour*, 28: 922–8.

Smith, P.K., Simon, T. and Emberton, R. (1985) 'Play, Problem-solving and Experimenter Effects', *British Journal of Developmental Psychology*, 3: 105–7.

Sodian, B. (1991) 'The Development of Deception in Young Children', *British Journal of Developmental Psychology*, 9: 173–88.

Somerindyke, J. (2000) Super cat girls, Symposium *AERA*.

Sorce, J.F. and Emde, R.N. (1981) 'Mother's Presence is Not Enough: Effect of Emotional Availability on Infant Exploration', *Developmental Psychology*, 17: 735–45.

Spencer, H. (1860) 'The Physiology of Laughter', *Macmillan's Magazine*, 1: 395–40.

Sroufe, A. and Wunsch, J.P. (1972) 'The Development of Laughter in the First Year of Life', *Child Development*, 43: 1326–44.

Stahmer, A.C. (1999) 'Using Pivotal Response to Facilitate Play in Children with Autism', *Child Language Teaching and Therapy*, 14: 29–40.

Stockinger Forys, S.K. and McCune-Nicolich, L.(1984) 'Shared Pretend: Socio-dramatic Play at 3 Years of Age', in H. Gitten (ed.) *Symbolic Play*, Academic Press, London.

Stone, G. (1981) *Social Psychology through Symbolic Interaction*, John Wiley, Chichester.

Sully, J. (1892) *The Human Mind*, Longman, Green, London.

Sutton-Smith, B. (1974) *Child's Play*, John Wiley, Chichester.

Sutton-Smith, B. (1983) 'Commentary on Social Class Differences in Sociodramatic Play in Historical Context: A Reply to McLoyd', *Developmental Review*, 3: 1–5.

Sutton-Smith, B. (2003) *The Ambiguity of Play*, Harvard University Press, Cambridge, MA.

Sutton-Smith, B. and Kelly-Byrne, D. (1984) 'The Phenomenon of Bipolarity in Play Theories', in T. Yawkey and A. Pellegrini (eds) *Child's Play, Developmental and Applied*, Lawrence Erlbaum, London.

Sylva, K., Bruner, J. and Genova, P. (1976) 'The Role of Play in the Problem-solving of Children 3–5 Years Old', in J.S. Bruner, A. Jolly and K. Sylva (eds) *Play*, Basic Books, New York.

Takkala, M. (1984) 'Family Way of Life and Interaction Patterns in Social Interaction', in W. Doise and A. Palmonam (eds) *Individual Development*, Cambridge University Press, Cambridge.

Thurber, J. (1936) *Let Your Mind Alone*, Hamish Hamilton, London.

Tower, R.B. and Singer, J.L. (1980) 'Imagination, Interest and Joy in Early Childhood', in P.E. McGhee and A.J. Chapman (eds) *Children's Humour*, Wiley, Chichester.

Trevelyan, G.M. (1942) *English Social History*, Longmans, Harlow.

Trew, K. and Kilpatrick, R. (1984) 'The Daily Life of the Unemployed', Psychology Department, Queen's University, Belfast.

Udwin, D. and Shmukler, D. (1981) 'The Influence of Sociocultural, Economic and Home Background on Play', *Developmental Psychology*, 17: 66–72.

Valentine, C.W. (1942) *The Early Life of the Child*, Methuen, London.

Valentine, C.W. (1968) *The Normal Child*, Penguin, Harmondsworth.

Vandell, P.E. (1979) 'The Effects of a Playgroup Experience', *Developmental Psychology*, 15: 397–85.

Vandermaas-Peeler, M., King, C., Clayton, A., Holt, M., Kurtz, K., Maestri, L., Morris, E. and Woody, E. (2001) 'Parental Scaffolding During Joint Play with Preschoolers', in J.L. Roopnarine (ed.) Conceptual, Social-Cognitive, and Contextual Issues in the Fields of Play. *Play and Culture Studies*, Vol. 4, Ablex, Westpoint.

Van Fleet (2001) *A Parent's Handbook of Play Therapy*, Play Therapy Press, Boulder, Colorado.

Washburn, R.W. (1929) 'A Study of the Smiling and Laughing of Infants in the First Year of Life', *Genetic Psychology Monographs*, 6: 397–535.

Watson, J.B. (1925) *Behaviourism*, Norton, New York.

Watson, M.W. and Fischer, K.W. (1977) 'A Developmental Sequence of Agent Use in Later Infancy', *Child Development*, 48: 828–36.

Watson, M.W. and Fischer, K.W. (1980) 'Development of Social Roles in Elicited and Spontaneous Behaviour', *Developmental Psychology*, 16: 483–94.

Wellman, A. (1985) 'The Child's Theory of Mind: The Development of Concept of Cognition', in S. Yussen (ed.) *The Growth of Reflection in Children*, Academic Press, London.

Wellman, H.D. (2000) The Emergence of Children's Causal Explanations and Theories, 37: 668–83.

Wells, G. (1981) *Learning through Interaction*, Cambridge University Press, Cambridge.

Whiting, B.B. and Edwards, C.P. (1988) *Children of Different Worlds: The Formation of Social Behavior*, Harvard University Press, Cambridge, MA.

Whiting, B.B. and Whiting, J.W.M. (1975) *Children of Six Cultures: A Psychocultural Analysis*, Harvard University Press, Cambridge, MA.

Winnicott, D.W. (1949) 'Why Children Play', in *The Ordinary Devoted Mother and her Baby*, *9*, broadcast talks.

Winnicott, D.W. (1964) *The Child the Family and the Outside World*, Penguin, Harmondsworth.

Winnicott, D.W. (1971) *Playing and Reality*, Penguin, Harmondsworth.

Wolf, T.M. (1973) 'Effects of Live Modeled Sex: Inappropriate Play in a Naturalistic Setting', *Developmental Psychology*, 9: 120–3.

Wolfberg, P.J. (1999) *Play and Imagination in Children with Autism*, Teachers College Press, New Yor.

Wolman, B.B. and Stricker, G. (1994) *Anxiety Related Disorders*, John Wiley, Chichester.

Wyre, R. (1991) Contribution to 'The Last Taboo', *Dispatches*, Channel 4.

Yarrow, L.J., Rubinstein, J.L. and Pedersen, F.A. (1975) *Infant and Environment*, Halsted, New York.

Yates, F. (1982) *The Art of Memory*, Ark, London.

Yawkey, T. and Pellegrini, A. (eds) (1984) *Child's Play, Developmental and Applied*, Lawrence Erlbaum, London.

Youngblade, L.M. and Dunn, J. (1995) 'Social Pretend with Mother and Sibling', in A. Pellegrini (ed.) *The Futur of Play Theory*, SUNY Press, New York.

Index